THE STUDY OF AMERICAN INDIAN RELIGIONS

American Academy of Religion

Studies in Religion

29

Editors
Charley Hardwick
James O. Duke

THE STUDY OF AMERICAN INDIAN RELIGIONS

ÅKE HULTKRANTZ

Edited by
CHRISTOPHER VECSEY

THE CROSSROAD PUBLISHING COMPANY
&
SCHOLARS PRESS

Published by
The Crossroad Publishing Company
575 Lexington Avenue
New York, NY 10022

Scholars Press
101 Salem St., P. O. Box 2268
Chico, CA 95927

299.7
H91
c.1

Library of Congress Cataloging in Publication Data
Hultkrantz, Åke
    The study of American Indian religions
    (Studies in religion / American Academy of Religion ;
no. 29)
    Includes bibliographical references.
    1. Indians   of   North   America—Religion   and
mythology—Study and teaching—History. 2. Religion—
Study and teaching—History. I. Title II. Series: Studies in
religion (American Academy of Religion) ; no. 29.
E98.R3H83 1982   299'.7'07   82-10533
ISBN 0-8245-0558-1 (Crossroad Publishing)
        0-89130-587-4 (Scholars Press)

Printed in the United States of America

Table of Contents

PREFACE

by Christopher Vecsey

We have gathered the following six essays by Åke Hultkrantz into a single volume in order to produce a major annotated bibliographical guide to American and European scholarship on North American Indian religions. The book supplements the wealth of references in Hultkrantz's recent publication, *Belief and Worship in Native North America*,[1] while providing a history and critique of the centuries-old interest in Indian religions. Used in conjunction with Ronda and Axtell's introduction to the study of Indian relations with Christian missions, and Turner's compendium of sources on "new" Indian religious movements,[2] *The Study of American Indian Religions* can give much needed and greatly appreciated direction to beginning students and scholars alike.[3]

We have arranged the essays and their references in a doubly chronological order. First, the essays appear in the serial place in which they were composed: the first four in the 1960s, the fifth in the 1970s, and the sixth in the 1980s. More importantly, they chronicle sequentially the study of native American religions from the seventeenth century to the present day, and as a result the bibliographies follow roughly a temporal progression, from the earliest missionary accounts to the most recent monographs. We hope that the book's organization—as well as its content—will prove useful to the reader.

Moreover, we hope that the collection of essays will stimulate further study of Indian religions by pointing to the masterworks in the field, by indicating the diverse approaches to the topic, by suggesting aspects of study hitherto neglected, and by demonstrating the value of native American religious scholarship to the study of world religions and to the study of humankind.

We wish to thank Carol Humphrey and Mary Lou Chilbert for typing

[1] Åke Hultkrantz, *Belief and Worship in Native North America*, Christopher Vecsey (ed.) (Syracuse: Syracuse University, 1981), pp. 295–330.

[2] James P. Ronda and James Axtell (eds.), *Indian Missions: A Critical Bibliography* (Bloomington: Indiana University, 1978); Harold W. Turner, *Bibliography of New Religious Movements in Primal Societies*, II: *North America* (Boston: G. K. Hall & Co., 1978).

[3] For a comparable guide to Eskimo religion, see John Fisher, "Bibliography for the Study of Eskimo Religion," *Anthropologica* XV (1973), pp. 231–71.

parts of the manuscript; Heidi Lichterfeld and Christine Walden for copyreading it; and series editor Charley D. Hardwick for promoting the project. In addition, we thank the following publishers for sharing Professor Hultkrantz's scholarship. The first four chapters of the present book are reprinted from "North American Indian Religion in the History of Research: A General Survey," 4 parts, *History of Religions* VI–VII (1966–67), by permission of the University of Chicago Press. Chapter five appears by permission of Harper & Row, Publishers, Inc., from *Seeing with a Native Eye*, edited by Walter Holden Capps (1976). A shorter version of chapter six is published as "The Study of Native American Religions and the Study of Religion" in *New Scholar* VIII (1982).

THE BEGINNINGS

INTRODUCTION

Everybody who becomes absorbed in the study of the research history on the North American Indian religion will sooner or later find that he profits twofold. First, he is informed of the changing ways in the scholastic interpretation of indigenous religions in North America, and second, he receives a historiographic survey of almost all the important schools of religious history and ethnology. In this connection he also becomes aware of an interesting cleavage between American and European thought on the subject. The Europeans have, on the whole, been more engaged in current ideas in the field of the history of religion than their American colleagues. The latter have, on the other hand, interpreted religion within the framework of American anthropological theories. This is exactly what could be expected, for the study of American Indian religion has always been an anthropological concern in the United States and Canada. In Europe, most students of American Indian religions have come from the ranks of ethnology, but, unlike their American colleagues, they have had a deep concern about religion as such outside of its cultural setting. During the last decades also professional historians of religion have become interested in North American aboriginal religions.

The following survey will certainly try to place both the European and the American contributions in their theoretical context, but most attention will here be paid to their achievements in illuminating North American religion.[1] In order to show the gradual changes in the research, a simple chronological method will be followed. Those who are particularly interested in the theoretical background of the authors and works mentioned here are referred to the historiographical works on religious and ethnological studies.[2]

---

[1] We are primarily concerned here with the religions of the Indians; works on Eskimo religion will only be mentioned occasionally. For a short appreciation of the research on Eskimo religion, see my "Les Religions du Grand Nord Américain," Ivar Paulson, Åke Hultkrantz, and Karl Jettmar (eds.), *Les Religions Arctiques et Finnoises* (Paris: Payot, 1965), pp. 346–47.

[2] For the history of religious research, consult, e.g., Wilhelm Schmidt, *Handbuch der Vergleichenden Religionsgeschichte* (Münster in Westfalen: Aschendorff, 1930), in particular pp. 153f., 156ff., 181ff., 194ff., 217f. For the history of ethnology in America, see Alexander A. Goldenweiser, "Recent Trends in American Anthropology," *American Anthropologist* XLIII (1941), pp. 151–63; Betty J. Meggers, "Recent Trends in American Ethnology," *American Anthropologist* XLVIII (1946), pp. 176–214; Robert H. Lowie, "Gegenwartsströmungen in der

MISSIONARIES, TRADERS, TRAVELERS AND THEORISTS

The first analyses of the aboriginal religions in North America were presented by the French Jesuit missionaries in Nouvelle France. Their descriptions of Iroquois and Algonkian cultures contain a treasure of materials on
the tribal religions which evidently fascinated them more than other cultural
expressions. Even today there is no work on American Indian religion which
in comprehensiveness can rival the seventy-one volumes of the *Jesuit
Relations*.[3] For a long time, the reports from Jesuit Fathers like Le Jeune,
Brébeuf, and Lallemand were considered to reflect Christian teaching, particularly in the domain of myths,[4] but the reverse is true; they represent the
earliest reliable sources of North American religion. On the other hand, the
Jesuits' analyses of the religious materials are inspired entirely by their own
religious and moral ideas.

A more detached position was taken by Father Lafitau, a Jesuit missionary who, in the beginning of the eighteenth century, worked for fifteen
years among the "savages" in French North America.[5] A modern connoisseur
of these Indians tells us that Lafitau and his younger colleague Charlevoix
(well known for his influence on Rousseau) "borrowed most of their material
from earlier accounts, usually without any acknowledgements, and were
eyewitnesses of very little that they related."[6] This is true, but credit must be
given to Lafitau on account of his methodical use of this material: if we
except the playful efforts of Lescarbot a hundred years earlier, Lafitau is the
first author who tries to present American Indian religion in relation to other
religions, in this case the religions of classical antiquity, through the method
of comparison.[7] Wilhelm Schmidt considers Lafitau as the founder of scientific ethnology; we may appreciate him as the first theorist in the field of
American Indian religion.

Amerikanischen Völkerkunde," *Mitteilungen aus dem Museum für Völkerkunde in Hamburg*
XXIII (1951), pp. 7–27; Lowie, "Contemporary Trends in American Cultural Anthropology,"
Sociologus V (1955), pp. 113–121; and A. Irving Hallowell, "The Beginnings of Anthropology in
America," Frederica de Laguna (ed.), *Selected Papers from the "American Anthropologist,"
1888–1920* (New York: American Anthropological Association, 1960), pp. 1–90.

[3] Rueben Gold Thwaites (ed.), *The Jesuit Relations and Allied Documents* (Cleveland,
Ohio: Burrows Bros., 1896–1901).

[4] Cf. Daniel G. Brinton, *Myths of the New World* (2d ed.; New York: H. Holt, 1876), p. 53.

[5] Most of the missionaries to New France were Jesuits, due to an early request from Cham-
plain to the Duke of Vendôme, viceroy of the territory.

[6] W. Vernon Kinietz, *The Indians of the Western Great Lakes 1615–1760* (Ann Arbor:
Occasional Contributions from the Museum of Anthropology of the University of Michigan X,
1940), p. x.

[7] Joseph François Lafitau, *Moeurs des Sauvages Ameriquains Comparées aux Moeurs des
Premiers Temps*, 2 vols. (Paris: Saugrain l'Aîné, 1724). For an appraisal of Lafitau's methodical
work in comparative religion, see Albert Bros, *L'Ethnologie Religieuse* (Paris: n.p., 1923), pp.
136ff. Lafitau's methods were, however, sometimes very superficial, for instance, when he
interpreted the Iroquoian god Areskoui with the Greek Ares (Lafitau, *op.cit.*, I, pp. 126ff. and
145).

Lafitau's picture of this religion became important, for it was generally accepted in eighteenth-century Europe. It was, on the whole, the information supplied by the missionaries which formed the basis of the knowledge in the subject in those days.[8] Modern anthropologists have often regarded mission reports in a condescending way because of their lack of objective judgments and methodical principles in research. However, most of the older missionaries were thoroughly trained in the indigenous languages, a competence which not too often characterizes the anthropologist of today. Religious research, moreover, has in many cases more to learn from old missionary documents than from present-day anthropological treatises.

Two Protestant missionaries from the latter part of the eighteenth century deserve particular mention because of their illuminating descriptions of American Indian religion: the Moravian brothers Zeisberger and Heckewelder, both of them engaged in the christianization of the eastern Indians, in particular the Delaware (Lenni-Lenape) and Iroquois.[9] Wissler considers them "the first great leaders in American ethnography" and points out that Heckewelder "regarded the beliefs and mythologies of Indians worth recording as a part of their social histories," an opinion which met some opposition in the American Philosophical Society, which was to publish his important book.[10]

In addition to the missionaries, travelers and merchants now started to spread information on the religion of the redskins. For instance, Nicolas Perrot, a Canadian *coureur de bois* who has been judged a keen and shrewd observer of Indian life, composed a most reliable description of Iroquois, Huron, and Ottawa religions,[11] and a merchant by the name of Long published an account of his travels in which he described the beliefs in guardian spirits amont the Ojibway.[12] He called these beliefs "totemism," a word which appears here for the first time in the literature.[13] Shortly afterward,

---

[8] Cf. how the Jesuit Father Chauchetiere, confessor of the "Iroquois Saint" Catherine Tegakouita, influenced Chateaubriand, the creator of "Atala," and how the Moravian missionary John Heckewelder (see n. 9 below) supplied the information on which James Fenimore Cooper based his famous novels.

[9] Archer Butler Hulbert and William N. Schwarze (eds.), *David Zeisberger's History of Northern American Indians* (Columbus: *Ohio Archaeological and Historical Quarterly* XIX/1–2, 1910); John Heckewelder, *An Account of the History, Manners and Customs of the Indian Nations Who Once Inhabited Pennsylvania and the Neighboring States* (Philadelphia: *Transactions of the American Philosophical Society* I, 1819).

[10] Clark Wissler, "The American Indian and the American Philosophical Society," *Proceedings of the American Philosophical Society* LXXXVI (1943), p. 197.

[11] Nicholas Perrot, "Memoir on the Manners, Customs, and Religion of the Savages of North America," Emma Helen Blair (ed.), *The Indian Tribes of the Upper Mississippi Valley and Region of the Great Lakes* I (Cleveland, Ohio: Arthur H. Clark, 1911).

[12] John Long, *Voyages and Travels of an Indian Interpreter and Trader, etc.* (London: by the author, 1791).

[13] Cf. Åke Hultkrantz, *Les Religions des Indiens Primitifs de l'Amérique* (Stockholm: Acta Universitatis Stockholmiensis, Stockholm Studies in Comparative Religions IV, 1963), pp. 68ff.

Lewis and Clark opened the road to the Indians of the Far West; their journals from the expedition to the Pacific Ocean in the years 1804–6 contain much information on the religions of the tribes whom they passed.[14]

In this connection it would be rather pointless to recapitulate all the contributions to the research on American Indian religion which have been made by different travelers during the first part of the nineteenth century. Two men, however, deserve particular attention: Catlin and the Prince of Wied. Both of them visited the Plains Indians in the 1830s, and both of them have given interesting sketches of the semisedentary Mandan Indians (although their evidence is sometimes mutually conflicting). George Catlin's vivid paintings of Indian cult scenes and medicine men provide us with significant ethnographical details and stir our imagination in spite of their poor artistic qualities. His text is more enlightening and actually more reliable.[15] A student of religion will find much material of interest in his description and interpretation of the Mandan anniversary rite, the *Okeepa*.[16] Prince Maximilian of Wied-Neuwied, accompanied by his skillful Swiss painter, Bodmer, gathered interesting information on religious ideas and practices among several Plains tribes.[17] As Lowie has pointed out, this information is sometimes characterized by exaggerations and subjective value judgments; but, as concerns the Crow Indians, "the record stands unscotched by later evidence."[18] Let us finally mention another traveler from Europe, Kohl, whose inspired accounts of Ojibway religion still can fascinate the reader.[19]

Among the most valuable documents on Indian religion from the first half of the nineteenth century—and there are many of great interest to students of religion[20]—we find some which were written by squaw men, that

[14] Rueben Gold Thwaites (ed.), *Original Journals of the Lewis and Clark Expedition 1804–1806*, 7 vols. (New York: Dodd, Mead, 1904–5). Cf. Verne F. Ray and Nancy O. Lurie, "The Contributions of Lewis and Clark to Ethnography," *Journal of the Washington Academy of Sciences* XLIV (1954), pp. 338–351.

[15] George Catlin, *Letters and Notes on the Manners, Customs, and Condition of the North American Indians*, 2 vols. (London: George Catlin, 1841).

[16] George Catlin, *O-Kee-Pa* (Philadelphia: J. B. Lippincott, 1867).

[17] Maxmilian Prinz zu Wied, *Reise in das Innere Nord-America in den Jahren 1832 bis 1834*, 2 vols. (Coblenz: J. Hoelscher, 1839–41; English ed., 1843).

[18] Robert H. Lowie, *The Crow Indians* (New York: Holt, Rinehart and Winston, 1935), pp. xiv–xv.

[19] Johann Georg Kohl, *Kitschi–Gami oder Erzählungen vom Obern See*, 2 vols. (Bremen: C. Schünemann, 1859; English ed., 1860).

[20] Cf. the manuscripts by Forsyth (on the Sauk and Fox), Trowbridge (on the Shawnee and Miami), Mary Eastman (on the Dakota), Father Boscana (Juaneño Shoshoneans), and others. See Thomas Forsyth, "An Account of the Manners and Customs of the Sauk and Fox Nations of Indians Tradition," Emma Helen Blair (ed.), *The Indian Tribes of the Upper Mississippi Valley and Region of the Great Lakes* II (Cleveland, Ohio: Arthur H. Clark, 1911), pp. 183–245; Charles Christopher Trowbridge, *Meearmeear Traditions* (Ann Arbor: Occasional Contributions from the Museum of Anthropology of the University of Michigan VII, 1938); *idem*,

is, whites who had taken residence among the Indians and married Indian girls. One of their file was Edwin Thompson Denig, married to an Assiniboin woman, and author of excellent descriptions of the religious and social life on the northern plains. The bulk of his contributions was without reference to the source incorporated in F. V. Hayden's ethnographical survey from this area;[21] it is only in the last decades that justice has been given to Denig by publishing his work to its full extent.[22] Another squaw man was Henry R. Schoolcraft who served as Indian agent at Sault Ste. Marie and was married to an Ojibway woman; his prodigious work in Indian ethnography marks a new phase in American anthropology.[23]

Schoolcraft was also a prominent figure from the point of view of comparative religion. His classical edition of Ojibway oral traditions, *Algic Researches, presents the* first collection of North American myths and legends.[24] W. Blackwood, 1875; Danish ed., 2 vols., Copenhagen, quite correct, since, to quote Thompson, "he reshaped the stories to suit his own literary taste."[25] As pointed out by Williams, however, this reworking has not invalidated the tales,[26] and there is certainly no reason to discard them as religious and mythological documents. (The confusion between the Algonkian culture hero Manabozho and the Iroquoian politician Hiawatha was brought about by Longfellow who used Schoolcraft's materials but interpreted them with *licentia poetica*.) Schoolcraft's work stood by itself for several decades; not until 1866 did there appear something similar, Rink's Eskimo tales and traditions,[27] and the first Indian myth collection of importance after Schoolcraft was Leland's Algonkian tales from New England in 1884.[28]

Many Indian legends and much information on beliefs, cults, and

Shawnese Traditions (Ann Arbor: Occasional Contributions from the Museum of Anthropology of the University of Michigan IX, 1939); Mary Eastman, *Dahcotah; or, Life and Legends of the Sioux around Fort Snelling* (New York: J. Wiley, 1849); Geronimo Boscana, *Chinigchinich* (new ed.; Santa Ana, California: Fine Arts, 1933).

[21] Ferdinand Vandeveer Hayden, *Contributions to the Ethnography and Philology of the Indian Tribes of the Missouri Valley* (Philadelphia: *Transactions of the American Philosophical Society* XII, 1862); cf. John C. Ewers's introduction to Edwin Thompson Denig, *Five Indian Tribes of the Upper Missouri* (Norman: University of Oklahoma, 1961), pp. xxxivff.

[22] Edwin Thompson Denig, *Indian Tribes of the Upper Missouri* (Washington, D.C.: Bureau of American Ethnology, 46th Annual Report, 1930), pp. 375–628; see also the work by Denig mentioned in n. 21 above.

[23] Cf. Hallowell, *op. cit.*, p. 42.

[24] Henry Rowe Schoolcraft, *Algic Researches, Comprising Inquiries Respecting the Mental Characteristics of the North American Indians*, 2 vols. (New York: Harper & Brothers, 1839).

[25] Stith Thompson, *Tales of the North American Indians* (Cambridge: Harvard University, 1929), p. xv.

[26] Mentor L. Williams (ed.), *Schoolcraft's Indian Legends* (East Lansing: Michigan State University, 1956), pp. xx-xxi.

[27] Hinrich Rink, *Tales and Traditions of the Eskimo* (Edinburgh: W. Blackwood, 1875; Danish ed., 2 vols., Copenhagen, 1866–71).

[28] Charles G. Leland, *The Algonquin Legends of New England* (Boston: Houghton, Mifflin, 1884). This work covers the Abnaki, Penobscot, Malecite, and Micmac Indians.

medicine men are included in Schoolcraft's famous six-volume work on the Indian tribes of the United States, where agents and missionaries have given their knowledge of the aborigines under their custody.[29] The credit for having collected this enormous material goes to Schoolcraft. It is a pity, however, that this first presentation of the different Indian religions east of the Rocky Mountains is so badly arranged and poorly digested.

Part of Schoolcraft's material in the latter work found its way into the first European contribution to the religious history of the American Indians, the Basel Professor Johann Georg Müller's *Geschichte der Amerikanischen Urreligionen*.[30] This is a comparative investigation divided into two parts, the first of which deals with the "savages," while the second and major part treats the "Kulturvölker." The chapter on "Die nordamerikanischen Rothäute" is the first effort to systematize North American religions. Thus, the author makes a distinction between the "Kulturreligion" in the southeren part of the continent, characterized by sun worship, temples, and priests, and the "Naturreligion" in the North, manifested in beliefs in spirits (guardian spirits) and fetishism (medicine bundles).[31] Oddly enough, Müller considers the first-mentioned type of religion as being the oldest. Many paragraphs are devoted to the Supreme Being who is interpreted as a personification of the natural forces and who owes his existence to the sun worship of the agricultural peoples.

Clearly Müller's work was composed before the evolutionistic doctrines of Lubbock, Tylor, and Spencer had revolutionized the ideas of religious development (Comte's contributions passed rather unnoticed outside of sociology, and Müller does not refer to him). It is interesting to note that the leading social evolutionist, Lewis Henry Morgan, some few years before had published his classical account of the Iroquois, still the best monograph on the subject, and the first thorough ethnographical description of an Indian tribe.[32] Apparently Müller was not acquainted with this work, but he would not have been surprised if he had read its three chapters on religion: there is no evolutionistic tendency there, and the Great Spirit stands first and foremost in

[29] Henry Rowe Schoolcraft, *Historical and Statistical Information Respecting the History, Condition and Prospects of the Indian Tribes of the United States*, 6 vols. (Philadelphia: J. B. Lippincott, 1851–57).

[30] Johann Georg Müller, *Geschichte der Amerikanischen Urreligionen* (Basel: Schweighausersche, 1855). As is well known, Müller was the first professor in the history of religion, and since 1837 he had regularly held lectures (between 6:00 and 7:00 A.M.!) in polytheistic religions at the theological faculty in Basel. Cf. Eberhard Vischer, "Die Lehrstühle und der Unterricht an der Theologischen Fakultät Basels Seit der Reformation," *Festschrift zur Feier des 450 Jährigen Bestehens der Universität Basel* (Basel: Universität Basel, 1910), p. 205.

[31] Müller, *op. cit.*, p. 51. Cf. Speck's division of North American religions in southern sun cult and northern animal worship, e.g., Frank G. Speck, *Naskapi* (Norman: University of Oklahoma, 1935), p. 87.

[32] Lewis H. Morgan, *League of the Ho-de-no sau-nee or Iroquois*, 2 vols. (New York: Dodd, Mead, 1851).

the pantheon as "creator, ruler and preserver."[33] As a matter of fact, Morgan underlines his important position among the Iroquois in a way which would scarcely be acceptable to present-day scholars in the field of Iroquois culture.

We find, on the other hand, in Schoolcraft's work and in separate articles from this time some examples which show that people who have been working with the Indians—in particular the missionaries—subscribe to the idea that the Great Spirit was no original Indian conception. Two missionaries with the Eastern Dakota, Riggs and Pond, cherished this idea: they maintained that Wakan Tanka, the Dakota godhead, was patterned on Christian concepts of God.[34] This standpoint was soon to be supported by the evolutionistic doctrine, and the pronouncements of Riggs and Pond were long indorsed by adherents of evolutionism.

While in this way a new view on Indian religion slowly grew forth, the material on Indian religion augmented in an accelerating tempo. It increased, as a matter of fact, as the frontier pushed further westward and new territories with Indian population were encircled by European civilization. Father De Smet visited the warlike tribes on the Northern Plains and penetrated Indian groups far up in the Plateau country, everywhere learning about their religions, and the army surgeon, Washington Matthews, collected preliminary information on the beliefs and ceremonies of the Hidatsa on the Missouri River.[35] The Southwest was still rather unknown. The same secrecy which still today keeps anthroplogists away from the cultic performances in the ceremonial chambers, *kivas* or *estufas*, was even more prevalent in the nineteenth century, preventing closer investigations. In California, however, a journalist by the name of Stephen Powers collected cultural and religious materials from almost all the different tribes and tribelets, and after having been printed in the *Overland Monthly* of San Francisco, all this information was published in a comprehensive volume, *Tribes of California*, which was, according to Kroeber, "the best introduction to the subject."[36]

Even from the far North, valuable information on Indian religion started to flow in. Shortly before the Alaskan purchase was made by the

---

[33] *Ibid.* (1901 ed.), p. 145.

[34] Gideon H. Pond, "Dakota Superstitions," *Minnesota Historical Collections* II/3 (1867), p. 34; Stephen Return Riggs, "The Theogony of the Sioux," *American Antiquarian* II/4 (1880), p. 265. Cf. also Samuel William Pond, "The Dakotas or Sioux in Minnesota as They Were in 1834," *Minnesota Historical Collections* XII (1908), pp. 424–25.

[35] Hiram Martin Chittenden and Alfred Talbot Richardson (eds.), *Life, Letters and Travels of Father Pierre-Jean De Smet, S.J.*, 4 vols. (New York: F. P. Harper, 1905); Washington Matthews, *Ethnography and Philology of the Hidatsa Indians* (Washington, D.C.: U.S. Geological Survey, Miscellaneous Publication VII, 1877). Matthews later wrote extensive papers on Navajo rituals and beliefs (see text and n. 52 below).

[36] Stephen Powers, *Tribes of California* (Washington, D.C.: Contributions to North American Ethnology III, 1877). Cf. Alfred Louis Kroeber, *Handbook of the Indians of California* (Washington, D.C.: Bureau of American Ethnology Bulletin LXXVIII, 1925), p. ix.

United States, a Russian subject, Holmberg, published notes on northern Tlingit and Alaskan Eskimo religion.[37] Thirty years afterward, a German traveler, Aurel Krause, wrote down his observations on Tlingit religion and shamanism from the northwestern Pacific Coast.[38] Farther down the same coast, James Swan investigated Haida and, even more, Nootka religion.[39] Petitot, a Catholic missionary, reported on the cultural and religious conditions of the Athapascan tribes in the Mackenzie River basin. He negotiated some of the finest accounts of northern Athapascan religion that we own today, contributions by modern investigators like Osgood and Honigmann not excepted.[40] In this connection, we discard his fantastic theories about a relation between the primitive religions of northern Canada and the biblical stories.[41] Petitot had a successor in another Catholic missionary, A. G. Morice, who wrote several informative papers on Athapascan, in particular Carrier, religion.[42]

The growing knowledge of the religions of western North America made it possible for the learned historian Hubert H. Bancroft of San Francisco to give a synopsis of these religions in his impressive publication set on the Indians of the Pacific territories.[43] It is true that this work mostly concerns the Mexican high cultures, but the primitive Indians are nevertheless treated extensively, and in the third volume of the series there is a systematic analysis of western Indian religions. The presentation is founded on current ideas in the study of religion, in particular the views of Herbert Spencer and Max Müller.

Hitherto a great deal of the extant knowledge of North American religion had been gathered from the works of dedicated amateurs or occasional observers. This situation was now about to change. Nevertheless, the amateurs continued to bring in valuable materials, although these soon were overshadowed by professional ethnological contributions. In some cases unjustifiably so, for there are amateurs' accounts which reveal a deeper insight into aboriginal religion than the works of their professional colleagues. In this connection, it is sufficient to bring to mind such amateur explorers as Grinnell and McClintock.

---

[37] Henrik Johan Holmberg, *Ethnographische Skizzen über die Völker des Russischen Amerika* (Helsinki: Acta Societatis Scientiarum Fennicae, 1855).

[38] Aurel Krause, *Die Tlinkit-Indianer* (Jena: H. Costenoble, 1885; English ed., 1956).

[39] James Gilchrist Swan, *The Indians of Cape Flattery* (Washington, D.C.: Smithsonian Institution, 1870).

[40] Émile F. S. Petitot, *Monographie des Déné-Dindjiés* (Paris: E. Leroux, 1876); and *Traditions Indiennes du Canada Nord-ouest* (Paris: Maisonneuve Frères et C. Leclerc, 1886).

[41] Émile F. S. Petitot, *Accord des Mythologies dans la Cosmogonie des Danites Arctiques* (Paris: É. Bouillon, 1890).

[42] Adrian Gabriel Morice, *The Western Dénés—Their Manners and Customs* (Toronto: Proceedings of the Canadian Institute VII 1889).

[43] Hubert Howe Bancroft, *The Native Races of the Pacific States*, 5 vols. (New York: D. Appleton, 1875–76).

George Bird Grinnell was a naturalist by profession and, among other things, founder of the Audubon Society. During his many trips to the western wilderness, he became acquainted with three important Plains Indian tribes, the Cheyenne, the Blackfoot, and the Pawnee. He had a rare gift of understanding these people, not least their religion. His books on Blackfoot and Pawnee tales and customs are invaluable to the students of religion.[44] His best success was, however, with the Cheyenne Indians who were his favorites; his well-known monograph on this tribe is also one of the best treatises on Plains Indian religion.[45]

Walter McClintock mediates to us the very atmosphere of Blackfoot religion.[46] It is true that the myths and tales he recounts are too freely rendered to satisfy scientific demands, but his accounts of rites and beliefs deserve much attention.

THE EARLY AMERICAN ANTHROPOLOGISTS

When the frontier had reached the Pacific, and the last great Indian uprising had been crushed on the Northern Plains, professional anthropology entered the scene, and a more systematic field research on Indian religions came about. True, the first anthropologists were not trained in their own domain but were recruited from other fields, and some of them cannot be considered academic in a right sense. Nevertheless, the organization of Indian investigations under the Bureau of Ethnology, founded in 1879 as a subsection of the famous Smithsonian Institution, marks a new era in the research on Indian religions.

It was largely due to the initiative of Major John Wesley Powell, first director of the Bureau, that the ethnological work became intensified. Mythology and "natural religion" were, according to Powell, integrating parts of the science of anthropology, and in the first annual report of the Bureau he presented an outline of Indian mythology characterized by a barbaric terminology of supposed mythological stages and accompanied by a few Ute and Paiute myths which he had noted down in the field.[47] Powell was an evolutionist, and he had the following to say about the North American Indians: "All these tribes are found in the higher stages of savagery, or the lower stages of barbarism, and their mythologics are found to be zoötheistic among the lowest, physitheistic/i.e., with gods of Nature/among the highest, and a great number of tribes are found in a transition stage; for zoötheism is found to be a characteristic of savagery, and physitheism of

---

[44] George Bird Grinnell, *Pawnee Hero Stories and Folk-Tales* (New York: Forest and Stream, 1889); and *Blackfoot Lodge Tales* (New York: C. Scribner's Sons, 1892).

[45] George Bird Grinnell, *The Cheyenne Indians*, 2 vols. (New Haven: Yale University, 1923).

[46] Walter McClintock, *The Old North Trail* (London: Macmillan, 1910).

[47] John Wesley Powell, *Sketch of the Mythology of the North American Indians* (Washington, D.C.: Bureau of Ethnology, First Annual Report, 1881).

barbarism, using the terms as they have been defined by Morgan."[48] Powell created four stages of "mythological philosophy" which he linked with Morgan's evolutionistic chain: Savagery–Barbarism–Civilization (to which he later added Enlightenment, a final stage of highest cultural refinement).

Far more important than the evolutionistic schemes were, however, the contributions to the factual knowledge of Indian religions which these early ethnologists and their non-professional cooperators made. The important series of tribal monographs under the auspices of the Bureau of Ethnology was now introduced, largely on Powell's initiative, and therewith a bulk of descriptions of Indian religions was presented within their cultural frame. Mrs. Matilda Coxe Stevenson, who for many years had associated with the otherwise inaccessible Pueblo Indians, wrote two informative papers on Sia and Zuni religion; the latter paper in particular has become a classical monograph.[49] Closer knowledge of Pueblo religion was now accumulating in articles by Mrs. Stevenson, F. H. Cushing, and J. W. Fewkes. Cushing investigated the Zuni and has given us several papers on their myths and their "fetishes," that is, sacred objects associated with the gods.[50] Fewkes wrote a large collection of articles on the Hopi (Tusayan) Indians of Arizona, most of them concerned with rituals and cultic paraphernalia.[51] The primitive neighbors of the Pueblo Indians, the Navajo, were at the same time described by the physician Washington Matthews (mentioned in the foregoing) who, among other things, gave good accounts of some of their myths and ceremonies.[52] McGee's monograph on the Seri in northwestern Mexico may also be mentioned in this connection. Most of the papers on the Southwest adduced hereto had an evolutionistic bias, and some of them—for instance those by Cushing and McGee—reveal the uncontrolled imagination of their authors.[53]

Also, Indian religions in other areas began to be covered through the publication of ethnographical monographs: MacCauley wrote on Seminole religion (Florida), Hoffman on Menomini religion (Wisconsin), Mooney on Kiowa religion (Oklahoma), Alice Fletcher on Teton Dakota religion (South Dakota and Wyoming), Gatschet on Klamath religion (Oregon), etc. Besides these tribal accounts there were other papers published which, because of

---

[48] *Ibid.*, p. 39.

[49] Matilda Coxe Stevenson, *The Zuñi Indians. Their Mythology, Esoteric Fraternities, and Ceremonies* (Washington, D.C.: Bureau of American Ethnology, 23rd Annual Report, 1904).

[50] Frank Hamilton Cushing, *Outlines of Zuñi Creation Myths* (Washington, D.C.: Bureau of Ethnology, 13th Annual Report, 1896).

[51] Jesse Walter Fewkes, *Hopi Katcinas* (Washington, D.C.: Bureau of American Ethnology, 21st Annual Report, 1903).

[52] Washington Matthews, *The Mountain Chant* (Washington, D.C.: Bureau of Ethnology, 5th Annual Report, 1887); and *Navaho Legends* (Boston: American Folklore Society Memoirs V, 1897).

[53] Robert H. Lowie, "Reminiscences of Anthropological Currents in America Half a Century Ago," *American Anthropologist* LVIII (1956), pp. 996, 999.

their exclusive concentration on religion, deserve our particular interest. To these works belong Bourke's account of Apache medicine men, J. O. Dorsey's careful analysis of Sioux religions, Hoffman's description of an Ojibway medicine ritual, and Mooney's vivid study of the Ghost Dance.[54] Dorsey's paper gives the whole range of rituals and religious ideas in the diverse Siouan groups. He relies extensively on missionary records and adopts, for example, Pond's and Riggs's views of the godhead, referred to in the foregoing. Hoffman is concerned with the initiation rites into the different degrees in the Grand Medicine Society of the Ojibway and produces informative birchbark drawings of the initiation scenes used by the Indians as mnemonic devices. Mooney's remarkable monograph on the Ghost Dance is the first and truly classical account of religious acculturation in an American Indian society. Mooney also published some accounts of Cherokee sacred formulas, myths, and cults, thereby paving the way for a deeper understanding of the Indian religions of the Southeast.[55] He was later followed in this topic by Bushnell and, in particular, by Swanton who made comprehensive contributions in this field (see below). Other early ethnological papers dealt with complex religious ceremonies, such as Alice Fletcher's description of the Pawnee Hako ritual,[56] or with burials and funerary customs, a subject introduced by Yarrow[57] (and later followed up by Bushnell, Moore, MacLeod, and others). Finally, let us also mention Colonel Mallery's extensive presentations of Indian picture-writing and underlying beliefs in two reports issued by the Bureau of Ethnology.[58]

The interest in Indian folklore and mythology now grew strong. First, two important myth collections were published by gifted amateurs: Rand's Micmac legends from Newfoundland and Curtin's Wintun mythologies from California.[59] Jeremiah Curtin was a journalist like his predecessor

[54] John G. Bourke, *The Medicine-men of the Apache* (Washington, D.C.: Bureau of Ethnology, Ninth Annual Report, 1892); James Owen Dorsey, *A Study of Siouan Cults* (Washington, D.C.: Bureau of Ethnology, 11th Annual Report, 1894); Walter James Hoffman, *The Midē'wiwin or "Grand Medicine Society" of the Ojibwa* (Washington, D.C.: Bureau of Ethnology, Seventh Annual Report, 1891); James Mooney, *The Ghost-Dance Religion and the Sioux Outbreak of 1890* (Washington, D.C.: Bureau of Ethnology, 14th Annual Report, Part 2, 1896).

[55] Cf. especially James Mooney, *The Sacred Formulas of the Cherokees* (Washington, D.C.: Bureau of Ethnology, Seventh Annual Report, 1891).

[56] Alice C. Fletcher, *The Hako: A Pawnee Ceremony* (Washington, D.C.: Bureau of American Ethnology, 22nd Annual Report, Part 2, 1904).

[57] H. C. Yarrow, *Introduction to the Study of Mortuary Customs among the North American Indians* (Washington, D.C.: Bureau of Ethnology, 1880); cf. Yarrow, *A Further Contribution to the Study of the Mortuary Customs of the North American Indians* (Washington, D.C.: Bureau of Ethnology, First Annual Report, 1881).

[58] Garrick Mallery, *Pictographs of the North American Indians* (Washington, D.C.: Bureau of Ethnology, Fourth Annual Report, 1886), in particular pp. 188ff.; and *Picture-writing of the American Indians* (Washington, D.C.: Bureau of Ethnology, Tenth Annual Report, 1893).

[59] Silas T. Rand, *Legends of the Micmacs* (New York: Longmans, Green, 1894); Jeremiah Curtin, *Creation Myths of Primitive America* (Boston: Little, Brown, 1898).

Powers, and he molded the Indian tales to conform to the romantic expectations of his public. Moreover, his statements on the Supreme Being (who is described as a lofty, ethical divinity), which have inspired Wilhelm Schmidt's interpretation of the North American high gods, emanate from only one informant, presumably a private philosopher.[60] Second, professional ethnologists and folklorists, who were also very often linguists as well, made careful recordings of myths, legends, and tales (unfortunately, they did not always keep the categories apart, particularly not if their aims were folkloristic in a general sense). One of these myth recorders was Mooney, another a diligent student of Iroquoian (Tuscarora) descent, Hewitt.[61] Many important myths were printed in the *Journal of American Folklore* and its memoir series which started to appear about this time (1888).[62]

The authors of the many papers on myth and religion did not always confine themselves to recording and editing. During these final decades of the last century, we discern a tendency to theorize on American Indian religion, for instance, in Powell's essay on mythology (cf. above). Powell's adversary in matters of anthropological principles, the first American professor of ethnology, D. G. Brinton, was, like Powell, an evolutionist, but presented different points of view on the question of religious development. Brinton was convinced that the American Indian idea of a Great Spirit was post-Christian. He claimed that the different terms for such a being "are entirely of modern origin, coined at the suggestion of missionaries, applied to the white man's God"[63] This theory had, as we know, a great following among later evolutionists. Brinton's argument suffered, however, from inconsistency in the handling of the materials, as Andrew Lang has demonstrated.[64] Thus, he considered—quite erroneously, for the rest—that the Algonkian culture hero Michabou ("the great Hare") was "the Father of All," and he further believed that his appellation "the great Hare" was a

---

[60] Cora Du Bois, *Wintu Ethnography* (Berkeley: University of California Publications in American Archaeology and Ethnology XXXVI/1, 1935), pp. 72–73. Cf. Curtin, *op. cit.*, pp. 3ff.

[61] James Mooney, *Myths of the Cherokee* (Washington, D.C.: Bureau of American Ethnology, 19th Annual Report, Part 1, 1900); J. N. B. Hewitt, *Iroquoian Cosmology* (Washington, D.C.: Bureau of American Ethnology, 21st and 43rd Annual Reports, 1903, 1908); Jeremiah Curtin and J. N. B. Hewitt, *Seneca Fiction, Legends, and Myths* (Washington, D.C.: Bureau of American Ethnology, 32nd Annual Report, 1918).

[62] In the first number of this journal, James O. Dorsey presented Sioux myths and tales. The dedication to Indian mythology and beliefs characterized the journal for many decades to come; cf. Tristram P. Coffin, *An Analytical Index to the Journal of American Folklore* (Philadelphia: Publications of the American Folklore Society VII, 1958), pp. 166ff. This interest, which was maintained by the anthropologists in the society, ceased, however, in the 1940s (see William N. Fenton *et al.*, "Report of the American Folklore Society to the Commission on Humanities," *Journal of American Folklore*, Suppl. (April, 1964), p. 32.

[63] Brinton, *op. cit.*, p. 53.

[64] Andrew Lang, *Myth, Ritual and Religion*, 2 vols. (2d ed.; London: Longmans, Green, 1899), I, pp. xxvii-xxviii; II, pp. 81ff.

linguistic misunderstanding of an earlier import "the great Light."[65] In other words, an aboriginal Great Spirit in spite of all!

Although he had written a monograph on Delaware Indian religion,[66] Brinton was not conscious of the importance of ethnic differences in religious expressions and interpretations. This was certainly due partly to the fact that he never conducted any field research but mainly to his inclination for speculation and "armchair theorizing." In any case, this man of "unusual erudition and exceptional cultivation," "deeply saturated with the European atmosphere"—I am here quoting Lowie[67]—applied viewpoints on aboriginal religions similar to those of Bastian. Thus, he considered that the same myth in neighboring tribes was the result of psychic unity.[68] Careless statements of this type make Brinton's study of New World mythology (which appeared as early as 1868) and other works of this prolific writer[69] less attractive from a scientific point of view.

Brinton's extreme doctrine of parallelism was challenged by such anthropologists as Putnam and Mason and definitely defeated by Boas in the latter's study of Northwestern Indian mythology.[70] Boas rejuvenated and reoriented the American Indian investigations which for so long had been under the sway of a farily crude evolutionism. Boas had a European background. Before discussing his contributions to our subject, let us glance at the European americanistic studies at this time.

THE EARLY EUROPEAN CONTRIBUTORS

In their outlook on Indian religions and in their theorizing, most of the American students quoted here had been influenced by European scentific progress, European thought, and European evolutionism. This impact of Europe on America can be discerned in American anthropology up to the 1930s when a slow severing of the unitive bonds set in. The tendencies in present-day American anthropology are in many respects far removed from European research on culture and religion.

With the exception of travelers like the Prince of Wied and Krause and the author of that unique book on New World religion, Müller, very few of the European students of the nineteenth century contributed to the study of

---

[65] Brinton, op. cit., pp. 176ff.

[66] Daniel G. Brinton, The Lenâpé and Their Legends (Philadelphia: Library of Aboriginal American Literature, V, 1885).

[67] Lowie, "Reminiscences," op. cit., p. 997.

[68] Daniel G. Brinton, Myths of the New World (1st ed.; New York: Leypoldt & Holt, 1868), pp. 172–73; see also Religions of Primitive Peoples (New York and London: G. P. Putnam's Sons, 1897), pp. 117–18.

[69] Cf. Daniel G. Brinton, American Hero-Myths (Philadelphia: H. C. Watts, 1882).

[70] Franz Boas, Indianische Sagen von der Nord-pacifischen Küste Amerikas (Berlin: A. Asher, 1895); a summary of the results of this investigation may be found in Boas, "The Growth of Indian Mythologies," Journal of American Folklore IX (1896), pp. 1–11.

American Indian religions. America was far away, and the religions of its primitive aborigines were not of the same paramount importance to comparative religion as the religions of the literate peoples, Semitic (Robertson Smith) and Indo-European (Max Müller) in particular. Nevertheless, the evolutionistic reconstructions of the latter part of the century required a perusal of the evidence in the field of primitive religion, and much material on American Indian religion—obtained from the Jesuits and Schoolcraft in the first place—was included in the pioneer works by Lubbock, Waitz, Tylor, Frazer, and others. North American religion was, in Europe, more or less a curious survival from the childhood of humanity, and in the writings of the historians of religion it was devoid of significant characterisitcs which set it apart from other primitive religions.

At the turn of the century, there were several European ethnologists who specialized in the field of Indian culture and religion, but their interests were mainly concentrated on South America (Ehrenreich, Koch-Grünberg, von den Steinen), or on Mexico (Preuss, Seler). Ehrenreich and Preuss made casual notes on North American religions, but these were not very significant. On the other hand, we find an incipient occupation with North America as manifested in treatises on burial customs by Preuss and Bahnson,[71] or in the series of articles on Algonkian ideas of life after death appearing in the *Revue de l'Histoire des Religions* in Paris.[72] Mostly, however, North American aboriginal religion was dealt with in connection with evidence from other religions and in order to prove certain presumed evolutionary stages. In several cases, the respective authors made interesting (if not always lasting) contributions to our understanding of Indian religions.

Let us look at some examples. Breysig, a Berlin professor with a very rigid idea of unilinear evolutionistic sequences, founded his theory of the origin and development of the "Heilbringer" (culture hero) on North American evidence. Proceeding from the conceptions of the Algonkian and Iroquoian Indians, he tried to demonstrate how the theriomorphic spirits turned into Heilbringer gods, now human, now animal-like, and how they finally resulted in monotheistic divinities.[73] In England, Frazer extensively discussed animal ceremonialism in North America in connection with his investigations of ritual killing.[74] He was also the first to put together and evaluate the material on American Indian totemism and guardian-spirit

---

[71] Konrad Theodor Preuss, "Die Begräbnisarten der Amerikaner und Nordostasiaten" (dissertation, Königsberg, 1894); Kristian Bahnson, "Gravskikke hos Amerikanske Folk," *Aarbog for Nordisk Oldkyndighed og Historie* (Copenhagen: Thieles, 1882), pp. 128–215.

[72] E. Laetitia Moon-Conard, "Les Idées des Indiens Algonquins Relatives á la Vie d'Outre-tombe," *Revue de l'Histoire des Religions* XLII (1900), pp. 9–49, 200–274.

[73] Kurt Breysig, *Die Entstehung des Gottesgedankens und der Heilbringer* (Berlin: G. Bondi, 1905).

[74] James George Frazer, *The Golden Bough*, 12 vols. (3rd ed.; London: Macmillan, 1912), Part 5, II, pp. 204ff.

beliefs and practices.[75] In Sweden, Reuterskiöld, later professor of the history of religions at Uppsala University, published a doctoral dissertation in which he analyzed the totemism of the Northwest Coast Indians, in particular the Kwakiutl.[76]

By this time, however, the tide had turned; ethnologists had largely refuted evolutionism or were slowly moving over toward historico-geographical studies. On the other hand, European students of religion remained in the grip of evolutionism for a long time, and it is characteristic that Reuterskiöld's evolutionistic treatise was founded on the materials and, partly, theories that had been presented by the antievolutionistic Boas.

The new historicism in European ethnology may be traced back to Ratzel (in the 1880s) and, above all, to Frobenius, Ankermann, and Graebner (at the turn of the century).[77] It is interesting, however, to find that the man who first proved the fallacies of unilinear evolutionism, already in the beginning of the 1890s, was Franz Boas, the German-born American scholar.

---

[75] James George Frazer, *Totemism and Exogamy* III (3rd ed.; London: Macmillan, 1910), pp. 370–456.

[76] Edgar Reuterskiöld, *Till Flågan om Uppkomsten af Sakramentala Måltider med Särskild Hänsyn till Totemismen* (Uppsala: Almqvist & Wiksells, 1908).

[77] See Robert Heine-Geldern, "One Hundred Years of Ethnological Theory in the German-speaking Countries: Some Milestones," *Current Anthropology* V (1964), pp. 407–18.

THE BOAS SCHOOL

THE WORK OF FRANZ BOAS

As is well known, Franz Boas rose to a towering eminence in American anthropology.[1] His influence was great in anthropological theory, and he also substantially contributed in the investigation of North American aboriginal cultures through his own fieldwork on the Northwest Coast, through his training of squaw men and Indians to record Indian traditions, and through the inspiration he gave his pupils to spend years among the Indians, learn their languages, and write down their culture contents.[2] We may also, with a certain justification, speak about a Boas period in the study of American Indian religion, roughly covering the years 1892–1925.[3]

This is not the place to judge Boas's contributions to anthropological theory and his importance as an anthropologist in the field. We are concerned here with his achievements in American Indian religion and his influence on comparative religious theory. Partly, of course, this influence was a consequence of his general anthropological finds and theories, since, as we shall see, he viewed religion as an expression of the same dynamic factors which operated on culture. According to the views of Boas, diffusion, for instance, was a mechanism in material culture, but it also played a role in religion, and partcularly in mythology.

It is interesting to note that Boas arrived in North America in 1888 at the instigation of E. B. Tylor, the father of "animism," who was then chairman of the British Association for the Advancement of Science. Boas was sent to the tribes on the coast of western Canada; his first report from this exploratory journey dealt with the religious ideas of the Tlingit, Haida, Tsimshian, Kwakiutl, Coast Salish, and Kutenai tribes.[4] This was not the first time Boas made fieldwork in the New World—he had visited the Central Eskimo five years earlier and composed a substantial paper on their culture

---

[1] Clyde Kluckhohn, "Developments in the Field of Anthropology in the Twentieth Century," *Cahiers d'Histoire Mondiale* III/2 (Neuchâtel, 1957), pp. 754–77.

[2] See the following works: Alfred Louis Kroeber *et al.*, *Franz Boas 1858–1942* (Menasha, Wisconsin: American Anthropological Association Memoirs LXI, 1943); Melville Herskovits, *Franz Boas* (New York: Scribner, 1953); Walter Goldschmidt (ed.), *The Anthropology of Franz Boas* (Menasha, Wisconsin: American Anthropological Association Memoirs LXXXIX, 1959).

[3] This time span for the domination of Boas and his pupils was suggested by Betty J. Meggers, "Recent Trends in American Ethnology," *American Anthropologist* XLVIII (1946), p. 176.

[4] Franz Boas, "Preliminary Notes on the Indians of British Columbia," *Report on the 58th Meeting of the British Association for the Advancement of Science* (1889), pp. 236–42.

and religion[5]—but from then on he worked almost exclusively among the Northwest Coast tribes, and stayed in America. The southern Kwakiutl (Vancouver Island and vicinity) soon emerged as his "special tribe."

It is not easy to judge Boas's contribution to religion, since, as mentioned before, this topic only occurred as a by-product in his work. His ideal of research was in 1896 "a detailed study of customs in their relation to the total culture of the tribe practising them, in connection with an investigation of their geographical distribution among neighboring tribes."[6] His object was "to find the *processes* by which certain stages of culture have developed."[7] Although in later years he reformulated the aims and methods of his research, their import remained the same. In an article written during his last years, Boas asserts that in his early teaching, when he fought evolutionism and other—as he says—"old speculative theories," he stressed the necessity of the study of dissemination. "When I thought that these *historical* methods were firmly established I began to stress, about 1910, the problems of cultural dynamics, of integration of culture and of the interaction between individual and society."[8] It matters little if, as Benedict thinks, the change in methods occurred at a later date,[9] the main thing is that Boas slowly and gradually altered his approach to the study of culture, laying more and more stress on functional problems (and thus contributing to the emergence of functionalism).

These theoretical trends are reflected in Boas's works on mythology. He found in the materials of myth and folklore excellent instruments to prove his theses of culture. His early monograph on Northwest Indian mythology, referred to above, demonstrated the diffusion of tales and motifs among the North Pacific Indians. In order to substantiate further investigations along the same line, Boas collected, interpreted, and published Bella Coola, Chinook, Kwakiutl, Tsimshian, and Kutenai myths and tales. The task which he set for himself was, in Jacobs' words, "to get the field research done, to publish it accurately, and to bring together evidence to display dissemination and amalgamation."[10] Jacobs has pointed out several deficiencies in the recording and presentation of Indian tales by Boas, for instance, the fact that "Boas's fieldwork did not always establish a narrative as myth or tale; in some instances he appears to have neglected to inquire how natives classified

---

[5] Franz Boas, *The Central Eskimo* (Washington, D.C.: Bureau of Ethnology, 6th Annual Report, 1888).

[6] Franz Boas, "The Limitations of the Comparative Method of Anthropology," Franz Boas, *Race, Language and Culture* (New York: Free Press, 1940), p. 276.

[7] *Ibid.*

[8] Franz Boas, "History and Science in Anthropology: A Reply," *ibid.*, p. 311.

[9] Ruth Fulton Benedict, "Franz Boas as an Ethnologist," *American Anthroplogical Association Memoirs* LXI (1943), p. 31.

[10] Melville Jacobs, "Folklore," *American Anthroplogical Association Memoirs* LXXXIX (1959), p. 120.

their stories."[11] This is an important objection and shows how little awareness Boas had of the viewpoints pertaining to the study of religions.

In his imposing work on Tsimshian mythology, Boas illustrated how mythological themes and plots were distributed and recombined in the Northwest Coast area. In a way, this important paper represents a perfection of his treatise on Indian mythologies from 1895. However, it goes further, for the author also demonstrates how Tsimshian mythology reflected Tsimshian culture.[12] The functionalistic perspective is thus evident here, and it was even more accentuated in a later work on Kwakiutl mythology.[13] Boas's pupils and followers further elaborated on this technique: Clara Ehrlich used it in her study of Crow mythology, Radin in his reconstruction of Winnebago history, Wittfogel and Goldfrank in their investigation of Pueblo mythology and society, and Katherine Spencer in her study of the Navajo origin myth.[14] Research along these lines has, of course, indirectly a certain value for the understanding of mythology. Radin, for instance, states that among the Winnebago the myth reflects the culture to a very slight extent, whereas the traditional tale is well integrated with aboriginal culture.[15] On the whole, however, emphasis is on culture in this type of studies, and this applies in particular to the studies made by Boas.

The criticism delivered here should not conceal the fact that, more than any other anthropologist, Boas has published a treasure of Indian myths and promoted the publication of such myths. We are indebted to him for bringing a whole corpus of Indian myths before the public in the memoir series of the American Folklore Society, in the publications of the American Ethnological Society, and in the publications of the Jesup North Pacific Expedition.

Boas stressed the importance of thorough fieldwork, in spite of the fact that he abhorred the experience of fieldwork.[16] He himself made, and trained his pupils to make, intense and varying collections of ethnographic materials. Says Reichard, "The strongest rocks in Boas's self-built monument are his texts, his belief that what people record of themselves in their own words will in the last analysis reveal their motivations and ideas most accurately."[17] The result of these efforts of Boas and his pupils is, as we

[11] *Ibid.*, p. 132.

[12] Franz Boas, *Tsimshian Mythology* (Washington, D.C.: Bureau of American Ethnology, 31st Annual Report, 1916).

[13] Franz Boas, *Kwakiutl Culture as Reflected in Mythology* (New York: American Folklore Society Memoirs XXVIII, 1935).

[14] See Katherine Spencer, *Reflection of Social Life in the Navaho Origin Myth* (Albuquerque: University of New Mexico Publications in Anthropology III, 1947), pp. 7ff.

[15] Paul Radin, "Literary Aspects of Winnebago Mythology," *Journal of American Folklore* XXXIX (1926), pp. 18–52.

[16] Jacobs, *op. cit.*, pp. 126–27.

[17] Gladys A. Reichard, "Franz Boas and Folklore," *American Anthropological Association Memoirs* LXI (1943), p. 55.

know, the finest series of monographs on primitive culture and religion that exists today.

As mentioned before, Boas's own contributions concerned mainly the Kwakiutl Indians on whom he published one volume after another. Besides the mythological texts, of which there are quite a few collections, we find accounts and texts referring to religious beliefs and religious rites. His famous paper on the secret societies, a classic in American anthropology, should be particularly mentioned in this connection.[18] It inspired him to psychological insights into the relationship between the religions of the philosopher and the layman—insights which a few years later stimulated Radin.[19] Some ten years after Boas died, the question was raised whether in his Kwakiutl papers he had described more than the culture and religion of the aristocracy (for these Indians had an interesting pseudo-stratified social system). Ray suggested that anthropologists should now concentrate on "the customs of the lower classes" and expected that "whole new complexes may be found, e.g., there may emerge a well-developed guardian spirit concept and quest similar to that of Puget Sound."[20] This interpretation of Kwakiutl society in terms of class concepts is, however, scarcely justified; as pointed out by Codere, the Kwakiutl had no class differentiation, but rank distinctions.[21] This means that their religion must have been fundamentally the same in all quarters, although modified in an esoteric direction in the secret societies.[22]

Boas did not publish any comprehensive survey of Kwakiutl religion. In fact, the work which is dedicated to the particular study of this religion contains, in a characteristic way, Kwakiutl texts and translations, like most of his other monographs on this tribe; the texts concern such topics as personal documents of shamans, and prayers. We seek in vain, however, for a cohesive treatment of the religion in all its aspects.[23] It is true that Boas attempted a systematic analysis of Kwakiutl religious concepts in a short paper in

[18] Franz Boas, "The Social Organization and the Secret Societies of the Kwakiutl Indians," *Report of the United States National Museum* (Washington, D.C.: Government Printing Office, 1897), pp. 311–738.

[19] Franz Boas, "The Ethnological Significance of Esoteric Doctrines," Franz Boas, *Race, Language and Culture, op. cit.*, pp. 312ff.

[20] Verne F. Ray, "Rejoinder," *American Anthropologist* LVIII (1956), p. 167.

[21] See Helen Codere, "Kwakiutl Society: Rank without Class," *American Anthropologist* LIX (1957), pp. 473–86.

[22] It is quite another matter whether the religious ideas of the slaves (for the Kwakiutl owned slaves) were the same as those of the freemen, in particular if the slaves had been captured in war and belonged to far off nations. This question needs further investigation (if it now can be solved at all).

[23] Franz Boas, *The Religion of the Kwakiutl Indians* (New York: Columbia University Contributions to Anthropology X/1–2, 1930). It ought to be observed that Boas here—as in many other works—published materials in his own name which had been collected by his Kwakiutl-speaking, half-breed assistant, George Hunt.

Festschrift Meinhof (1927), but the perspective is one of linguistic terminology, not of religion.[24] Boas obviously disliked generalizations, even, so it seems, generalizations of Kwakiutl religion.[25] His method was particularistic insofar as that he restricted himself to a careful sifting of religious facts, posing problems rather than solving them. This notwithstanding, he did produce some important generalizing studies, for instance, a lengthy article on North American mythology.[26] Although this paper gives an outline of Indian myths, it is first and foremost a methodological treatise, perhaps "Boas's best writing on method."[27] However, despite his vast writing on Kwakiutl religion, he never summed it up in the same way as he comprehended Kwakiutl social organization.

It is possible that Boas's avoidance of generalized and comparative accounts has something to do with his inability to preclude inconsistencies in his research and in matters of opinion. Lowie, for instance, has noticed how, in one paper, Boas credited the Northwest Coast Indians with a belief in possession, whereas in another report he attributed possesssional phenomena exclusively to the Old World.[28] Boas has certainly not helped in clarifying the role of possession in America, a difficult but intriguing issue which still awaits an adequate treatment.[29]

Kroeber may be right when, in an assessment of Boas's influence in America, he says that Boas stood for a sound approach, not a dogma.[30] One of Boas's critics, Wax, considers that it was an extreme empiricism, negativistic in its consequences, and fateful for the development of anthropology.[31] This is undoubtedly true. However, Boas placed American investigations of Indian religions on a solid, factual, and empirical basis. It is due to his influence that the speculative and uncontrolled ideas about Indian religions gave way to a sound, descriptive-analytical research on these religions. Boas

[24] Franz Boas, "Religious Terminology of the Kwakiutl," Franz Boas, *Race, Language and Culture, op. cit.*, pp. 612ff.

[25] See his statements in the article "Some problems of Methodology in the Social Sciences," *ibid.*, p. 268, and his refutation of Locher's systematic interpretation of Kwakiutl mythology (also in *Race, Language and Culture*, pp. 446ff.). Cf. also Reichard, *op cit.*, p. 56.

[26] Franz Boas, "Mythology and Folk-Tales of the North American Indians," *Anthropology in North America* (New York: G. E. Stechert, 1915), pp. 306–49.

[27] Jacobs, *op. cit.*, p. 125.

[28] Robert H. Lowie, *The History of Ethnological Theory* (New York: Farrar & Rinehart, 1937), pp. 152–53. Kroeber's opinion that Boas's enormous output does not contain "even minute instances of error" is, against this background, surprising. See Alfred Louis Kroeber, "Franz Boas: The Man," *American Anthropological Association, Memoirs*, LXI (1943), p. 22.

[29] Cf. Åke Hultkrantz, *Les Religions des Indiens Primitifs de l'Amérique* (Stockholm: Acta Universitatis Stockholmiensis, Stockholm Studies in Comparative Religions IV, 1963), pp. 96ff.

[30] Kroeber, *Franz Boas: The Man, op. cit.*, p. 24. See also Leslie Spier, "Some Central Elements in the Legacy," *American Anthropological Association Memoirs* LXXXIX (1959), p. 146.

[31] Murray Wax, "The Limitations of Boas's Anthropology," *American Anthropologist* LVIII (1956), pp. 63–74.

founded, as Goldenweiser expresses it, "the American school of anthropology."[32] In doing so, he also influenced the American approach to primitive Indian religions.

THE "BOASIANS": THE PUPILS OF BOAS

As mentioned before, Boas and his pupils dominated research on North American religions for several decades. That meant, above all, that penetrating field work and a cautious attitude to generalizations (particularly as regards environmental influences and evolution) characterized most achievements. Most, but not all: Goldenweiser, for instance, was not a good field researcher, and Kroeber made historical reconstructions of Pueblo and Californian religions of which his teacher disapproved.[33] Boas's skeptical attitude toward far-reaching historical reconstructions was shared by Lowie, whereas Radin lightheartedly made the Southeastern temple culture originate from Mexican emigrants who had crossed the Gulf of Mexico.[34] Other audacious propositions on historical reconstruction were suggested by Wissler, a psychologist from the start who soon became entangled in his studies of culture area and cultural intenstity, key concepts in his diffusionistic approach.[35] Wissler's scheme of cultural and religious development guided many American papers on Indian religions in the 1920s and 1930s. More careful reconstructive rules were subsequently put forward by the ingenious linguist Sapir and the penetrating field researcher Cooper; the latter was, as we shall see in the sequence, a remarkable student of American Indian religion.[36]

Our main attention is, however, attached to the accomplishments in the field research. Here Boas's pupils followed their master who, as Kroeber says, was negativistic in his concern about premature explanations but was "a constructive positivist as regards data" and one who "tirelessly collected data from unknown cultures and languages in his search for a better understanding of processes."[37] Field research was the signum of this period in

[32] Alexander Goldenweiser, "Recent Trends in American Anthropology," *American Anthropologist* XLIII (1941), p. 157.

[33] Alfred Louis Kroeber, *The History of Native Culture in California* (Berkeley: University of California Publications in American Archaeology and Ethnology XX, 1923), pp. 123–42; and his *Native Culture of the Southwest* (Berkeley: University of California Publications in American Archaeology and Ethnology XXIII, 1928).

[34] Paul Radin, *The Story of the American Indian* (New York: Liveright, 1944), pp. 38, 201.

[35] Clark Wissler, *The Relation of Nature to Man in Aboriginal America* (New York: Oxford University, 1926); cf. in particular the discussions of the sun dance (pp. 82ff.), the visions and guardian-spirit complex (pp. 90ff.), and the peyote cult (pp. 189ff.).

[36] Edward Sapir, *Time Perspective in Aboriginal American Culture: A Study in Method* (Ottawa: Canada Department of Mines, Geological Survey, Memoir XC, 1916); John M. Cooper, *Temporal Sequence and the Marginal Cultures* (Washington, D.C.: The Catholic University of America Anthropology Series X, 1941).

[37] Alfred Louis Kroeber, "The History and Present Orientation of Cultural Anthropology," *The Nature of Culture* (Chicago: University of Chicago, 1952), p. 146.

anthropology. It is even possible to say that the results of Boas and his pupils have no parallels in this respect in any other country; nowhere on earth may the student of religion find as many thorough field reports on primitive religions as in this American corpus of works, published and unpublished. We may take exception to the way in which the interpretations have been done, but the facts and the texts are usually of a high quality. In this respect, things changed after the 1930s, when a new generation of anthropologists, less interested in facts and more preoccupied with theories, made their entry.

Some of the "Boasian" (as they have been called) field reports reveal a genuine interest and true feeling for religion and the role it plays in the life of the indiviual and in society and culture. Others, however, view religion as a denomination of a varied lot of cultural expression, superstitious in effect but essentially motivated by behavioristic causes. Therefore, ritual actions are more intensely described than religious ideas, the latter not infrequently being grouped together under headings such as "miscellaneous beliefs." In all fairness, however, it must be admitted that many American Indian religious systems at least superficially lend themselves to such an interpretation, for, as clearly emerges from Lowie's analysis of North American ceremonialism, among these Indians ritually regulated performances have been an obsession.[38] In many places, in fact, the intricate ceremonial structure has survived the religious beliefs which once were associated with it.[39] Nevertheless, the temptation has been great for many students in the field to limit religion to ritual acts and behavior (see below concerning the sun-dance studies).

The field work which was produced by Boas's pupils covered almost all of the North American culture areas (as these had been defined by Wissler).[40] Thus, Kroeber, Barrett, Dixon, and Goddard penetrated California; Sapir made some contributions to mythology and religion in the southern part of the North Pacific Coast area; Wissler, Lowie, and Linton, and several others investigated the Plains area; Parsons, Haeberlin, Spier, Bunzel, Reichard, and Underhill visited the Southwestern Indians; Michelson, Goldenweiser, Speck, Radin, and Skinner turned to the Eastern Woodland area; and Swanton and Bushnell studied the religions of the Southeastern Indians. Swanton's work was prevailingly ethnohistorical, that is, he made extensive use of older documentary sources; the reason was, of course, that these Indians had already changed their aboriginal cultures. The most thorough field work was done on the Plains, since the Plains Indians had

[38] Robert H. Lowie, "Ceremonialism in North America," *Anthropology in North America* (New York: G. E. Stechert, 1915), pp. 229ff. Many students of comparative religion have been frustrated when trying to disentangle religious attitudes from the web of ceremonial activities.

[39] Cf., for instance, James H. Howard, "The Compleat Stomp Dancer," *South Dakota Museum News* XXVI (1965), pp. 5–6.

[40] Clark Wissler, *The American Indian* (3d ed.; New York: Douglas C. McMurtie, 1938), p. 221.

been the last conquered Indians (the Ghost Dance in 1890–91), and their culture and religion remained rather intact for a long time afterward.

The field work on religion was, as has been pointed out, part of the field work on culture, and it is therefore interesting to compare the contributions made from the viewpoints of ethnology and comparative religions, respectively. It is apparent that such a great anthropologist as Kroeber, Boas's successor as leading figure in the science, stands back for Lowie, Radin, and Speck from the point of view of comparative religion. Although none of the latter directly specialized in the field of religion (Radin perhaps partly excepted), they developed a keen interest in the subject, and their field reports on religion are in many ways excellent.

Robert H. Lowie spent a long series of seasons with the Crow Indians in Montana (1907, 1910–16, 1931). Their old inherited culture was then, as he says, a living culture, and their aboriginal religion was still persisting. Lowie conducted field research also in other quarters (among the Basin Shoshoni, Chipewyan, Blackfoot, Washo, Hopi, and others), but it is through his intense and sober work among the Crow that he made his substantial contributions to the study of primitive religion. Although unable to experience it himself, Lowie was fascinated by the "religious thrill," as he termed it,[41] and the visionary experiences and individual religious reactions take first place in his descriptions of Crow religion.[42] If, in these papers, we lack a systematic treatment of Crow religion as a functioning whole, this deficiency has probably to do with Lowie's skeptical attitude to cultural systems. We find this mistrust clearly demonstrated in his classical work, *Primitive Religion*, in which he annihilates pretentious theoretical systems but scarcely presents other theoretical constructions.[43] Lowie's refusal to deal with such general schemes was certainly not, as Goldenweiser thought, dependent upon a "markedly unimaginative" nature,[44] rather it was provoked by a careful, sifting attitude and a rigor in method which he had taken over from Boas. Incidentally, he always frantically defended Boas against the latter's adversaries in the 1950s.

[41] See Robert H. Lowie, *Primitive Religion* (2d ed.; New York: Liveright, 1948), p. v. Concerning Lowie's own reaction to religion, see his posthumous work, *Robert H. Lowie, Ethnologist: A Personal Record* (Berkeley and Los Angeles: University of California, 1959), pp. 99ff., 134, and the likewise posthumously published article, "Dreams, Idle Dreams," *Current Anthropology* VII (1966), p. 379.

[42] Robert H. Lowie, *The Religion of the Crow Indians* (New York: Anthropological Papers of the American Museum of Natural History XXV/2, 1922); and his *The Crow Indians* (New York: Holt, Rinehart and Winston, 1935), pp. 237ff.; "Crow Religion," *Primitive Religion, op. cit.*, pp. 3ff.; and "Die Religion der Crow-Indianer," *Beiträge zur Völkerkunde Nordamerikas* (Hamburg: n.p., 1951), pp. 28–42.

[43] Lowie, *Primitive Religion, op. cit.*, Parts 2 and 3. Lowie felt that this book was neglected, at least by anthropologists.

[44] Goldenweiser, "Recent Trends," *op. cit.*, p. 159. Cf. Lowie's reply in *Robert H. Lowie, Ethnologist, op. cit.*, p. 133.

To return to Lowie's work among the Crow, he was not the first to give details of their religion. Besides Catlin and Maximilian, referred to in Part I, we may mention in particular Simms and Curtis among the earlier reporters.[45] Lowie was, however, the first anthropologist to delve into the particulars of Crow religion and to try to understand it from within. In this respect he differed from his master, Boas, and also from most of the anthropologists of his own generation. As Radin remarks, Lowie's Crow work is in a class by itself.[46] It is not the quantity of texts which is so remarkable—both Boas and Radin had more to offer—but the skilful analysis, the true "religious insight."

Lowie also recorded myths, tales, cults, and ceremonies among the Crow. His interest in myths was in no way outstanding, although (rather much against his own wishes) he had started his career with an article on mythology.[47] Later in life, however, he returned to this subject.[48] Lowie's articles on cultic activities engaged him more, since their theme was close to problems of social organization for which he had a lifelong interest.[49] Radin considers that Lowie's paper on the Plains age-societies (the societies which sponsored the sun dance) "for its completeness, its clear-cut recognition of the problems involved, and its admirable solution, has never been excelled."[50] Whereas I doubt that the solutions would be accepted by present-day structuralists, it is obvious that this paper represented a high mark in its day, and we are still impressed by the author's elegant reasoning. In this work, Lowie for once appears as a master connoisseur of Plains Indian religion and society in general. Otherwise, he himself has stated that he had never been a specialist on the Plains area as Boas was on the North Pacific and Kroeber on the Californian areas.[51] As a matter of fact, in many respects he refuted the

---

[45] Stephen C. Simms, *Traditions of the Crows* (Chicago: Field Museum Publication LXXXV/2, 1903); Edward S. Curtis, *The North American Indian*, 20 vols. (Cambridge: Harvard University, 1909), IV.

[46] Paul Radin, "Robert H. Lowie 1883–1957," *American Anthropologist* LX (1958), p. 361.

[47] Robert H. Lowie, "The Test-Theme in North American Mythology," *Journal of American Folklore* XXI (1908), pp. 97–148.

[48] Cf. Robert H. Lowie, *Studies in Plains Indian Folklore* (Berkeley: University of California Publications in American Archaeology and Ethnology XL/1, 1942).

[49] Cf. Robert H. Lowie, *The Sun Dance of the Crow* (New York: Anthropological Papers of the American Museum of Natural History XVI/1, 1915), his *The Tobacco Society of the Crow Indians* (New York: Anthropological Papers of the American Museum of Natural History XXI/2, 1919), and his *Minor Ceremonies of the Crow Indians* (New York: Anthropological Papers of the American Museum of Natural History XXI/5, 1924).

[50] Radin, "Robert H. Lowie 1883–1957," *op. cit.*; Lowie's paper was titled: *Plains Indian Age-Societies: Historical and Comparative Summary* (New York: Anthropological Papers of the American Museum of Natural History XI/13, 1916). Cf. also Radin's review in: Paul Radin, *The Method and Theory of Ethnology: An Essay in Criticism* (New York and London: McGraw-Hill, 1933), pp. 148ff.

[51] *Robert H. Lowie, Ethnologist, op. cit.*, p. 168.

area approach.[52] This notwithstanding, he has presented a synthesis of Plains Indian religion in one of his last major works.[53]

One thing remains to be said about Lowie's investigations of Crow religion: He was never keen on studying acculturation, cultural or religious. It was, he says, the reconstruction of the ancient primitive life which interested him.[54] It was left to later students, Voget for example, to penetrate the religious acculturation of the Crow Indians.

While Lowie's papers on Crow religion constitute the finest anthropological achievements in the study of Plains religion, Paul Radin contributed the finest data from the Woodland area. "His" tribe, the Winnebago, are linguistically akin (Siouan) to the Crow Indians but participate in another cultural type and live in another ecological environment. The Crow Indians once separated from the Hidatsa at the Missouri River, a tribe which Lowie visited for that reason. Radin found his Winnebago closer affiliated to the Omaha, another tribe at the Missouri River, and therefore took part in Alice Fletcher's investigations of this tribe with a vivid interest (see below). Radin also paid attention to two Canadian Woodland tribes, the Ojibway and Ottawa, from whom he secured valuable materials on dreams and visions.[55] He extended his field trips to the Mexican Zapotecs, for whom he had a lifelong interest, and some Indian groups in California. But it was as a specialist on the Winnebago that he acquired a worldwide reputation in anthropology, literature, and comparative religion.

Paul Radin visited the Winnebago (of Wisconsin and Oklahoma) during the years 1908–13. Like his old friend Robert Lowie, he learned the language of the tribe. Whereas, however, Lowie turned to studies of social and ritual organization, Radin, from the very beginning, became interested in the literary and religious aspects of Winnebago oral traditions, and in the life-stories of single individuals. In his classical monograph on the Winnebago tribe, Radin characteristically dismisses their material culture in a few pages. Their clan organization is extensively treated, with preference given to clan myths and songs, and the detailed accounts of religious beliefs and ceremonies fill up two-thirds of the volume. All through this work, myths, tales, prayers, and recitals have a domineering place; a ceremony, for instance, is often described by reference to an Indian account of it or the

[52] Cf. Robert H. Lowie, "The Culture Area Concept as Applied to North and South America," *Proceedings of the 32nd International Congress of Americanists* (1958), pp. 73–78.

[53] Robert H. Lowie, *Indians of the Plains* (New York: McGraw-Hill, 1954), pp. 154ff.; the chapter is called, strange to say, "Supernaturalism."

[54] *Robert H. Lowie, Ethnologist, op. cit.,* p. 169.

[55] See Paul Radin, *Some Aspects of Puberty Fasting among the Ojibwa* (Ottawa: Canada Geological Survey, Museum Bulletin II, 1914), pp. 517ff.; and his "Ojibwa and Ottawa Puberty Dreams," *Essays in Anthropology Presented to A. L. Kroeber* (Berkeley: University of California, 1936). pp. 233–64.

speeches given.[56] In short, the book was written as if Winnebago culture consisted solely of oral literature and religious beliefs. Herein lies its limits, but also its force, for it is the ethnographical monograph on North American religions that has gained most attention from the students of religion.

All the interests and themes that were brought forth in this monograph engaged Radin for the rest of his life. We need not here discuss his provocative papers on literary style among the Winnebago and other Indian tribes, although they have an indirect bearing on the evaluation of mythology.[57] Of more immediate interest to us are his analyses of the religious value of literary documents. Radin, particularly in his later years, published many important myths, recorded in the Winnebago language and thoroughly commented upon.[58] There are still many manuscripts of his on this subject which await publication; quite a few of them were not directly recorded by Radin but sent to him by knowledgeable informants whom he had trained during his field visits.[59] The careful analysis of the texts of this enormous mythological material contrasts in an unfortunate way with the rather lighthearted conclusions as regards the religious import associated with them. Goldenweiser has stressed, quite justly, that Radin was a talented man with sudden insights, but: "The companion vice of this virtue is a certain impatience as to certainty. . . . Radin accepts, or at least gives official status to a hunch, though he may not be able to make it more than probable."[60] In short, Radin was a man of much imagination, and his imagination—or intuition—sometimes ran wild, although it was connected with great learning and wide reading.[61]

It is this quality of Radin's which often makes it so difficult to accept his theses in his general books on religion and culture.[62] The same tendency is, however, also obvious in his interpretations of Winnebago myths. For

---

[56] Paul Radin, *The Winnebago Tribe* (Washington, D.C.: Bureau of American Ethnology, 37th Annual Report, 1923).

[57] Cf. Paul Radin, *Literary Aspects of North American Mythology* (Ottawa: Canada Geological Survey, Museum Bulletin XVI, 1915); and his "Literary Aspects of Winnebago Mythology," *Journal of American Folklore* XXXIX (1926), pp. 18ff.

[58] See, for instance, Paul Radin's following works: "The Winnebago Myth of the Twins," *Papers of the Southwestern Anthropological Society* I (1915), pp. 1–56; "Winnebago Myth Cycles," *Primitive Culture* I (1926), pp. 8–86; "The Thunderbird Warclub: A Winnebago Tale," *Journal of American Folklore* XLIV (1931), pp. 143–65; *Winnebago Hero Cycles: A Study in Aboriginal Literature* (Baltimore: Waverly, International Journal of American Linguistics Memoirs I, 1948); *The Evolution of an American Indian Prose Epic: A Study in Comparative Literature*, 2 vols. (Basel: Ethnographical Museum, 1954, 1956).

[59] Goldenweiser, *op. cit.*, pp. 160f.

[60] *Ibid.*, p. 160.

[61] A completely different judgment of Radin's speculations may be found in J. D. Sapir, "Paul Radin 1883–1959," *Journal of American Folklore* LXXIV (1961), pp. 66–67.

[62] See, in particular, Robert H. Lowie's works, *Primitive Religion* (New York: Liveright, 1937) and *The World of Primitive Man* (London, New York, and Toronto: Henry Schuman, 1953). Cf. my criticism in *Man* LXIII/230 (1963), p. 181.

instance, the culture hero of the Winnebago is treated as a fictive trickster created by literary imagination, embodying some primal needs. "I think it safe to assume," says Radin, "that it began with an account of a nondescript person obsessed by hunger, by an uncontrollable urge to wander and by sexuality."[63] This person is then the creation of the gifted raconteur, a figure to whom Radin repeatedly returns in his works and by whom he was obviously fascinated (see below). This theory of the trickster is undoubtedly a pure fancy in view of extant mythological materials from other Indian tribes.[64] It was, however, more or less accepted and further elucidated by Kerényi (adducing Greek tricksters) and, from a psychological angle, by C. G. Jung. Radin had studied under Jung and was certainly stimulated by him, but never became a Jungian.[65]

Radin's preference of subjective judgments in cultural and religious studies reflected his own inclination toward a humanistic approach and his denunciation of quantitative methods.[66] He thought it possible to reconstruct Winnebago religious history through an analysis of internal evidence in personal documents and accounts of religious rites, in myths and legends.[67] His ambitions were certainly laudable, but his canons of procedure did not safeguard a correct interpretation.

Radin's conspicuous interest in personal documents, apparent in his Winnebago monograph, paved the way for biographical and autobiographical accounts of religious experiences among North American Indians.[68] Although the impetus to such studies originally came from Boas (and, perhaps, Emelie Demant-Hatt in Denmark), Radin had a direct personal interest in regarding individuals as creators, as the moving forces behind the wheels of history. His ambitions were in this respect directed against the French sociologists and psychologists and against the old evolutionistic dogmas about societies without history and without philosophers. Radin's presentation in 1920 of the life-history of a Winnebago Indian provided students of religion with first-class religious materials.[69] This concentration on

[63] Paul Radin, The Trickster: A Study in American Indian Mythology (New York: Bell, 1956), p. 165.

[64] Hultkrantz, Les Religions des Indiens Primitifs de l'Amérique, op. cit., pp. 36ff.

[65] Cora DuBois, "Paul Radin: An Appreciation," Stanley Diamond (ed.), Culture in History, Essays in Honor of Paul Radin (New York: Columbia University, 1960), p. xiii. Cf. Paul Radin, The Dreams of an American Indian: Their Meaning and Function (Zürich: Studien zur Analytischen Psychologie C. G. Jung II, 1955), pp. 146ff.; Radin, "History of Ethnological Theories," American Anthropologist XXXI (1929), pp. 9–33.

[66] Radin, The Method and Theory of Ethnology, op. cit.

[67] Ibid., pp. 31ff., 183ff.

[68] See Clyde Kluckhohn, The Personal Document in Anthropological Science (New York: Social Science Research Council Bulletin LIII, 1945), pp. 79ff.

[69] Paul Radin, The Autobiography of a Winnebago Indian (Berkeley: University of California Publications in American Archaeology and Ethnology XVI/7, 1920); later reissued as Crashing Thunder (New York and London: D. Appleton, 1926).

the individual, his abilities and inabilities, formed the basis for Radin's well-known differentiation between the priest-thinker and the man of action.[70]

The Winnebago Indian whose autobiography Radin published ended up as a peyotist. Radin gave a sketch of the new Peyote religion in his Winnebago monograph. In an earlier paper he had proved in a masterly way how the Peyote cult was fitted into the native religious scheme of the Winnebago Indians.[71] This was one of the first studies ever made in cultural and religious process among primitive peoples.

The medicine society of the Winnebago constituted the subject of another historical investigation by Radin. His first paper on the medicine dance was a quantitative analysis of the type then popular in American anthropology; Radin followed here the same pattern as Kroeber, Golden-weiser, Spier, and other contemporary students.[72] True to his inmost attitude in methodological questions, Radin later repudiated this article.[73] He returned, however, to the theme itself with a thorough study which not only presents the authentic ritual in all its detail but also aims at elucidating its historical development. Thus, Radin found out that the medicine ritual originated in an old shamanistic ceremony to which the shooting feature characteristic for the Algonkian medicine ceremoney (midewiwin) had been added.[74] We cannot judge here whether he was right in his reconstruction;[75] the important thing is that he tried to reveal religious history in a "primitive" tribe at an early date and that his chief method was the use of internal evidence and the study of neighboring tribes.[76]

Radin was called "the trickster" by his close colleagues in his last years. And he was indeed a capricious culture hero among those American anthropologists who were concerned with religious studies: He changed his opinion from one book to another and was quite open about it. Nevertheless, his factual contributions to our knowledge of American Indian religions were outstanding, and not one of his colleagues did as much as he did to further the interest in these religions.

Next to Lowie and Radin, Frank Speck was the researcher who was most dedicated to the study of Indian religions. He was a congenial field student and had a rare gift of tracing important religious materials

[70] Paul Radin, Primitive Man as Philosopher (New York: D. Appleton, 1927).

[71] Paul Radin, "A Sketch of the Peyote Cult of the Winnebago: A Study in Borrowing," Journal of Religious Psychology VII (1914), pp. 1–22.

[72] Paul Radin, "The Ritual and Significance of the Winnebago Medicine Dance," Journal of American Folklore XXIV (1911), pp. 149–208.

[73] Radin, The Method and Theory, op. cit., pp. 139ff.

[74] Paul Radin, The Road of Life and Death (New York: Pantheon, Bollingen Series, 1945), pp. 74ff.

[75] Modern research based on the study of documents seems to corroborate his account. See Nancy O. Lurie, "Winnebago Protohistory," Stanley Diamond, op. cit., p. 797.

[76] Cf. also Paul Radin, The Origin Myth of the Medicine Rite: Three Versions (Baltimore: Special Publications of Bollingen Foundation II, 1950).

pertaining to the little known Algonkian groups in the East, the Iroquois, the Yuchi and the Eastern Sioux. His first great work on the Yuchi produced information on totemism which has proved to be of considerable value to comparative religion.[77] His later investigations in the field of religion mostly concerned Algonkian myths, religious beliefs, and rites. He collected myths and tales from widely scattered Algonkian Indians, many of them in text (he mastered Algonkian dialects in a marvelous way);[78] he published the first close analysis of American shamanism in function;[79] and he wrote a substantial report on the religious beliefs of a New England tribe.[80]

His finest contribution to comparative religion was without doubt the monograph on the Naskapi-Montagnais Indians of the Labrador peninsula, a work which is concerned solely with the religious beliefs and rituals of these "savage hunters."[81] Speck has presented here an interesting picture of a religion dominated by beliefs in animal masters, bear ceremonialism, and rites of divination. Another first-rank monograph contains detailed accounts of the Delaware Indian house of ceremonies and of the spirits and annual rites connected therewith.[82] This work was later supplemented by a study of religious ceremonies among the Delaware of Oklahoma.[83] A third important book on the same Indians described their bear ceremonies.[84] Speck's last great work dealt with the midwinter rites of the Iroquois.[85]

Speck not only wrote on religion—he was, for instance, very interested in arts and crafts—but he was, deeply concerned with the problems of Algonkian religion and had the profoundest sympathy for the religious expressions of his native friends. His accounts are factual and reliable and do not contain much personal speculation. "He was never primarily concerned with high-level generalizations or interpretations, but rather with putting

---

[77] Frank G. Speck, *Ethnology of the Yuchi Indians* (Philadelphia: University of Pennsylvania, Anthropological Publications of the University Museum I/1, 1909); see, in particular, pp. 70ff.

[78] See, e.g., Frank G. Speck, *Wawenock Myth Texts from Maine* (Washington, D.C.: Bureau of American Ethnololgy, 43rd Annual Report, 1928).

[79] Frank G. Speck, *Penobscot Shamanism* (Lancaster, Pennsylvania: American Anthropological Association Memoirs VI/4, 1919).

[80] Frank G. Speck, "Penobscot Tales and Religious Beliefs," *Journal of American Folklore* XLVIII (1935), pp. 1–107.

[81] Frank G. Speck, *Naskapi: The Savage Hunters of the Labrador Peninsula* (Norman: University of Oklahoma, 1935).

[82] Frank G. Speck, *A Study of the Delaware Indian Big House Ceremony* (Philadelphia: Publications of the Pennsylvania Historical Commission II, 1931).

[83] Frank G. Speck, *Oklahoma Delaware Ceremonies, Dances, and Feasts* (Philadelphia: American Philosophical Society Memoirs VII, 1937).

[84] Frank G. Speck, *The Celestial Bear Comes Down to Earth* (Reading, Pennsylvania: Reading Public Museum and Art Gallery, 1945).

[85] Frank G. Speck, *Midwinter Rites of the Cayuga Long House* (Philadelphia: University of Pennsylvania, 1949).

well attested facts on record."[86] His descriptions of Indian religions belong to the finest of the American anthropoligical tradition.

In comparison with Lowie, Radin, and Speck, the other pupils of Franz Boas were less outstanding in the field of religion. Still, many of them have composed field reports which are of great importance to the students of religion.

Thus, Alfred Louis Kroeber published much folkloristic and ethnological material on Plains and Californian Indians in which religious ideas, rites, and myths had a conspicuous place. Kroeber was himself convinced that his early contributions on some Plains tribes, Arapaho and Gros Ventre, were less satisfactory due to his lack of training in the field.[87] His account of Arapaho religion is sometimes bewildering. There is, for example, no description or discussion of the land of the dead (nor is there in his myth collection), but there are references to ghosts and, characteristically, to objects which may be associated with ghosts.[88] Similar observations can be made in other connections in this early paper. In other words, beliefs are occasionally described, but most attention is given to rituals and ritual symbols.[89] Kroeber's book on the Gros Ventre, close kinsmen of the Arapaho, is slightly better.[90] His recordings of myths and tales from both tribes were published separately, in the true American tradition—for such materials have mostly been considered as pure narratives without having any deeper religious implications.[91]

Kroeber's numerous books and articles on the Californian Indians, on whose culture he was the specialist *par préférence,* contain extremely valuable information on religion. Even if we also find here an uneven presentation of the material, this is largely a consequence of the situation in the field, for the Californian Indians represented only remnants of once-functioning religions. Nevertheless, Kroeber wrote informative accounts of aboriginal Californian religion on such diverse ethnic groups as the Yuki, the Patwin, the Nisenan, the Cahuilla, and the Mohave. His work on Patwin religion is noteworthy because it includes a very enlightening discussion of the Californian Kuksu cult system.[92] Kroeber's analysis of Mohave myths is rewarding to the student of

[86] A. Irving Hallowell, "Frank Gouldsmith Speck, 1881–1950," *American Anthropologist* LIII (1951), p. 68.

[87] Alfred Louis Kroeber, "The Place of Boas in Anthropology," *American Anthropologist* LVIII (1956), p. 153.

[88] Alfred Louis Kroeber, "The Arapaho, IV: Religion," *American Museum of Natural History Bulletin* XVIII/4 (1907), pp. 317, 323, 342, 437, 447, 452.

[89] Cf. Alfred Louis Kroeber's "The Arapaho, III: Ceremonial Organization," *American Museum of Natural History Bulletin* XVIII/2 (1904).

[90] Alfred Louis Kroeber, *Ethnology of the Gros Ventre* (New York: Anthropological Papers of the American Museum of Natural History I/4, 1908).

[91] For a new trend in this respect, see William Bascom, "The Forms of Folklore: Prose Narratives," *Journal of American Folklore* LXXVIII (1965), pp. 3–20.

[92] Alfred Louis Kroeber, *The Patwin and Their Neighbors* (Berkeley: University of California Publications in American Archaeology and Ethnology XXIX/4, 1932), pp. 391ff. Cf. Loeb,

religion, illustrating how lore picked up here and there takes form as circumstantial myths through the medium of dreams.[93] Descriptions and analyses of myths figure, on the whole, very often in Kroeber's publications, not least in those which concern Californian Indians. His concept of "myth" is, of course, very inclusive.[94]

Kroeber's classical handbook of the Californian Indians, published in 1925, contains *inter alia* a sketch of the aboriginal "cultural provinces" (culture areas).[95] Steward remarks that "whereas his contemporary, Clark Wissler, delineated native New World culture areas about this same time mainly in terms of technological adaptations to distinctive environments, Kroeber tended to emphasize religious organization and belief."[96] Kroeber had earlier presented an outline of Indian religion in California.[97] With the exception of myths and tales, Kroeber paid more attention to religion in the formative days of his career, although during his last years he told the present writer that he had become more and more intrigued by the role played by the shaman in aboriginal society. It was during these years that he published texts, including religious texts and myths, which he had written down in his notebooks when he visited the Yurok and Mohave Indians at the turn of the century. Together with Gifford, another indefatigable scholar at Berkeley, he issued a well-known book on the world-renewal rites of northwest California; Kroeber's contributions cover the Yurok and Wiyot, Gifford's the Karuk and Hupa facts.[98]

Kroeber's interest in Californian Indians remained with him throughout his life, whereas his earliest commitments, Eskimo and Plains Indians, ceased to attract him after 1910 (not counting a study of Arapaho dialects published in 1916). For a time, the Zuni Indians in the Southwest caught his attention, also from the religious angle.[99] However, when not writing on

---

whose works on the Kuksu cult will be mentioned later.

[93] Alfred Louis Kroeber, *Seven Mohave Myths* (Berkeley and Los Angeles: Anthropological Records XI/1, 1948), pp. 1f. Cf. his "Preliminary Sketch of the Mohave Indians," *American Anthropologist* IV (1902), pp. 279f.; and *Handbook of the Indians of California* (Washington, D.C.: Bureau of American Ethnology Bulletin LXXVIII, 1925), pp. 754ff.

[94] One of Alfred Louis Kroeber's best known myth collections concerns the Yokuts Indians: *Indian Myths of South Central California* (Berkeley: University of California Publications in American Archaeology and Ethnology IV/4, 1907).

[95] Kroeber, *Handbook of the Indians of California, op. cit.*, pp. 898ff.

[96] Julian H. Steward, "Alfred Louis Kroeber 1876–1960," *American Anthropologist* LXIII (1961), p. 1056.

[97] Alfred Louis Kroeber, *The Religions of the Indians of California* (Berkeley: University of California Publications in American Archaeology and Ethnology IV/6, 1907).

[98] Alfred Louis Kroeber and E. W. Gifford, *World Renewal: A Cult System of Native Northwest California* (Berkeley and Los Angeles: Anthropological Records XIII/1, 1949).

[99] Alfred Louis Kroeber, "Thoughts on Zuñi Religion," *Anthropological Essays Presented to William Henry Holmes* (Washington, D.C.: privately printed, 1916), pp. 269–77; and his "Zuñi," James Hastings (ed.), *Encyclopaedia of Religion and Ethics* XII (New York: Scribner's, 1922), pp. 868–73.

Californian Indians he mostly turned to studies of culture and culture processes, and these studies have made him as famous as his teacher Boas. On the other hand, they have not rendered him a distinguished place among theorists on religion. This is unfortunate for, indirectly, Kroeber's cultural analyses have a profound bearing on the study of religion.

Another first-rank anthropologist among Boas's pupils was Edward Sapir, a man who was "brilliantly endowed," according to Benedict's and Goldenweiser's judgments.[100] Although his paramount interests were concentrated on linguistics and individual psychology, where his contributions were of a markedly high order, he also paid some attention to religion. Besides the presentation of myths in text collections from the Nootka, Yana, Southern Paiute, and Navajo Indians, he published an account of Takelma religious ideas and field notes on religious beliefs and rites among the Nootka, Wishram, and Yana.[101] Sapir had the linguist's approach to the myth, and idea systems probably appealed to him from the psychologist's point of view; but there are indications that he was also perceptive of the religious implications of such materials.[102]

A prominent anthropologist who was more genuinely interested in religious problems was John R. Swanton, himself a devoted spiritualist (something which provoked the scorn of his otherwise admiring fellow anthropologists).[103] His first field work was done among the Tlingit and Haida Indians of the Pacific Northwest and resulted in a series of papers on, among other things, myths, legends, and beliefs of these tribes. After 1905 he turned, surprisingly, to investigations among the Indians of the Southeast, and in this field he continued to specialize to such a degree, says Kroeber, "that it remains undisputedly his, and that mention of the area automatically brings to all of us the association of his name."[104] Two earlier ethnologists, J. O. Dorsey and Gatschet, had done some work here, but it remained for Swanton to put together what meager information he could get from the acculturated, small, and dispersed surviving groups, more or less absorbed by the white or Negro populations. Beside this field work which brought together remnants of religious beliefs and scraps of myths and tales, Swanton dived into the archives and perused, as the first of American ethnologists, the most authentic data on these Indians, the old written records. He was a master in

---

[100] Ruth Fulton Benedict, "Edward Sapir," *American Anthropologist* XLI (1939), p. 468; Goldenweiser, *op. cit.*, p. 158.

[101] See, in particular, Edward Sapir, "Religious Ideas of the Takelma Indians," *Journal of American Folklore* XX (1907), pp. 33–49.

[102] Cf. Edward Sapir, "The Meaning of Religion," David G. Mandelbaum (ed.), *Selected Writings of Edward Sapir* (Berkeley and Los Angeles: University of California, 1949), pp. 346ff.

[103] William N. Fenton, "John Reed Swanton 1873–1958," *American Anthropologist* LXI (1959), p. 667.

[104] Alfred Louis Kroeber, "The Work of John R. Swanton," *Smithsonian Miscellaneous Collections* C (1940), p. 2.

the use of these documents from past centuries and is regarded as the first "ethnohistorian."

Swanton's first important paper on the Southeast, in which he combined information from field work and archival sources, was his classical treatise on the Natchez and their neighbors, a book which contains much valuable material on the last remnants of the Mississippian temple-mound religions.[105] His later production on the Southeast included such papers as studies of Creek and Chickasaw religions, a source book on Choctaw ceremonies, an analysis of southeastern sun cults and general surveys of southeastern Indian religion.[106] His personal interest in problems of religious history may be discerned in a couple of articles on religion and magic (see below). Swanton's accounts of Indian religion are sober and sound, although perhaps slightly unimaginative.

In the Southwest area, Elsie Clews Parsons paved the way for the study of Pueblo religion. Parsons started out with a fervent sociological interest, and one has the impression that, even in those books and articles which treat Pueblo religion, she was more interested in clans and ceremonial details than in religion.[107] Parsons had, however, a keen sense of historic change in religion, in clear distinction from most of her colleagues who—as Kroeber has pointed out—saw history in a "flat perspective."[108] Her contributions to the study of Pueblo religion are numerous, beginning with some short articles on the Zuni and ending with the bulky work on Pueblo Indian religion in its entirety. She has written articles on sacred shrines,[109] on ceremonialsim,[110] and on the sacred clowns (an intriguing subject which was also dealt with by J H. Steward).[111] She has published myths and tales, for instance origin

---

[105] John R. Swanton, *Indian Tribes of the Lower Mississippi and Adjacent Coast of the Gulf of Mexico* (Washington, D.C.: Bureau of American Ethnology Bulletin XLIII, 1911).

[106] John R. Swanton, *Religious Beliefs and Medical Practices of the Creek Indians* (Washington, D.C.: Bureau of American Ethnology, 42nd Annual Report, 1928); and, *Social and Religious Beliefs and Usages of the Chickasaw Indians* (Washington, D.C.: Bureau of American Ethnology, 44th Annual Report, 1928); and, *Source Material for the Social and Ceremonial Life of the Choctaw Indians* (Washington, D.C.: Bureau of American Ethnology Bulletin CIII, 1931); and, "Sun Worship in the Southeast," *American Anthropologist* XXX (1928), pp. 206–13; and *Aboriginal Culture of the Southeast* (Washington, D.C.: Bureau of American Ethnology, 42nd Annual Report, 1928); and, *The Indians of the Southeastern United States* (Washington, D.C.: Bureau of American Ethnology Bulletin CXXXVII, 1946), pp. 742ff.

[107] Cf., for instance, Elsie Clews Parsons, "The Religion of the Pueblo Indians," *Proceedings of the 21st International Congress of Americanists* I (1924), pp. 140–61.

[108] Kroeber, "The History and Present Orientation," *op. cit.*, p. 151.

[109] Elsie Clews Parsons, "War God Shrines of Laguna and Zuñi," *American Anthropologist* XX (1918), pp. 381–405.

[110] Elsie Clews Parsons, *Notes on Ceremonialism at Laguna* (New York: Anthropological Papers of the American Museum of Natural History XIX/4, 1920); and *Hopi and Zuñi Ceremonialism* (Menasha, Wisconsin: American Anthropological Association Memoirs XXXIX, 1933).

[111] Elsie Clews Parsons and Ralph L. Beals, "The Sacred Clowns of the Pueblo and Mayo-Yaqui Indians," *American Anthropologist* XXXVI (1934), pp. 491–514. Cf. Julian H. Steward, "The

myths.[112] Finally, she has analyzed the ways in which certain tales, witch-craft, and *kachina* ceremonies have been influenced by Spanish sources,[113] and she found ritual and other parallels to Pueblo religion in Plains and even Aztec religions.[114] Her great comprehensive opus on Pueblo religion brings together a mass of material which she had not published elsewhere.[115] It is a pity, however, that the reader is drowned in a sea of facts without always glimpsing the religious themes and motivations.

In spite of these shortcomings, it must be said that no one has had such a knowledge of Pueblo religion as Miss Parsons. Her investigations all over the Pueblo area, from Hopi in Arizona to Taos in New Mexico, inaugurated a new era in the research on southwestern religions. As a partial result of her activity, there followed quite a few publications on Pueblo religion by Bunzel, Dumarest, Goldfrank, Stirling, White, and others.

In this connection, we should also mention another of Boas's disciples, the early deceased Herman Haeberlin, who pointed out in a provocative paper that Pueblo religion was dominated by the idea of fertilization.[116] With the possible exception of Lowie's monograph on Plains age-societies, this was the first attempt at the pattern approach which was later so emphatically used by another of Boas's pupils, Ruth Benedict (see below).[117] Haeberlin's other works dealt with myths and religious customs of the Puget Sound area. He wrote, among other things, an interesting account of a shamanistic ceremony which has been much quoted.[118] His premature death

---

Ceremonial Buffoon of the American Indian," *Papers of the Michigan Academy of Science, Arts and Letters* XIV (1930), pp. 187–207.

[112] Elsie Clews Parsons, "The Origin Myth of Zuñi," *Journal of American Folklore* XXXVI (1923), pp. 135–62.

[113] Elsie Clews Parsons, "Witchcraft among the Pueblos: Indian or Spanish," *Man* XXVII (1927), pp. 106–12, 125–28; and "Spanish Elements in the Kachina Cult of the Pueblos," *Proceedings of the 23rd International Congress of Americanists* (1928), pp. 582ff.

[114] Elsie Clews Parsons, "Ritual Parallels in Pueblo and Plains Cultures, with a Special Reference to the Pawnee," *American Anthropologist* XXXI (1929), pp. 642–54: and "Some Aztec and Pueblo Parallels," *American Anthropologist* XXXV (1933), pp. 611–33, Concerning the connections between the Pueblo and Plains Indians, see also Parsons, *Pueblo Indian Religion* II (Chicago: University of Chicago, 1939), pp. 1029ff., as well as the article by Charles H. Lange, "Plains-Southwestern Inter-Cultural Relations during the Historic Period," *Ethnohistory* IV (1957), pp. 150–73.

[115] Parsons, *Pueblo Indian Religion, op. cit.*

[116] Herman Karl Haeberlin, *The Idea of Fertilization in the Culture of the Pueblo Indians* (Lancaster, Pennsylvania: American Anthropological Association Memoirs III/1, 1916).

[117] According to Lowie, Haeberlin might have been influenced by Wundt's ideas; see Robert H. Lowie, "Reminiscences of Anthropological Currents in America Half a Century Ago," *American Anthropologist* LVIII (1956), p. 1012.

[118] Herman Karl Haeberlin, "SbEtEtda'q, a Shamanistic Performance of the Coast Salish," *American Anthropologist* XX (1918), pp. 249–57.

deprived American research on primitive religion of one of its most promising talents.[119]

Clark Wissler was a great anthopologist in his day. Not only did he deeply influence his science through his development of the culture-area concept (and his ideas of diffusion, touched upon above), he also organized most of the ethnological expeditions to North American Indian reservations, and he mastered Plains Indian ethnography as had no one else. Many students have received their first impression of North American religions from his famous introduction to New World anthropology;[120] others have become acquainted with Plains Indian religion through the study of his handbook on these Indians.[121] Wissler was, however, first and foremost interested in material culture, and his contributions to Indian religion are not outstanding. He wrote some papers on Teton Dakota mythology and Pawnee rituals, but most of his work on culture and religion emanated from field studies among the Blackfeet (before a serious illness in 1909, which put an end to his intensive field research).[122] With the aid of a native Blackfoot, D. C. Duvall, Wissler recorded texts on Blackfoot myths, prayers, visionary experiences, and rituals.[123] Although he had originally been trained as a psychologist, Wissler does not evince any interest for the religious experiences as such in his publications. He was more taken in by problems of convergence and diffusion in the sphere of rituals and ritual objects.[124]

Wissler's occupation with the Pawnee rituals is perhaps most obviously manifested by the aid he gave to James R. Murie when the latter prepared his manuscript on Pawnee ceremonies. Murie, a native Pawnee who had earlier assisted both Miss Fletcher and the Chicago anthropologist George A. Dorsey during their Pawneee researches,[125] was himself eager to record the entire religion of his people, and he was thereby helped by Wissler who arranged and edited the enormous manuscript (which is, however, still unpublished).[126]

[119] Franz Boas, "In Memoriam: Herman K. Haeberlin," *American Anthropologist* XXI (1919), p. 71.

[120] Wissler, *The American Indian, op. cit.*, pp. 193ff.

[121] Clark Wissler, *North American Indians of the Plains* (3rd ed.; New York: American Museum of Natural History, 1941), pp. 106ff.

[122] It has been hinted that Wissler's interest in the Blackfoot (and the Pawnee?) was inspired by Grinnell; see N. C. Nelson, "Clark Wissler 1870–1947," *American Antiquity* XIII (1948), p. 245.

[123] Clark Wissler and D. C. Duvall, *Mythology of the Blackfoot Indians* (New York: Anthropological Papers of the American Museum of Natural History II/1, 1908); Wissler, *Ceremonial Bundles of the Blackfoot Indians* (New York: Anthropological Papers of the American Museum of Natural History VII/2, 1912).

[124] Clark Wissler, "Comparative Study of Pawnee and Blackfoot Rituals," *Proceedings of the 19th Congress of Americanists* (1915), pp. 335–39.

[125] Cf. George A. Dorsey, *The Pawnee: Mythology* (Washington, D.C.: The Carnegie Institution, 1906); and his *Traditions of the Skidi Pawnee* (Boston: American Folklore Society Memoirs VIII, 1904).

[126] J. R. Murie, "The Ceremonies of the Pawnee," (MS in the Bureau of American Ethnology); cf. Gene Weltfish, *The Lost Universe* (New York and London: Basic Books, 1965), pp. 480f.

Wissler was curator at the American museum of Natural History, New York, and here he was assisted by a staff of able men, most of them students under Boas: Lowie, Spinden, Skinner, Goddard, Spier, and others. Some of these men, and Lowie of course first of all, contributed considerably to the study of North American Indian religions. Alanson Skinner was a diligent field worker among the Menomini, Ojibway, Cree, Iowa, Sauk, Potawatomi, and other tribes of the Middle West, and has written on the Menomini medicine ceremony and sacred bundles.[127] He has also illuminated the hunting religion of the Northern Algonkian groups in several papers.[128] Pliny Earle Goddard investigated religious life among the Hupa of California and collected myths among some Apache groups.[129] Leslie Spier made excellent ethnographical monographs of the Klamath in Oregon and some Yuman tribes in the Southwest (Havasupai, Maricopa); religion is here treated in its cultural context, and religious features are, in a characteristic way, linked with similar features in other Indian tribes.[130] This "plotting" procedure reached its culmination in Spier's study of the sun-dance distribution (see below). As will emerge from the sequence, Spier later made important research on phenomena of religious contact.

Many more pupils of Boas's could be mentioned who, like the ones presented here, wrote accounts of Indian religions within the framework of culture. There was Roland Dixon, critical and exeedingly learned, whose monograph on the Maidu Indians of northern California, "the first strictly scientific investigation of a Californian tribe" according to Lowie, was a model monograph.[131] S. A. Barrett is known, among other things, for his descriptions of Pomo medicine men and Central Algonkian religious dances,[132] Truman

---

[127] Alanson Skinner, *Medicine Ceremony of the Menomini, Iowa, and Wahpeton Dakota* (New York: Indian Notes and Monographs IV, 1920); and his *Social Life and Ceremonial Bundles of the Menomini Indians* (New York: Anthropological Papers of the American Museum of Natural History XIII/1, 1913).

[128] See, e.g., Alanson Skinner, *Notes on the Eastern Cree and Northern Saulteaux* (New York: Anthropological Papers of the American Museum of Natural History IX/1, 1911).

[129] Pliny Earle Goddard, *Life and Culture of the Hupa* (Berkeley: University of California Publications in American Archaeology and Ethnology I/1, 1903); see also his *Jicarilla Apache Texts* (New York: Anthropological Papers of the American Museum of Natural History VIII, 1911); *Myths and Tales from the White Mountain Apache*, and *White Mountain Apache Texts* (New York: Anthropological Papers of the American Museum of Natural History XXIV/2, 4, 1919, 1920).

[130] See, e.g., Leslie Spier, *Havasupai Ethnography* (New York: Anthropological Papers of the American Museum of Natural History XXIX/3, 1928), pp. 261ff. and 275ff.

[131] Roland B. Dixon, *The Northern Maidu* (New York: American Museum of Natural History Bulletin XVII/3, 1905); cf. Robert H. Lowie, "Franz Boas 1858–1942," Cora DuBois (ed.), *Lowie's Selected Papers in Anthropology* (Berkeley and Los Angeles: University of California, 1960), p. 428.

[132] S. A. Barrett, *Pomo Bear Doctors* (Berkeley: University of California Publications in American Archaeology and Ethnology XII/11, 1917); and his *The Dream Dance of the Chippewa and Menominee Indians of Northern Wisconsin* (Milwaukee: Publications of the Museum of

Michelson, prominent linguist, contributed to our knowledge of Fox myths and rituals,[133] and so on. In the sequence, we shall discuss the later "Boasians": Lesser, Linton, Bunzel, Benedict, Reichard, Underhill, and Gunther, and others who mainly operated after 1925 and who partly changed the course of studies of Indian religions.

Some words, finally, about the Indians and squaw men whom Boas trained, not only to record texts, but also to handle the collected material in a scientific way. George Hunt, his Kwakiutl collaborator, has been mentioned. A keen observer was James Teit, whose excellent descriptions of religious beliefs and rites in ethnographical monographs on different Salishan Indians—Thompson River, Lillooet, Shuswap, and Okanagon in the Columbia-Fraser Plateau area—constitute a treasure trove for the student of North American religion.[134] Teit was also active in recording the myths and legends of the tribes mentioned. William Jones, a part Fox Indian, became a good linguist and ethnologist on his own cultural heritage. His analysis of Fox religion deserves our attention.[135]

---

the City of Milwaukee Bulletin I, 1911).

[133] Cf., for example, the papers on ceremonies and fetishes brought together in Truman Michelson, *Contributions to Fox Ethnology*, 2 vols. (Washington, D.C.: Bureau of American Ethnology Bulletins LXXXV and XCV, 1927, 1930).

[134] See, e.g., James Teit, *The Thompson Indians of British Columbia* (New York: American Museum of Natural History Memoirs II, 1900), pp. 326ff., 337ff., 368ff.

[135] William Jones, *Ethnography of the Fox Indians* (Washington, D.C.: Bureau of American Ethnology Bulletin CXXV, 1939), pp. 10ff. The book was edited by Margaret W. Fisher. Jones was killed by the Ilongots of Luzon while performing field research among them in 1909.

ISSUES RAISED BY BOASIAN ANTHROPOLOGY

INTRODUCTION

The field research performed by Boas and his pupils broadened the knowledge of American Indian religion immensely. New scientific problems emerged and were courageously attacked—and allegedly explained—by the field investigators themselves, and old issues were resumed and illustrated in the light of the new experiences. Problems posed by European theoreticians, such as the priority of animism and the validity of the high-god concept, were also reflected in this debate. Historical perspectives dominated, and culture-historical procedures founded on Boas's insights slowly replaced evolutionistic ones.

To a certain extent also, European ethnologists and historians of religion contributed to the debate. Their points of view were still partly evolutionistic, although strong historical winds now started to blow from Vienna and Frankfurt. Also sociologists and social psychologists appeared on the scene. For natural reasons the main debate was, however, conducted in America.

INDIAN RELIGIOUS CONCEPTS

At the same time as, in Europe, R. R. Marett developed his thoughts on pre-animistic religion (with specific reference to Bishop Codrington's writings on the *mana* of Melanesia), the Iroquois ethnologist, J. N. B. Hewitt, presented an article in which he asserted that the notion of *orenda* among the Iroquois corresponded in fact to the ideas of "mystic potence" which might be found, he said, in all religions.[1] Moreover, he suggested that *orenda* should be the *terminus technicus* for this power.[2] It is obvious that at that time Hewitt was ignorant of Codrington's and Marett's works, for *mana* is not mentioned in his article. Many theorists later on, when the concept of *mana* fell into disrepute in scientific quarters, questioned Hewitt's interpretation of *orenda* as an impersonal power. However, they have done so in vain, for *orenda* is one of the most convincing proofs of such a conception that can be found.[3]

---

[1] J. N. B. Hewitt, "Orenda and a Definition of Religion," *American Anthropologist* IV (1902), pp. 33–46.

[2] *Ibid.*, pp. 37ff. Actually, the classicist Pfister adopted the term as a substitution for *mana*, and the folklorist C. W. von Sydow followed his example.

[3] See Åke Hultkrantz, *Les Religions des Indiens Primitifs de l'Amérique* (Stockholm: Acta Universitatis Stockholmiensis, Stockholm Studies in Comparative Religion IV, 1963), pp. 17ff.

Hewitt thought he could find a counterpart to Iroquoian *orenda* in the *manitou* of the Algonkian Indians. This suggestion evidently struck William Jones, for in an article on the Algonkian *manitou* published a few years later, he identified this concept with the idea of a mysterious cosmic power to be found everywhere in Nature.[4] Jones's opinion of the import of the word, although grounded on linguistic materials, has not convinced other students. Allowing for a variation of meaning in different Algonkian tribes[5]—Jones's data mainly referred to the Fox Indians—it may be stated that *manitou* indicates rather a supernatural quality than supernatural power.[6] A *manitou* is a supernatural being, which mostly means: a spirit.[7]

Whereas Hewitt saw in *orenda* a distinctive power in each individual situation, Jones developed the idea that it was an "abstract conception of a diffused, all-pervasive, invisible, manipulable, and transferable life-energy, or universal force." This interpretation was certainly motivated by his identification of *manitou* as a power with the highest *manitou*, in some Algonkian languages, for instance, in Cree dialects, named Manitou.[8] Swanton, too, thought that he had discovered the concept of universal supernatural energy in an Indian tribe, the Tlingit Indians of western Canada and Alaska. He found that the language of these Indians was so constructed that "instead of thinking of so many different objects, they think of one diffused into many." Each spirit is, consequently, a manifestation of "the ocean of supernatural energy."[9] Among the Siouan Omaha, finally, the celebrated anthropologist Alice C. Fletcher, closely collaborating with the tribal member Francis La Flesche, found a similar meaning attached to the concept of *wakonda*. *Wakonda*, she stated, "is the name given to the mysterious all-pervading and life-giving power to which certain anthropomorphic aspects are attributed," and the same name "is also applied to objects or phenomena regarded as sacred or mysterious."[10] We need not here further develop Miss Fletcher's interpretation which, particularly after the publication of her remarkable monograph on the Omaha, drew much

[4] William Jones, "The Algonkin Manitou," *Journal of American Folklore* XVIII (1905), pp. 183–90.

[5] Erminie Wheeler-Voegelin, "Manitu, Manito, or Manitou," *Standard Dictionary of Folklore, Mythology, and Legend* I (New York: Funk & Wagnalls, 1950), p. 674.

[6] Hultkrantz, *op. cit.*, pp. 16f.

[7] Cf. Fisher's comment in William Jones, *Ethnography of the Fox Indians* (Washington, D.C.: Bureau of American Ethnology Bulletin CXXV, 1939), p. 11, n. 6.

[8] John M. Cooper, "The Northern Algonquian Supreme Being," *Primitive Man* VI/3–4 (1933), pp. 46, 48, 50, 60, 74, 106.

[9] John R. Swanton, *Social Condition, Beliefs, and Linguistic Relationship of the Tlingit Indians* (Washington, D.C.: Bureau of American Ethnology, 26th Annual Report, 1908), p. 451, note.

[10] Alice C. Fletcher, "Wakonda," *Handbook of American Indians* II (Washington, D.C.: Bureau of American Ethnology Bulletin XXX, 1910), p. 897.

attention from the scientific world.[11]

The reaction to the interpretations referred to above was very different in different quarters. Boas, sober as usual, was convinced that the belief in "magic power" was a fundamental concept in American Indian religion, but did not accept the view that it denoted universal power.[12] Radin refuted entirely the idea that Indians believed in such a thing as supernatural power. Belief in such a power was, in his opinion, not a fact but an interpretation without foundation in facts.[13] To Radin, concepts such as *manitou* and *wakan* (among the Dakota) revealed a belief in spirits. "Animism, then, in the old Tylorian sense of the term, is the belief of the Indians," he declared.[14] This was obviously no correct interpretation. First, Lowie showed that Radin gave evidence of "a quite un-Tylorian indifference," since he did not derive his concept of spirit from the concept of soul.[15] Second, both *manitou* and *wakan* stand for supernatural (being) and thus cover more than the spirit idea.

The discussion around *orenda*, *manitou*, and *wakonda* was not confined to America but went on also in Europe where researchers such as Preuss, F. R. Lehmann, Söderblom, Schmidt, Beth, and Arbman wrestled with these concepts. The idea of *manitou* and *wakonda* as a general, cosmic energy represented in individual instances appealed to Preuss; he found that this cosmic energy was supposed to penetrate all life on earth and cause it to move.[16] A similar standpoint was taken by Beth, whereas Lehmann, Söderblom, Schmidt, and Arbman defended the view that the concepts adduced expressed a quality, not a universal potency. The latter interpretation gained ground among the students in both hemispheres, and no researcher today would subscribe to Preuss's and Beth's opinion. Nevertheless, the latter had a certain foundation in the materials supplied by Miss Fletcher and Swanton—if these materials were not, as Radin thought, formed by the field investigators' own leading ideas.

The last-mentioned hypothesis was shared by Arbman. He considered that Miss Fletcher's description of Omaha religion evinced an idealizing tendency which was due partly to the fact that these Indians had been influenced by Christianity.[17] Arbman found that such a concept as *wakonda*

---

[11] Alice C. Fletcher and Francis La Flesche, *The Omaha Tribe* (Washington, D.C.: Bureau of American Ethnology, 27th Annual Report, 1911).

[12] Franz Boas, "Religion," *Handbook of American Indians* II (Washington, D.C.: Bureau of American Ethnology Bulletin XXX, 1910), p. 366.

[13] Paul Radin, "Religion of the North American Indians," *Anthropology in North America* (New York: G. E. Stechert, 1915), p. 276.

[14] *Op. cit.*, p. 278.

[15] Robert H. Lowie, *Primitive Religion* (New York: Liveright, 1924), pp. 123f.

[16] Konrad Theodor Preuss, *Glauben und Mystik im Schatten des Höchsten Wesens* (Leipzig: C. L. Hirschfeld, 1926), pp. 29ff. In earlier works Preuss showed a less decided opinion.

[17] Ernst Arbman, "Seele und Mana," *Archiv für Religionswissenschaft* XXIX (1931), p. 345.

partly denoted a quality, as well as beings provided with this quality, and meant partly the totality of gods, or at least a category of gods; and it was in the latter sense that *wakonda* had been misunderstood by Miss Fletcher.[18] Arbman could here adduce the physician J. R. Walker's excellent monograph on the sun dance of another Siouan tribe, the Oglala (Dakota), in which the ideas of the gods and the universe were presented together with the description of the dancing ritual. Walker's informants, the medicine men, provided him with remarkable materials on the classification of gods, and working on this basis Walker thought he could identify a kind of mythological system which, according to him, was accepted as true by the Indians.[19] He thus worked out the presumed shamanistic doctrine of the Oglala, characterized by mythological combinations based on the sacred number four.[20] According to the same doctrine, Wakan Tanka, "the great mystery," was one, and yet dissolved in a plurality of divinities.[21]

As is readily seen, there are two limitations in Walker's data: first, they refer only to the beliefs of the medicine men; and second, the final systematization is Walker's own.[22] Other information, supplied by, *inter alia*, the celebrated ethnomusicologist Frances Densmore, makes it more than probable that Wakan Tanka was a Supreme Being, vaguely manifested in phenomena which also pertain to other gods, such as the sun or the thunder.[23] Wakan Tanka corresponds to Wakonda among the Omaha. The idea of *wakonda* alternates, as Miss Fletcher has shown (see above), between a personal god and a quality belonging to the gods.[24] Because of its vagueness, the concept of the Supreme God was difficult to analyze for early ethnologists (Swanton) and was mistaken for a universal *mana* by some theorists (Preuss, Beth), and a collective name for gods by others (Arbman).

As a matter of fact, aboriginal North America supplies us with some of the best examples of a belief in Supreme Beings that can be found. In particular did new information from the Californian Indians impress students of religion during the first decades of our century. Curtin's records from the Wintun, Dixon's from the Maidu, Kroeber's from Central California show the existence of a belief in a lofty Creator and a *creatio ex nihilo*. These

[18] *Ibid.*, p. 342.

[19] J. R. Walker, *The Sun Dance and Other Ceremonies of the Oglala Division of the Teton Dakota* (New York: Anthropological Papers of the American Museum of Natural History XVI/2, 1917), p. 56.

[20] *Ibid.*, pp. 78ff.

[21] *Ibid.*, pp. 57, 79f.

[22] The Dakota Indian linguist Ella Deloria has many unpublished materials which illuminate another interpretation of the religious system than the one given by Walker.

[23] Frances Densmore, *Teton Sioux Music* (Washington, D.C.: Bureau of American Ethnology Bulletin LXI, 1918), pp. 85f., 96. Cf. my discussion in Åke Hultkrantz, *Conceptions of the Soul among North American Indians* (Stockholm: Statens Etnografiska Museum Monograph Series I, 1953), pp. 196ff.

[24] Cf. Åke Hultkrantz, *Les Religions des Indiens Primitifs, op. cit.*, pp. 18f.

records were later supplemented by field material from other Indian groups, particularly the Pawnee (Grinnell, G. A. Dorsey) and Algonkian tribes (Grinnell, Skinner, Dorsey, Speck, and others). In an early paper on Californian Indian religion, Kroeber underlined the fundamental importance of the Creator concept and its antithesis, the concept of the Trickster (Coyote).[25] It is remarkable, however, that in a later paper the same author attributed these beliefs to a relatively recent time.[26]

Whatever their age, the American Indian ideas of the Supreme Being attracted wide interest among theoreticians on primitive religion and religious genesis. Lang had already presented the Australian high gods to the educated public; some students had rejected his evidence while others, like for instance Marett, interpreted these gods as a late development in primitive religion. The new evidence from America strengthened Lang's position that the belief in high gods belonged to a very early phase in human history.[27]

The North American material also stimulated Wilhelm Schmidt who, in the second and fifth volumes of his great work on the origin of the idea of god, included lengthy quotations from the field reports on Californian Indian, Algonkian, Salish, and Eskimo religions.[28] A condensed treatise on the North American high gods was also written by the same author.[29] To Schmidt, these materials constituted proofs of his general idea that the high-god concept preceded in time any other religious concept—an idea which he tried to base on the cultural-historical position of the tribes involved. There is no reason here to dwell upon his *Kulturkreislehre* which, in the form he gave it, has long ago been dismissed as a scientific tool. Allowing for the many mistakes in the control of sources and other technical shortcomings in Schmidt's literary production we may, however, say that he succeeded in proving the extensive occurrence of the belief in high gods among primitive societies. Some of his finest examples have been obtained from the Indians of North America.

Schmidt's investigations of the North American high gods served as a basis for his efforts to establish a temporal differentiation of North American

[25] Alfred Louis Kroeber, *The Religion of the Indians of California* (Berkeley: University of California Publications in American Archaeology and Ethnology IV/6, 1907), p. 343; cf. also by the same author, *Types of Indian Culture in California* (Berkeley: University of California Publications in American Archaeology and Ethnology II/3, 1904), p. 97.

[26] Alfred Louis Kroeber, *The History of Native Culture in California* (Berkeley: University of California Publications in American Archaeology and Ethnology XX, 1923), p. 134.

[27] Here it must be admitted that in his accounts of North American theism Lang did not clearly recognize the difference between Supreme Beings and culture heroes; see, e.g., Andrew Lang, *Myth, Ritual and Religion* II (2d ed.; London: Longmanns, Green, 1899), pp. 60ff. Cf. Söderblom, below.

[28] Wilhelm Schmidt, *Der Ursprung der Gottesidee* II, V (Münster in Westfalen: Aschendorff, 1929, 1934).

[29] Wilhelm Schmidt, *High Gods in North America* (Oxford: Oxford University, 1933).

religions. The Yuki, Kato, and other Northwest Central Californian tribes and tribelets had, according to him, the oldest religious pattern, characterized by a Supreme Being closely associated with the thunder and the rainbow, and by a creative assistant, usually the First Ancestor.[30] In the eastern parts of northern central California the Maidu and other groups represented the next historical layer: the high god had here an antagonist, the Coyote, and the creation of the world included the diving of birds and animals into the primeval sea to fetch earth. Since the latter pattern could also be found among the Algonkian tribes, Schmidt supposed there had once been contact between Californian and Algonkian groups in the Canadian forest region. Because of certain religious and mythological affinities, the Salishan tribes were also referred to the same original area. The religions of the Californians, Algonkians, and Salish were finally linked with the religions of the "Arctic primeval culture" (*Urkultur*), represented by Caribou Eskimo, Samoyeds, and other Arctic groups.[31]

Schmidt's interpretations of the American data were questioned from many quarters, and an intensive discussion of the validity of his material also followed. Alternative suggestions of the import of the American high-god concepts were presented, for instance, by Nathan Söderblom. He defined these great gods as "originators" (*Urheber*), but in describing them he confused them with the culture heroes.[32] The connections between the Supreme Being and the culture hero in North America puzzled many students of religion in Europe, but also American anthropologists found them complicated. In an essay on primitive "monotheism," with most examples obtained from aboriginal North America, Radin assures us that if we find a Supreme Being with the attributes of a culture hero this reprsents a secondary development.[33] As to the concept of the culture hero, Boas considered, in opposition to Brinton, that the sexual and egotistical motifs in the culture-hero tales are primary and that there is a gradual transition to a clearly altruistic series.[34] It is interesting to note that Dixon found these ideas evolutionistic and therefore challenged them.

The enigmatic position of the Supreme Being in North American native religion intrigued in particular two American anthropologists, Radin and

---

[30] Cf. Wilhelm Schmidt, "Donner und Regenbogen beim Höchsten Vesen der Yuki," *Essays in Anthropology Presented to A. L. Kroeber* (Berkeley: University of California, 1936), pp. 299–308.

[31] Josef Haekel, "Prof. Wilhelm Schmidts Bedeutung für die Religionsgeschichte des Vorkolumbischen Amerika," *Saeculum* VII/1 (1956), pp. 1–39; here pp. 6ff.

[32] Nathan Söderblom, *Gudstrons Uppkomst* (Stockholm: H. Gebers, 1914), pp. 128ff.

[33] Paul Radin, *Monotheism among Primitive Peoples* (1st ed.; London: G. Allen & Unwin, 1924; Basel: Ethnographical Museum, 1954), p. 12.

[34] Franz Boas, "Introduction" to James Teit, *Traditions of the Thompson River Indians of British Columbia* (Boston and New York: American Folklore Society Memoirs VI, 1898), pp. 4ff., 9.

Lowie.[35] In his article on North American Indian religions already quoted, Radin maintained that the Supreme Being is a rare phenomenon in these religions; he is best represented among the Pawnee.[36] Radin developed here, for the first time, the idea that "the single deity" is "a thoroughly shamanistic construction."[37] Ten years later, in his lecture on monotheism already referred to, Radin ascribed the belief in the Supreme Being to the creative thinking of "devoutly religious" individuals who sought for a First Cause of things. The common people, the realists, have secondarily brought about the fusion between this lofty concept and the amoral culture hero.[38] Similar views were expressed in Radin's *Primitive Man as Philosopher*.[39] Later on in his work on primitive religion, Radin changed his opinion to the extent that he did not allow the belief in high gods to be called monotheism any longer. Still more important was his new statement that wherever such a god exists "it is the belief either of a few individuals or of a special group," namely, the religious thinkers.[40] This accounts for the otiose character of these high gods. In his last books on the subject, Radin went even further: the high gods of North America are all, with one exception, the Tirawa of the Pawnee, explained as developments from Christian stimuli.[41] As was so often the case, however, Radin was not consistent in his points of view: the Winnebago Earthmaker is said to antedate Christian teachings.[42]

In contradistinction to Radin, Lowie was very careful in his evaluation of the North American data on Supreme Beings. As noted down by Bidney, he finally accepted, with certain modifications, Schmidt's proofs of a quite common belief in such beings among primitive peoples.[43] It is apparent, however, that Lowie hesitated to generalize the evidence insofar as it concerned North American Indians.[44] Never interested in patterns and systems, he preferred to adduce the single cases without combining them into an integrated picture.

We may say with certain justification that americanists were inclined to accept the North American high-god ideas as genuine, but with few

---

[35] Cf. David Bidney, "The Ethnology of Religion and the Problem of Human Evolution," *American Anthropologist* LVI (1954), pp. 1–18.

[36] Cf. George Bird Grinnell, "Pawnee Mythology," *Journal of American Folklore* VI (1893), pp. 113–30; and *Pawnee Hero Stories and Folk-Tales* (New York: Forest and Stream, 1889), pp. 352ff.

[37] Radin, "Religion of the North American Indians," *op, cit.,* p. 293.

[38] Radin, *Monotheism among Primitive Peoples, op. cit.,* pp. 25f.

[39] Paul Radin, *Primitive Man as Philosopher* (New York: D. Appleton, 1927), pp. 342ff.

[40] Paul Radin, *Primitive Religion* (New York: Viking, 1937), p. 257.

[41] Paul Radin, *Die Religiöse Erfahrung der Naturvölker* (Zürich: Rhein, Albae Vigiliae XI, 1951), p. 108.

[42] Paul Radin, *The Trickster: A Study in American Indian Mythology* (New York: Philosophical Library, 1956), p. 115.

[43] Robert H. Lowie, *Primitive Religion* (2d ed.; New York: Liveright, 1948), p. vi.

[44] Cf. Robert H. Lowie, *Indians of the Plains* (New York: McGraw-Hill, 1954), pp. 165f.

exceptions—Radin, Swanton[45]—did they care to formulate a high-god theory. The interest was greater in Europe where Preuss, Söderblom, Schmidt, and others co-ordinated the North American findings with similar conceptions from other regions. The theistic concepts were also analyzed in Loewenthal's study of Eastern Algonkian religion.[46] This and Kroeber's account of Californian Indian religion were the first treatises on regional North American native religion. Loewenthal also produced an initiated article on the culture hero in eastern North America.[47]

Most American anthropologists were less interested in the culture hero as a metaphysical concept than in his activities as a trickster in the myths. Indeed, the trickster cycle looms large in North American myth collections, assembled and published during this period. Some tales contain decidedly religious motifs, but even if these occasionally were observed, as in Kroeber's footnotes to his collection of Arapaho traditions,[48] they were mostly overlooked and drowned in the huge mass of epic materials.

MYTHOLOGY

This leads us to the problem of the place of myths and legends during the Boasian regime. The past period of research had been characterized by a genuine interest in the religious aspects of myths and legends. We may distinguish three major lines in interpretation before the appearance of Boas: first, the evolutionistic approach as manifested in Powell's and Brinton's myth analyses, discussed in the foregoing; second, the "naturistic" theories of Max Müller and his school, evinced in Brinton's writings and in several other papers, for instance, in Wardle's interpretation of the Eskimo Sedna cycle as a symbolic rendering of the day cycle (with later additional symbolism);[49] and third, the ritual approach to myth, represented by Matthews.[50] The evolutionistic myth interpretations disappeared with the doctrine of cultural evolutionism, and the "eclipse of solar mythology" had begun already in the 1880s and was *de facto* finished with Müller's death in 1900.[51] American

---

[45] John R. Swanton, "Three Factors in Primitive Religion," *American Anthropologist* XXVI (1924), pp. 358–65. Cf. also the same author, "Some Anthropological Misconceptions," *American Anthropologist* XIX (1917), pp. 459–70.

[46] John Loewenthal, *Die Religion der Ostalgonkin* (Berlin: W. & S.. Loewenthal, 1913), pp. 59ff.

[47] John Loewenthal, "Der Heilbringer in der Irokesischen und Algonkinischen Religion," *Zeitschrift für Ethnologie* XLV (1913), pp. 65–82.

[48] George A. Dorsey and Alfred Louis Kroeber, *Traditions of the Arapaho* (Chicago: Field Columbian Museum Anthropological Series V, 1903).

[49] H. Newell Wardle, "The Sedna Cycle: A Study in Myth Evolution," *American Anthropologist* II (1900), pp. 568–80.

[50] Washington Matthews, *The Night Chant, A Navaho Ceremony* (New York: American Museum of Natural History Memoirs VI, 1902).

[51] Richard M. Dorson, "The Eclipse of Solar Mythology," Thomas E. Sebeok (ed.), *Myth: A Symposium* (Bloomington: Indiana University, 1958), p. 37.

students of North American mythology were only slightly affected by the new "astral mythology" which took form in Germany after the turn of the century (with Siecke, Lessmann, and others). On the other hand, German americanists were affected by it, in particular Hugo Kunike.[52] One leading German americanist, Paul Ehrenreich, found good evidence that the South American myths lent themselves to an interpretation along solar-mythological lines.[53]

The final blow to naturist mythology in America was thrust by Waterman in his examinaion of etiological myths in North America. Waterman found that hundreds of explanations of natural phenomena were scattered throughout the North American Indian tales, but that in most cases they were loosely added to the tales without being important parts of them.[54] Waterman's essay was clearly in line with the general trend at that time among American anthropologists—notably Boas, Lowie, Dixon, and Goldenweiser—to tear to pieces former assumptions and reconstructions within their science which lacked a sound foundation in reality.

Matthews's aforementioned studies of the conjunction between myth and ritual, finally, had no immediate effects on mythological theory. His insistence on the priority of myth over ritual ran counter to contemporary trends in Europe as represented by Frazer, Robertson Smith, and, later on, Harrison. Harrison's *Themis* (1912), which became so influential as the first exposition of the myth-and-ritual school, proceeded from the presumption that myths arise out of rites, and not the other way round. Boas and his followers seem to have embraced a similar view. Indeed, it may be a matter of a strange convergence that already in 1898 Boas could pronounce that "ritual moulds the explanatory myth."[55] In the same connection, he claimed that "oft-repeated actions which are the expression of social laws . . . may be expected to be more stable than traditions that are not repeated in a pre-scribed form or ritual."[56] However, the problem did not attract much attention with Boas whose main concern was the diffusion of myths and tales.

As a matter of fact, although Boas deserves our praise for the inspiration he gave to myth collectors, and for the extensive myth collections he recorded himself in native languages, his approach to myths was clearly a regression from an earlier period as far as concerns the religious point of view. Myths were not any more primarily observed with respect to their

---

[52] H. Kunike, "Zur Astralmythologie der Nordamerikanischen Indianer," *Internationales Archiv für Ethnographie* XXVII (1926), pp. 1–29, 55–78, 107–34.

[53] Paul Ehrenreich, "Die Mythen und Legenden der Südarmerikanischen Urvölker und Ihre Beziehunger zu denen Nordamerikas und der Alten Welt" (Berlin: A. Asher, *Zeitschrift für Ethnologie* XXXVII, Supplement, 1905).

[54] T. T. Waterman, "The Explanatory Element in North American Mythology," *Journal of American Folklore* XXVII (1914), pp. 1–54.

[55] Franz Boas, *Race, Language and Culture* (New York: Free Press, 1940), p. 423.

[56] *Ibid.*

religious contents. As a genre they were not differentiated from other oral narratives.[57] Their value lay in the contribution they could give to our understanding of the diffusion mechanisms and, at least in the eyes of Boas's pupils, to the reconstruction of American Indian culture history. Boas was also, as we have seen, keenly interested in the ways in which myths mirrored culture, and he distinguished (although not consequently, as shown by Barbeau) between the esoteric tales of the common tribesman and the esoteric tales of the specialist, the medicine man or member of a secret society.[58] (This fruitful line was later further developed by Radin.) Boas's surprising indifference to the religious import of myths and legends is reflected in the fact that he, with so many later folklorists, primarily stressed their literary quality: "The one-sided emphasis laid upon the intimate relation between religion and mythology obscures the imaginative play that is involved in the formation of myths."[59] He shared this general attitude with Radin, as we have also seen.

Boas and his circle of anthropologists made a great impression on folklorists, and it is no exaggeration to say that they even domineered the American Folklore Society. Stith Thompson was a folklorist, not an anthropologist, but his work on North American Indian traditions is marked by the double heritage from Boas and the Finnish folklorist school (Krohn, Aarne). His foremost work was a representative corpus of North American tales.[60] It is still the best presentation of its kind, although we now have a modern anthology written along similar lines.[61] Thompson's mythological investigations are primarily diffusion studies of the classical type and scarcely touch on the problem of the religious functions of the tales.[62]

Quite apart from the diffusionistic and behavioristic concerns of most American anthropologists, the philosopher Hartley B. Alexander analyzed Indian beliefs and myths as testimonies of a religious philosophy. Interested initially in the art and mythology of the Pawnee, Alexander soon became absorbed by American Indian mythology in general. He wrote a learned work on North American mythology which is still a helpful source of reference to students of American Indian religion;[63] it was later followed by a

---

[57] Cf. Franz Boas, "Mythology and Folklore," Franz Boas (ed.), *General Anthropology* (New York: D. C. Heath, 1938), p. 609.

[58] Boas, *Race, Language and Culture, op. cit.*, pp. 306, 312–15, 447f.; Charles Marius Barbeau, "Review of *Tsimshian Mythology* by Franz Boas," *American Anthropologist* XIX (1917), pp. 548–63.

[59] Boas, "Mythology and Folklore," *op. cit.*, p. 611.

[60] Stith Thompson, *Tales of the North American Indians* (Cambridge: Harvard University, 1929).

[61] Tristram P. Coffin, *Indian Tales of North America* (Philadelphia: American Folklore Society, Bibliographical and Special Series XIII, 1961).

[62] Stith Thompson, "The Star Husband Tale," *Studia Septentrionalia* IV (1953), pp. 93–163.

[63] Hartley Burr Alexander, *North American Mythology* (Boston: Marshall Jones, Mythology of All Races X, 1916). A predecessor of this work was Lewis Spence, *Myths and Legends: The*

similar book on Central and South American aboriginal mythology.[64] Some years afterwards he issued a paper on Pueblo Indian ritual dances.[65] His later works were mostly more subjective, endeavouring to reveal the eternal values of North American Indian mythical and ritual speculation. One book appeared as a result of his activities as a guest lecturer on American Indian art and philosophy at the Sorbonne;[66] another was published posthumously and communicates to us his over-all view of "the white pages of American Indian thought and understanding."[67] Alexander's approach to his subject reminds us of the Santee Indian doctor Charles Alexander Eastman's ("Ohiyesa") *Einfühlung* into Plains Indian religion,[68] and his concepts of univeralism and symbolism point forward to recent ideas among historians of religion (Eliade), anthropologists (Redfield, Brown), and philosophers of religion (Schuon).

It is impossible to review here all books and articles which, during the Boas period and its immediate sequence, were published on North American myths and legends. Suffice it to say, with Thompson, that "of all groups of peoples outside our own Western civilization, none have been so thoroughly studied as the North American Indians," and this applies unreservedly to their myths and legends.[69] The greatest collector of all was Franz Boas, and next to him came Hewitt and Radin, Sapir and Swanton. A wealth of folk-lore material was also recorded by the Canadian ethnologist Marius Bar-beau, whose early publications include works on Iroquoian myths and legends, as well as analyses of Iroquoian myths and religious ideas.[70] In later years Barbeau has written monographs on such topics as Haida myths (the Haida are the Indians of Queen Charlotte Islands) and totem poles.[71] The latter work, a study of North Pacific totem poles and their associated

North American Indians (Boston: D. D. Nickerson, 1914). The latter work contains, *inter alia*, a chapter on the phenomenology of North American Indian religion, pp. 80–140.

[64] Hartley Burr Alexander, *Latin American Mythology* (Boston: Marshall Jones, Mythology of All Races XI, 1920).

[65] Hartley Burr Alexander, *The Ritual Dances of the Pueblo Indians* (Denver: Denver Art Museum, 1927).

[66] Hartley Burr Alexander, *L'Art et la Philosophie des Indiens de l'Amérique du Nord* (Paris: E. Leroux, 1926).

[67] Hartley Burr Alexander, *The World's Rim: Great Mysteries of the North American Indians* (Lincoln: University of Nebraska, 1953).

[68] Charles Alexander Eastman, *The Soul of the Indian* (Boston and New York: Houghton Mifflin, 1911).

[69] Stith Thompson, *The Folktale* (New York: Holt, Rinehart and Winston, 1946), p. 297. Cf. the extensive list of printed myth collections in *ibid.*, pp. 475ff.

[70] Charles Marius Barbeau, *Huron and Wyandot Mythology* (Ottawa: Canada Department of Mines, Geological Survey, Memoirs XLVI, 1915). Cf. the same author, "Supernatural Beings of the Huron and Wyandot," *American Anthropologist* XVI (1914), pp. 288–313.

[71] Charles Marius Barbeau, *Haida Myths* (Ottawa: National Museum of Canada, Bulletin CXXVII, 1953); the same author, *Totem Poles*, 2 vols. (Ottawa: National Museum of Canada, Bulletin CXIX, 1951).

as well as the same author's paper on Northwestern Indian totemism,[72] bring us to our next subject, the issue of totemism.

TOTEMISM, GUARDIAN SPIRITS, AND VISIONS

Next to such topics as *orenda*, the Great Spirit, the culture hero and the myths relating to him, totemism was a favorite theme with Boas and his followers. The interest in totemism, started by MacLennan (1866), had been revived by Frazer and Robertson Smith.[73] American field ethnologists soon found that totemistic phenomena occurred in many Indian societies, often associated with what has later been called "manituism" or "individual totemism": the belief in a personal guardian spirit. As Alice Fletcher could point out for the Omaha, there were many similarities between totems and guardian spirits, and the human attitude to them was also similar. Therefore, she concluded, the totem of the social group (in this case a *gens* or patrilineal sib) must have come into existence in the same manner as the personal guardian spirit, and must have represented the manifestation of an ancestor's vision.[74] Boas stated that among the Kwakiutl the personal tutelary had once been acquired by a mythical ancestor and that it was now handed down from generation to generation.[75] Without presenting the facts, Morice and Merriam held the opinion that among the Canadian Athapascans and the Californian Indians, respectively, clan totemism had developed out of individual totemism.[76] Hill-Tout, an ethnologist who specialized in the Plateau Indians, went so far that he postulated the general development of totemism from guardian-spirit beliefs.[77] This theory, which has been called "the American theory of totemism," was not accepted by all American anthroplogists— Benedict, for instance, thought that it even contradicted North American data. However, the theory is still considered probable by many scholars, particularly in Germany (for instance, by Baumann and Haekel).

[72] Charles Marius Barbeau, "Totemism, A Modern Growth on the North Pacific Coast," *Journal of American Folklore* LVII (1944), pp. 51–58.

[73] Cf. above pp. 3f., 14f., for early research on North American totemism.

[74] Alice C. Fletcher, "The Import of the Totem: A Study from the Omaha Tribe," *Proceedings of the American Association for the Advancement of Science* XLVI (1897), pp. 325–36.

[75] Franz Boas, "The Social Organization and the Secret Societies of the Kwakiutl Indians," *Report of the United States National Museum* (Washington, D.C.: Government Printing Office, 1897), p. 336. It should be observed, however, that Boas did not generalize his findings among the Kwakiutl; on the contrary, he believed in the diversification of the totemistic processes (see Boas, "The Origin of Totemism," *Race, Language and Culture, op. cit.*, pp. 316ff.).

[76] Adrian Gabriel Morice, "The Canadian Dénés," *Ontario Provincial Museum, Annual Archaeological Report for 1905* (1906), pp. 187–219; Clinton Hart Merriam, "Totemism in California," *American Anthropologist* X (1908), pp. 558–62.

[77] Charles Hill-Tout, "Totemism: A Consideration of Its Origin and Import," *Transactions of the Royal Society of Canada* IX (1903–4), pp. 61–99. Hill-Tout even defined totemism as the doctrine of guardian spirits in *British North America, I: The Far West, the Home of the Salish and Déné* (London: A. Constable, 1907), p. 174.

While this theory was being formed, new viewpoints on totemism were presented in important Australian field monographs. Their effect on European theoreticians in culture and religion was considerable. To Durkheim and Freud, Australian totemism became the beginning of religion. American thinkers reacted differently. Goldenweiser, working with both American and Australian data, refuted Durkheim's ideas and even challenged the concept of totemism. Not only did he prove that totemism is not a typical phenomenon among very primitive peoples, but he also questioned its character as an integral phenomenon. Such features as clan exogamy, animal names of social groups, and beliefs in descent from an animal have, Goldenweiser opined, a complex historical and psychological derivation. Under special psychosociological conditions they enter into intimate association with one another, thus constituting a totemic complex.[78] There followed an intense discussion among Goldenweiser, Lowie, Boas, Wallis, and Andrew Lang which we cannot review here since it does not primarily concern the North American Indians.

If totemism, for a time at least, seemed to have lost its substance and to have evaporated in the eyes of many American anthropologists, the belief in guardian spirits remained as a simple and undeniable fact. Indeed, it was so widespread in North America that in some measures it colored the general idea of Indian religions. Radin, for instance, called it "the most characteristic feature of Indian religion."[79] Earlier students of aboriginal religion had observed the importance of this belief, and in its most extreme form, as "nagualism" (where the client takes part of its tutelary's life and character), it had been analyzed, *inter alios*, by Brinton.[80] The indefatigable Frazer collected a treasure trove of evidence of guardian-spirit beliefs and the associated vision quest.[81] However, it was Ruth Benedict, a pupil of Boas's, who undertook the first penetrating analysis of this complex of beliefs and attitudes.[82] In her work, which has become a classic in anthropology and religious ethnology, she pays particular attention to the types of guardian-spirit experience and to the relation of this spirit concept to other cultural and religious features: ancestor spirits, puberty ordeals, totemism, shamanism, etc. Although oriented from the quantitative methods of her teacher,

---

[78] Alexander Goldenweiser, "Totemism: An Analytical Study," *Journal of American Folklore* XXIII (1910), pp. 179–293; "The Origin of Totemism," *American Anthropologist* XIV (1912), pp. 600–607; "Form and Content in Totemism," *American Anthropologist* XX (1918), pp. 280–95; "Totemism: An Essay on Religion and Society," Victor Francis Calverton (ed.), *The Making of Man: An Outline of Anthropology* (New York: Modern Library, 1931), pp. 363–92.

[79] Radin, "Religion of the North American Indians," *op. cit.*, p. 294.

[80] Daniel G. Brinton, *Nagualism: A Study in Native American Folk-lore and History* (Philadelphia: MacCalla, Proceedings of the American Philosophical Society XXXIII, 1894).

[81] James George Frazer, *Totemism and Exogamy* III (London: Macmillan, 1910), pp. 370ff.

[82] Ruth Fulton Benedict, *The Concept of the Guardian Spirit in North America* (Menasha, Wisconsin: American Anthropological Association Memoirs XXIX, 1923).

Benedict's investigation still makes a versatile impression and conserves many points of view which can be profitably used by modern students of religion. Also other American anthropologists dealt with guardian-spirit ideas, for instance, Lowie in his studies of Crow religion.

Benedict was, however, more interested in social psychology than in religious phenomenology. She therefore made much out of the fact that she found the vision more inclusive and more universal than the guardian-spirit concept. She spoke of "the social recognition of the vision as the fundamental and typical religious fact of North America."[83] The vision experience was the common element behind the changing figures of guardian spirits, but it was also patterned according to local historical presuppositions, as Benedict showed in a study of Plains Indian visions.[84] Another anthropologist, Blumenshohn, demonstrated that one of the elements of the vision quest, the fasting, was peculiar to the Central Algonkian Indians; and, further, "that the fast and the pitiful suppliant are two essentially unconnected elements of religion in North America."[85] Blumensohn's paper was written in the 1930s, but the problems defined belonged to the Boas period (and could have been posed by Boas.)

The distribution studies which characterized most of the studies on totemism, guardian spirits, and vision were brought into a wider frame when A. I. Hallowell published his well-known monograph on bear ceremonialism.[86] The contacts between northern Asia and northern North America, including those of religious and magic import, had partly been established by the Jesup North Pacific Expedition at the turn of the century. Bogoras, one of the members of the expedition, had written an important study of the myths and religious beliefs common to both continents at their junction in the North.[87] The same subject fascinated several other scholars, for instance, Speck and Lowie,[88] and reached its climax with Hallowell's investigation. From another point of view, Hallowell's work is the first treatise on the hunters' religion in North America, if we exclude Frazer's preoccupation with animal ceremonialism in one of the volumes of the *Golden Bough*.[89] As

---

[83] *Ibid.*, p. 28.

[84] Ruth Fulton Benedict, "The Vision in Plains Culture," *American Anthropologist* XXIV (1922), pp. 1–23.

[85] Jules Blumensohn, "The Fast among North American Indians," *American Anthropologist* XXXV (1933), pp. 451–69; quotation from p. 468.

[86] A. Irving Hallowell, "Bear Ceremonialism in the Northern Hemisphere," *American Anthropologist* XXVIII (1926), pp. 1–175.

[87] Waldemar Bogoras, "The Folklore of Northeastern Asia, as Compared with that of Northwestern America," *American Anthropologist* IV (1902), pp. 577–683.

[88] See, in particular, Robert H. Lowie, "On the Historical Connection between Certain Old World and New World Beliefs," *Proceedings of the 21st Congress of Americanists* (1925), pp. 546–49; "Religious Ideas and Practices of the Eurasiatic and North American Areas," *Essays Presented to C. G. Seligman* (London: Kegan Paul, Trench, Trubner, 1934), pp. 183–88.

[89] Cf. above, p. 14f.

such, Hallowell's paper has stimulated later studies on the bear cult in Siberia and in North America; as concerns North America, we may think of contributions made by Speck, Barbeau, and others.[90]

CEREMONIALISM

In addition to the hunting rites and allied concepts, the ceremonialism around the fish and sea animals also came into focus. The beginning was made with Erna Gunther's analyses of salmon rites.[91] The main attention was here, as in Hallowell's investigation, paid to the distribution of cult elements. Thus, the dissemination of the salmon ceremonial was compared to that of the bear cult. Later on, Margaret Lantis illuminated the whale ceremonialism in Alaska,[92] and Kroeber and Gifford finally analyzed the Northwest Californian salmon rites in their wider setting as world-renewal rites (cf. Part II of the present paper). We shall later list some European contributions to this and adjoining problem complexes.

Besides the Jesup Expedition, the greatest ethnological undertaking of the Boas era was the series of investigations of the sun-dance ceremonial of the Plains Indians sponsored by the American Museum of Natural History. Some work on this ritual had already been accomplished, notably by the Chicago anthropologist George A. Dorsey. The latter made circumstantial accounts of the Arapaho and Cheyenne dances with some observations of the myths and beliefs surrounding them.[93] In comparison with these works, the investigations under the auspices of Clark Wissler and the American Museum of Natural History appear perhaps more technical, but also more sterile. Wissler's interest was less directed toward the religious system and symbolism than toward the ritual elements of the dance, for these elements could be arranged in diffusional series and serve as building pieces in his culture-area theory. This does not mean to say that the series of papers on the dance which Wissler introduced was as such deficient. There were particular difficulties: some of the dances described had not been performed for a long time. Lowie, for instance, had to rely on the faithful memories of his Crow informants, for the last Crow sun dance of the old style was held in

---

[90] See Frank G. Speck, *The Celestial Bear Comes Down to Earth* (Reading, Pennsylvania: Reading Public Museum and Art Gallery, 1945); and Charles Marius Barbeau, "Bear Mother," *Journal of American Folklore* LIX (1946), pp. 1–12.

[91] Erna Gunther, "An Analysis of the First Salmon Ceremony," *American Anthropologist* XXVIII (1926), pp. 605–17; "A Further Analysis of the First Salmon Ceremony," *University of Washington Publications in Anthropology* II/5 (1928), pp. 129–73.

[92] Margaret Lantis, "The Alaskan Whale Cult and Its Affinities," *American Anthropologist* XL (1938), pp. 438–84.

[93] George A. Dorsey, *The Arapaho Sun Dance* (Chicago: Field Columbian Museum Anthropological Series IV, 1903); *The Cheyenne*, II: *The Sun Dance* (Chicago: Field Columbian Museum Anthropological Series IX/2, 1905).

the 1870s.[94] One contributor, the above-mentioned J. R. Walker, was, as we have found, particularly aware of the mythology and religious beliefs associated with the dance of the Oglala Teton Dakota.[95] Even if he failed to see the dance in a wider religious perspective, he managed to give us a glimpse of its religious implications.[96]

Nevertheless, some of the papers were rather limited in scope and vision. Wissler, for instance, paid only casual attention to the mythological frame of the Blackfoot sun dance. The subject was pushed aside under the heading "mythological notes" at the end of his paper, and only two out of fifty pages were given to it.[97]

The last contribution in the series was Spier's comparative investigation of the Plains sun-dance complex.[98] It has for a long time been considered a model of the ethnological methods used by Wissler and his generation. Spier listed the ritual elements according to their quantitative distribution; and by analyzing their diffusion, their climax, and their "measure of coherence," he found that the Central Plains tribes, the Arapaho, Cheyenne, and Oglala, must have originated the ceremony. By the same distributional operation he was able to establish that the dance was originally organized under individual leadership, not under fraternities. Spier's plotting procedure, built upon Wissler's and Sapir's methodological assumptions, was typical of the mechanistic, "flat" historical perspective which, as we have seen, dominated American ethnology in those days. His paper was admirably worked out, but it had to stand up to much criticism.[99] It is no surprise that the sober and critical-minded author later denounced his methods and results.[100]

This did not mean that the quantitative and statistical approaches to the history of the sun dance had come to an end, for ten years after the appearance of Spier's study Clements published a paper on the correlation of tribes with sun-dance data.[101] However, this paper opened up a new path to

---

[94] Robert H. Lowie, *The Sun Dance of the Crow Indians* (New York: Anthropological Papers of the American Museum of Natural History XVI/1, 1915), p. 5. The present-day sun dance among the Crow Indians was introduced in 1941 from the Wind River Shoshoni. See Fred W. Voget, "Individual Motivation in the Diffusion of the Wind River Shoshone Sundance to the Crow Indians," *American Anthropologist* L (1948), pp. 634–46.

[95] See the reference above, n. 19.

[96] Ella Deloria (cf. above) has written a later study of the same sun dance, "The Sun Dance of the Oglala Sioux," *Journal of American Folklore* XLII (1929), pp. 354–413.

[97] Clark Wissler, *The Sun Dance of the Blackfoot Indians* (New York: Anthropological Papers of the American Museum of Natural History XVI/3, 1918), pp. 268ff.

[98] Leslie Spier, *The Sun Dance of the Plains Indians: Its Development and Diffusion* (New York: Anthropological Papers of the American Museum of Natural History XVI/7, 1921).

[99] Cf., for instance, Paul Radin's criticism in his *The Method and Theory of Ethnology: An Essay in Criticism* (New York and London: McGraw-Hill, 1933), pp. 142ff.

[100] See H. W. Basehart and W. W. Hill, "Leslie Spier 1893–1961," *American Anthropologist* LXVII (1965), p. 1263.

[101] Forrest Clements, "Plains Indian Tribal Correlations with Sun Dance Data," *American Anthropologist* XXXIII (1931), p. 216–27.

cultural analysis.

Looking back at the sun-dance papers written by Wissler and his colleagues, one cannot but regret that the meaning and function of the dance was so completely neglected. Latter-day anthropologists are aware of this deficiency. Eggan thus declares that "despite all the studies of the Sun Dance we still do not have an adequate account giving us the meaning and significance of the rituals for the participants and for the tribe. One such account would enable us to revalue the whole literature of the Sun Dance."[102] This view seems quite correct.[103] Perhaps a student of religion with ethnological background would be the best man to unveil the sundance ideology.

Meanwhile, we can proceed from the hypothesis put forth by Wilhelm Schmidt and later elaborated by Werner Müller that the sun dance represents, from its start, a yearly thanksgiving to the Supreme Being.[104] Even if this hypothesis does not fit all the facts of the "ethnographical present," it explains the dance as a whole and thereby fulfils some of the more essential demands which a student of comparative religion might present.[105]

There are other themes which were discussed by Boas and his disciples, and subsequently treated by European ethnologists and historians of religion (mostly in general reference works and phenomenological surveys). Some of them figured in passing in our preceding account of Boas and his pupils. We may here mention the ritual organizations, some of which functioned in connection with the sun dance; the secret societies of the North Pacific Coast, the Southwest, and the Great Lakes area; the religious practitioners (shamans and priests); the religious and areligious individualists, etc. Most of these themes kept their actuality in ethnological debate long after the Boas period had ended, since they were a natural outcome of the field research. In this way they differ markedly from the themes introduced by European scholars, such as animism, animatism, monotheism, etc. To be sure, such items may turn up in the field materials, but they seldom occur as clear-cut as some theoreticians assume. Lowie once told the present writer that if his European colleagues really had experienced Indian fieldwork they would not have committed themselves so easily to all-explaining theories.

It is no wonder that the carefully collected North American Indian data of the Boas period frequently appeared in contemporaneous European comparative studies. The cultural historians of Germany and Austria, the

---

[102] Fred Eggan, "Social Anthropology and the Method of Controlled Comparison," *American Anthropologist* LVI (1954), p. 757.

[103] Cf. my own criticism in *Current Anthropology* I/1 (1960), p. 57; and in "The Study of North American Indian Religion," *Temenos* I (1965), p. 88.

[104] Wilhelm Schmidt, *Der Ursprung der Gottesidee, op. cit.*, II, pp. 815ff.

[105] Cf. to the foregoing discussion John W. Bennett, "The Development of Ethnological Theory as Illustrated by Studies of the Plains Sun Dance," *American Anthropologist* XLVI (1944), pp. 162–81.

extreme diffusionists of Britain, and the sociologists and social psychologists of France alike often drew on the American Indian materials to illustrate their points of view. Similar works were only to a slight extent published in the United States, for the empiricism and skepticism of Boas had become a virtue among American anthropologists, and consequently far-reaching generalizations on religion had a suspect reputation.

AN APPRAISAL

If we should characterize the theoretical work on North American Indian religion performed during the first decades of this century, we might say that the American approach suffered from the writers' behavioristic bias and, usually, secondary interest for religion, but profited from their first-hand knowledge of aboriginal religion. The Europeans, on the other hand, were shut off from this immediate contact with the field, and consequently had not always a clear picture of what Indian religions were like. In discussing them they made theoretical generalizations which were often unacceptable to their better-informed American colleagues. Still, they were, in contradistinction to the latter, on the whole more genuinely interested in religion as such.

There were, of course, exceptions to this general rule. We have met some American anthropologists who had an open sense for religion, for instance, Lowie, Radin, Speck, and Swanton. Several monographs on Indian religions by these and other authors have been mentioned in the foregoing, and more could be cited.[106] Also, not all of the Europeans writing on North American native religions were armchair students any longer. We have already referred to Preuss, who made ethnographical field trips to tribes in the Mexican Sierra Madre area (which, liberally, may be grouped with North America).[107] Another name to remember is C. C. Uhlenbeck, a Dutch linguist who worked among the Blackfoot.[108]

In spite of many shortcomings, the achievements in the knowledge of North American Indian religion were considerable during the time that Boas

---

[106] See in particular, Cora DuBois, *The Religion of the Luiseño Indians of Southern California* (Berkeley: University of California Publications in American Archaeology and Ethnology VIII/3, 1908); T. T. Waterman, *The Religious Practices of the Diegueño Indians* (Berkeley: University of California Publications in American Archaeology and Ethnology VIII/6, 1910); Arthur C. Parker, *The Code of Handsome Lake, the Seneca Prophet* (Albany: New York State Museum Bulletin CLXIII, 1912); Morris Wolf, *Iroquois Religion and Its Relation to Their Morals* (New York: Columbia University, 1919); M. R. Harrington, *Religion and Ceremonies of the Lenape* (New York: Museum of the American Indian, Heye Foundation, Indian Notes and Monographs, 1921).

[107] Konrad Theodor Preuss, *Die Nayaritexpedition*, I: *Die Religion der Coraindianer in Texten nebst Wörterbuch* (Leipzig: B. G. Teubner, 1912).

[108] Cf., e.g., Christianus Cornelius Uhlenbeck, "The Origin of the Otter-Lodge," *Festschrift Vilhelm Thomsen* (Leipzig: Otto Harrossowitz, 1912), pp. 74–77.

guided American research, and most contributions were, of course, coming from the United States and Canada. At the end of the period it was possible to write comprehensible surveys of Indian religions, surveys which still may considered useful. In this category of works belong Alexander's book on mythology, Lowie's study of primitive religion (which largely deals with North American data), and Krickeberg's account of North American ethnography, inclusive of religion.[109] A remarkably well-informed series of sketches of Indian religion was presented in Curtis's bulky and beautifully illustrated work on the North American Indian.[110] And in the well-known *Encyclopaedia of Religion and Ethics* a staff of American anthropologists, including Goddard, Gray, Kroeber, Lowie, Prince, Sapir, Skinner, Spence, and Swanton, presented the salient facts of North American aboriginal religions.[111]

Some final words must be said about an outstanding semi-popular book from this time. E. C. Parsons edited a collection of essays on North American Indian culture written by practically all the leading American ethnologists of the day. In this work informative notes on Indian religion were presented in a fictional form by such eminent experts as Harrington, Lowie, Radin, Skinner, Swanton, and Wissler. In his introduction to the volume Kroeber wrote, *inter alia*: "The book is likely to make the impression that some sixty per cent of Indian life must have been concerned with religion. This imbalance is due to the fact that religion has become the best known aspect of Indian life. Ritual and ceremony follow exact forms which the native is able to relate with accuracy from memory, long after the practices have become defunct. Moreover, once his confidence is gained, he often delights in occupying his mind with the matters of belief and rite that put an emotional stamp on his youth."[112]

This quotation gives us, in a nutshell, the achievements brought about by the Boasians in the field of religion. Religion was not their prime interest, but religious facts were easier to record than other social facts. For obvious reasons, most of these religious facts concerned rites and ceremonies. This notwithstanding, more work was dedicated to religious subjects in those days than ever afterward in American anthropology. There is quite a gap between the anthropological work in the early twenties and the corresponding work of the present day, when religion often figures only in the periphery of the investigations. The old generation of anthropologists could not of course anticipate this development. At the end of the Boas era they thought that the real study of Indian religions was now about to start. As Wissler

---

[109] Walter Krickeberg, "Amerika: Die Völker Nord- und Mittelamerikas," Georg Buschan (ed.), *Illustrierte Völkerkunde* I (Stuttgart: Strecker und Schröder, 1922), pp. 27–164.

[110] Edward S. Curtis, *The North American Indian*, 20 vols. (Cambridge: Harvard University, 1907–30).

[111] James Hastings (ed.), *Encyclopaedia of Religion and Ethics*, 12 vols. (Edinburgh: T. & T. Clark, 1908–26).

[112] Elsie Clews Parsons (ed.), *American Indian Life* (New York: B. W. Huebsch, 1922), p. 14.

expressed it: "The whole subject of mythical thought, philosophical, and religious conceptions as a New World contribution to man's history is still before us."[113]

[113] Clark Wissler, *The American Indian* (3rd ed.; New York: Douglas C. McMurtie, 1950), p. 217.

RESEARCH APPROACHES AFTER 1925

AMERICAN SCHOLARS

Until the 1920s the investigations of North American Indian religions were mainly concentrated to American anthropology, and were carried out according to the approaches and methods of the Boas school. During the period that followed, two major changes occurred: the intense preoccupation with religion slackened in American anthropology at the same time as methods and approaches changed; and the professional interest of European ethnologists—later also European and American students of religion—in Indian religions was strengthened. We may consider the period 1925–45 as an era of decline in American anthropological studies of Indian religions; whereas the period from 1945 until the present day is marked by a certain revival of this kind of studies, particularly in the history of religions where such studies earlier achieved only a marginal interest.[1]

The change in outlook which took place in American anthropology after 1925 (or, according to some authorities, after 1930) was rather conspicuous.[2] Boas lived for twenty years more, but his influence waned at the same time as new methods and directions for research came to the fore.[3] His pupils continued to play a role until about 1960, but more and more they changed their attitudes and scientific methods, in particular Kroeber, Sapir, Spier, and the younger generation of Boasians. And the new adepts of the anthropological discipline were not americanists to the same degree as the preceding generations.

There is a close correspondence between the fading interest in americanistics and the receding preoccupaion with native American religions. Also in this field the period that followed after Boas meant a major break with past tendencies. Studies of Indian religions were no longer in vogue in many

---

[1] For a closer analysis of the postwar investigations, see Åke Hultkrantz, "The Study of North American Indian Religion," *Temenos* I (1965), pp. 87–121.

[2] Meggers gives 1925 as the year when the great reorientation was started, and so does Kroeber. See Alfred Louis Kroeber, *The Nature of Culture* (Chicago: University of Chicago, 1952), p. 147.

[3] It may be remarked here that the functionalistic approaches of Malinowski's stamp which dominated anthropological perspectives in the 1920s and 1930s had, as a matter of fact, some roots in Boas's anthropology. Cf. Ruth L. Bunzel, "Introduction," Margaret Mead and Ruth L. Bunzel (eds.), *The Golden Age of American Anthropology* (New York: George Braziller, 1960), p. 402; and Alexander Goldenweiser, "Recent Trends in American Anthropology," *American Anthropologist* XLIII (1941), p. 162.

anthropological quarters, and new outlooks and new methods redirected the focal interests of research. If the anthropological concern had been religion, or rather primitive forms of religion, during the late 1800s, and if it had been religion, particularly religious ritual, as an expression of cultural dynamics during the Boas period, it became psychology and sociology during the new era after 1925.[4] Still later, after World War II, studies of culture based on economic and sociological analyses received a wide application. Religion, in aboriginal North America and elsewhere, was of course dealt with in many works, but it was rated as secondary information. If, as Kroeber said, religious factors had been overdimensioned in past ethnology, they were now often overlooked.

There were several reasons for this change in perspectives. One was that traditional Indian societies had altered and that old forms of social and ritual organization had disintegrated. The supposedlly "pure" cultures were gone by 1920, only "contaminated" cultures remained—at least this was the general idea.[5] True, some pueblos in New Mexico and isolated tribal communities in Alaska and northern Canada still offered opportuinites for field research of the old model, but for this type of work most anthropologists now turned to distant, virgin places such as South America, Oceania, and Africa. And, as Lowie pointed out, this trend was strengthened after World War II.[6] To a student of comparative religion this abolition of the home market may seem farily surprising, for, although the material and social dimensions of North American Indian cultures have disintegrated, traditional religion still flourishes in many places. Thus, after a revisit to the Winnebago Indians in 1958, Paul Radin told the present author that the religion of these Indians was practically the same as the one he had found among them fifty years earlier. Despite the deterioration of the vision complex, the religion of the Wind River Shoshoni as I experienced it in 1948 was basically identical with the one which was reported in sources of the late 1800s. Dusenberry's material on the Cree in the 1960s corroborates the persistence of religion in Plains Indian societies.[7] Moreover, rituals which on account of their bloodshed were forbidden by the whites around 1880 have again come to the surface after the removal of the bans on Indian ceremonies by the Roosevelt administration.[8]

---

[4] Cf. Betty J. Meggers, "Recent Trends in American Ethnology," *American Anthropologist* XLVIII (1946), pp. 176–214.

[5] Bunzel in Mead and Bunzel, *op. cit.*, p. 574.

[6] Robert H. Lowie, "Contemporary Trends in American Cultural Anthropology," *Sociologus* V/2 (1955), p. 114.

[7] See below, n. 122.

[8] Åke Hultkrantz, "Spirit Lodge, a North American Shamanistic Séance," Carl-Martin Edsman (ed.), *Studies in Shamanism* (Uppsala: Scripta Instituti Donneriani Aboensis I, 1967), pp. 32–68. Cf. also Iron Eyes Cody, "Sioux Sun Dance," *The Branding Iron of the Los Angeles Corral of the Westerners* (Los Angeles: n.p., 1965).

Such testimony incites some few dedicated scholars, but to the majority of American anthropologists it is of little consequence, for religion as such does not attract their attention any longer. This brings us to the second main reason for the anthropologists' lack of interest in American Indian religions.

As pointed out above, during the Boas era, religion had gained importance as part of culture. However, during the time that followed, culture was increasingly understood as a "construct" and as "an 'abstraction' from the ultimate realtiy, the behavior of individuals."[9] Although this tendency with its emphasis on "culture-and-personality" problems changed in the 1940s, when Kroeber's and White's revitalization of the culture concept came about, it certainly contributed to reducing the image of American Indian religions as fixed systems of beliefs and rituals. In a path-breaking article, in which he pleads for our considering culture (and religion!) as a statistical fiction and the individual relations as the basic reality behind the screen of culture, Sapir has, among other things, the following to say about Bella Coola mythology, as it had been recorded by Boas.[10] "What shall we do, for instance, with the cosmogenic system of the Bella Coola Indians of British Columbia? The five superimposed worlds which we learn about in this system not only have no close parallels among the other tribes of the Northwest Coast area but have not been vouched for by any informant other than the one individual from whom Boas obtained his information. Is this cosmogenic system typical Bella Coola religious belief? Is it individual fantasy construction or is it a peculiar individual elaboration on the basis of a simpler cosmogenic system which belongs to the community as a whole?"[11] Here, then, the dissolution of the culture concept creates problems for the interpretation of tribal religion.

The social-psychological "pattern" approach, inaugurated by Ruth Benedict (cf. below), certainly helped to maintain, or even to restore, the idea of definable religious profiles; but the religious accent was sometimes lost, for religion was, to a large extent, cast in a psychological mold where it withstood the risk of disappearing. To the psychiatrists, myths were wishful dreams, beliefs were projections of personality disorders, and rituals were mechanisms for the release of anxiety.

Other reasons for overlooking religion could also be adduced, for instance, the irreligious or even antireligious backgound of many leading anthropological personalities. However, it is only fair to state that, even if religion is part of the anthropological study, it is not by any means its main object. Therefore, we cannot blame the modern American anthropologists

---

[9] Meggers, op. cit., p. 177.

[10] Franz Boas, The Mythology of the Bella Coola Indians (New York: Anthropological Papers of the American Museum of Natural History II/2, 1900). Cf. below, n. 143.

[11] Edward Sapir, "Cultural Anthropology and Psychiatry," Journal of Abnormal and Social Psychology XXVII (1932), p. 230.

for their disinterest in forming new syntheses of Indian religious forms and developments. We can possibly reproach them for not having been too eager to assemble satisfactory religious facts when the information is so easily available. Modern American anthropology seems to be more concerned with theory than with facts. It follows Malinowski's early advice that one cannot collect facts without a theory.

What has been said in the foregoing also applies, more or less, to the folkloristic studies. William Fenton remarks, referring to American Indian folklore studies: "From Schoolcraft to Boas's insistence on collecting texts in the native languages, folkloristic studies underwent a gradual metamorphosis, reached intensity in the 1920s, and then declined with a shift of interests to other topics."[12] New myth collections were composed by talented anthropologists like Reichard, Beckwith, Opler, and Goodwin. But the old fervor was gone, and the religious factor in folktales was largely disregarded. A summing up of what was achieved in mythological research in different areas of Indian North America until the end of World War I may be found in a number of the *Journal of American Folklore*, where distinguished anthropologists and folklorists like Gayton, Fenton, Flannery, Lowie, Haas, and Ray have guided their pens.[13] Mythological publications after this time have been comparatively scarce, thus reflecting the general tendency to abandon the North American Indian field. Furthermore, the modern concentration on style, structure, and other formal aspects of the tales cannot make up for the loss of insight into their religious values. It is most ironical that in a time when the approach to values is of paramount importance to anthropology (cf. Redfield, Bidney, Ladd, and others) so little attention is paid to the distinctive religious values of American Indian folktales.[14] Only very recently a renewed interest in belief analyses of oral prose traditions can be discerned in the United States.[15]

In spite of a generally unfavorable situation after the end of the Boas era, much new information on Indian religions and mythologies has crept forth in American anthropological and folkloristic publications. It is perhaps impossible to point at any new "classical" monographs. Still, in the middle of all the books and articles on law, education, economics, Oedipus complexes, kinship, and social transformation there are some intriguing papers on North American religions, and quite a few smaller articles have bearing on these

[12] William N. Fenton, "Ethnohistory and Its Problems," *Ethnohistory* IX/1 (1962), p. 8.

[13] A. H. Gayton *et al.*, "Folklore Research in North America," *Journal of American Folklore* LX (1947), pp. 350–55.

[14] There are, on the other hand, value studies in the field of American native religious systems. A good example is Robert N. Rapoport, *Changing Navaho Religious Values: A Study of Christian Missions to the Rimrock Navahos* (Cambridge: Papers of the Peabody Museum of American Archaeology and Ethnology XLI/2, 1954).

[15] Cf. William Bascom, "The Forms of Folklore: Prose Narratives," *Journal of American Folklore* LXXVIII (1965), pp. 3–20.

religions. In the following we shall give a selection of this literature, and at the same time present more closely some of the authors concerned.

Several of these persons who have contributed to our stock of knowledge of native North American religions during the last decades have been leading figures in American anthropology and folklore. Many of them were originally Boas's disciples, and, at least partly, they have done research in his spirit. At the same time, however, they have broken new paths in the anthropological study of religion and become closely connected with the research programs that have characterized the period after 1925: personality in culture, cultural patterns and values, culture change (acculturation), social structure, and ethnohistory.[16] It is well known that some of the figureheads of the preceding era also continued their important research, and even took part in formulating the new perspectives. They will not be presented here again, with three exceptions: Benedict, Spier, and Hallowell. These anthropologists stand out as connecting links between the past and the present in the study of North American Indian religions.

The following review will follow up the research from area to area. It is obvious that many students did not confine their research activities to one area, for instance, Spier and Cooper; they will then be dealt with in connection with the culture area which they mostly frequented. In spite of more global orientations than before (cf. below), American anthropologists still favor such specialization in one area. We start with the Southwest, desert home of the Pueblo Indians, the Pima-Papago, and the Apache and Navajo.

After her preoccupation with guardian-spirit phenomenology and visions, Ruth Benedict turned to fieldwork among the Serrano, Cochiti, and Zuni Indians of California and New Mexico. The results of this fieldwork are embodied in her publications of myths and legends of these Indians.[17] More important, however, was her growing concern with the idea "that culture is not an aggregate of traits, but is meaningfully structured in and through organizing patterns."[18] She presented her new insights—which were inspired by anthropologists like Boas, Haeberlin, Sapir, and Malinowski; culture philosophers like Dilthey and Spengler; and configurational psychologists like Wertheimer and Stern—in two famous papers. One, an introductory article to the subject, contrasts the different ways in which the bereavement situation is handled in different aboriginal ("realistic," "Dionysian," and "Apollonian") North American cultures. Each "configuration" or "pattern" exhibits a selected series of traits which has been promoted in the society.[19] In her

[16] Cf. Åke Hultkrantz, "Historical Approaches in American Ethnology," *Ethnologia Europaea* I/2 (1967), pp. 96–116.

[17] See, e.g., Ruth Fulton Benedict, *Zuni Mythology*, 2 vols. (New York: Columbia University Contributions to Anthropology XXI, 1935).

[18] Alfred Louis Kroeber *et al.*, *Ruth Benedict: A Memorial* (New York: Viking Fund, 1949), p. 32.

[19] Ruth Fulton Benedict, "Configurations of Culture in North America," *American*

Patterns of Culture, similar points of view are brought forth and are at least partly supported by religious materials from the Pueblo area and the North Pacific Coast.[20] It was, as we know, the latter book that became "an anthropology for the common man." It showed, among other things, how religion functioned within the confines of American Indian cultural patterns. Boas, Hsu, and Codere have rightly pointed out that Benedict exaggerated the differences among culture patterns and also the possiblity of describing such patterns in terms of dominant themes.[21] Still, no student of the American Indian can avoid observing the peculiarity of religious patterns, and these may be related to cultural styles and leading cultural motifs.

In an earlier paper, Benedict had called attention to the mental differences between agriculturalists and hunters of the Southwest.[22] This recourse to psychological evaluations represented something new in American anthropology. It is no coincidence that such views should have appeared at this time, for the configurational and deep psychological approaches were gaining ground in the 1920s. In combination with anthropological theories, they stimulated studies of the personality-and-culture type. Psycho-analytical analyses within the frame of anthropology (and, much later on, folklore) became fashionable—some anthropologists, like Kroeber, turned into psychoanalysts for a time. Following the pattern set by Malinowski in England eight years earlier, Sapir stressed, in 1932, the necessity of combining anthropology with psychiatry.[23] This new approach took form in the writings of anthropologists like DuBois, Hallowell, Opler, Kluckhohn, and Devereux, and since these authors mostly worked with North American Indians, their papers occasionally contained important passages on Indian religions.

The use of psychological tests was transferred from psychology to anthropology, and the versatile Leslie Spier was among the first anthropologists who applied them.[24] Using Havasupai data, Spier tried to establish the association test as a means of revealing religious concepts. If, for instance, a Havasupai Indian (Arizona) thinks of the North—where the afterworld is supposed to be situated—his associated thought is "hunting." In other words, the occupation of the dead is hunting.[25] Spier was, however, clear about the

---

Anthropologist XXXIV (1932), pp. 1–27.

[20] Ruth Fulton Benedict, *Patterns of Culture* (Boston and New York: Houghton Mifflin, 1934).

[21] See, e.g., Helen Codere, "The Amiable Side of Kwakiutl Life," *American Anthropologist* LVIII (1956), pp. 334–51.

[22] Ruth Fulton Benedict, "Psychological Types in the Cultures of the Southwest," *Proceedings of the 23rd International Congress of Americanists* (1928), pp. 572–81.

[23] Sapir, *op. cit.*, pp. 229ff.

[24] Leslie Spier, "The Association Test as a Method of Defining Religious Concepts," *American Anthropologist* XXIX (1927), pp. 267–70. Meggers's information that Margaret Mead introduced psychological tests in anthropology in her Samoa investigation (1928) is thus not correct. See Meggers, *op. cit.*, p. 184.

[25] Spier, *op cit.*, p. 269.

3Check Out Receipt

Main - Elkhart Public Library (Main)
574-522-2665
www.elkhart.lib.in.us
Wed, Dec 05, 2007 07:11:18 PM

Item: 33080001313280
Title: The study of American Indian rel
igions
Due: 12/26/2007

Total Items: 1

Thank You!

limitations of this method, since associated words are not the same as associated ideas.

Spier introduced a more rewarding approach to American Indian religion with his reopening of the Ghost Dance analyses. As we remember, Mooney had discussed the Ghost Dance in a work which is now rated as a classic.[26] The theme had since then only been treated in passing by Kroeber, Gifford, and other scholars. With a fine feeling for new scientific needs, Spier revived the subject in his detailed paper on one northern Californian tribe, the Klamath.[27] In a later investigation, he proved the predeccessor of the Ghost Dance to be the Prophet Dance of the Plateau.[28] Mastering an immense store of historical materials, he could point out that the ideas of the Paviotso Indian, Wovoka, founder of the Ghost Dance, ultimately originated in the Prophet Dance, and that the doctrine of Smohalla and the western Plateau Shakerism represented a christianized version of the same dance. Spier's findings revolutionize our knowledge of the religious history in the Basin, Plateau, and western Plains areas. He also stimulated subsequent papers on the prophet movements by such writers as Gayton, DuBois, Barnett, and Suttles.

From the methodological point of view, Spier anticipates in the two papers we have quoted here the new anthropological approach of acculturation and culture change which was defined in 1936 by Redfield, Linton, and Herskovits.[29] By using historical documents for the reconstruction of religious developments, he furthered the ethnohistorical approach which had already been used by Swanton.[30] Studies of changing religions became fashionable as an aspect of these new approaches.

The strict historical perspective which Spier favored, and which proves so fertile in studies of American Indian religions whenever it can be applied, has another devotee in Ruth Underhill. Like Benedict and Spier an original pupil of Franz Boas, she dedicated much interest to straightforward ethnographical descriptions of different western North American tribes. Her main fieldwork was, however, concentrated on the Papago and Navajo Indians of the Southwest. Her papers on Papago Indian religion offer interesting reading to students of religion and are extremely lucid and informative.[31]

---

[26] See above, p. 11.

[27] Leslie Spier, *The Ghost Dance of 1870 among the Klamath of Oregon* (Seattle: University of Washington Publications in Anthropology II/2, 1927).

[28] Leslie Spier, *The Prophet Dance of the Northwest and Its Derivatives* (Menasha, Wisconsin: General Series in Anthropology I, 1935).

[29] Robert Redfield, Ralph Linton, and Melville Herskovits, "A Memorandum for the Study of Acculturation," *American Anthropologist* XXXVIII (1936), p. 149–52.

[30] See above, p. 33f.

[31] Ruth M. Underhill, *Singing for Power: The Song Magic of the Papago Indians* (Berkeley: University of California, 1938); *Papago Indian Religion* (New York: Columbia University Contributions to Anthropology XXXIII, 1946).

Through her intimate knowledge of Southwestern Indian archaeology, ethnology, and religion, Underhill was well equipped to write a synthesis of the religious manifestations of the area.[32] In contradistinction to Miss Parsons, she deals with religious patterns, and contrasts the individualistic hunting religions of the camp-dwelling tribes with the collectivistic ceremonial attitudes of the agricultural Pueblo settlers. Recently she has published the first modern American survey of the religions of North America.[33] This well-balanced work, composed for the general public, is, like the foregoing paper, anchored in an ecological and ritual perspective. She reiterates Radin's interpretation that religious beliefs were the specialty of the thinker and seer, while the ritual was essential for the layman. Underhill is today the leading American authority on North American Indian religions.

Underhill is not the first anthropologist to have used archaeological facts in her approach to North American religion. Forty years ago David Bushnell, an ethnohistorian at the Bureau of American Ethnology, brought together all the then extant informaion on burials and cemeteries east of the Rocky Mountains.[34] His works are, however, no longer up to date, for the archaeological discoveries during the last decades have changed the picture. But, as Underhill's investigations show, the approach to religion through archaeology is more valid today than before. Moreover, archaeologists are now themselves preoccupied with solving the problems of prehistoric North American religions.[35]

In Gladys Reichard, also a pupil of Boas, we find another scholar who, like Spier and Underhill, aimed at what Kroeber has called "descriptive integration" of Indian religions. Her particular tribe was the Navajo, and in studying their tribal language and religion she tried to determine the peculiarly Navajo aspects of these subjects.[36] Her interest in religion was motivated by her conviction that "it is religion which integrates all phases of Navajo culture."[37] Reichard held the functionalistic view that each religious element operates in the highly elaborated whole of Navajo culture and religion. For instance, in one of her works she describes the function and

[32] Ruth Underhill, *Ceremonial Patterns in the Greater Southwest* (New York: Monographs of the American Ethnological Society XIII, 1948).

[33] Ruth Underhill, *Red Man's Religion: Beliefs and Practices of the Indians North of Mexico* (Chicago: University of Chicago, 1965).

[34] David I. Bushnell, Jr., *Native Cemeteries and Forms of Burial East of the Mississippi* (Washington, D.C.: Bureau of American Ethnology Bulletin LXXI, 1920); *Burials of the Algonquian, Siouan and Caddoan Tribes West of the Mississippi* (Washington, D.C.: Bureau of American Ethnology Bulletin LXXXIII, 1927).

[35] William H. Sears, "The Study of Social and Religious Systems in North American Archaeology," *Current Anthropology* II (1961), pp. 223–46.

[36] Marian W. Smith, "Gladys Armanda Reichard," *American Anthropologist* LVIII (1956), p. 914.

[37] Gladys A. Reichard, *Prayer: The Compulsive Word* (New York: Monographs of the American Ethnological Society VII, 1944), p. 2.

meaning of Navajo sandpainting as one phase of a ceremonial whole which also includes myths, without which the paintings would be devoid of meaning.[38] Speaking of the Navajo ceremonial chants, she asserts that "a full understanding of any one chant can be secured only by witnessing its performance and correlating it with the myth which is the narrative script of the drama, as it were, and the verbal description of the rites and acts of the complex."[39] Reichard's overemphasis of function carried her here to a position which was later challenged by another Navajo specialist (Kluckhohn).

Reichard wrote a provocative book on the function, content, and struc-ture of Navajo prayers, which she saw as a fundamental feature of their rituals.[40] By linguistic analysis of the ceremonial language, she arrived at the same conclusion as in her other papers on the Navajo, namely, that no Navajo classification can be valid in our own terms. The same stress on the distinctive qualities of Navajo religion is to be found in her introductory paper to this religion.[41] In this article, and particularly in her bulky work on Navajo religion which sums up her field investigations with this tribe, Reichard arrives at the conclusion that all features of Navajo rituals are interwoven and co-ordinated by symbolic association. Similar conditions for the Zuni had already been pointed out long ago by Cushing,[42] but indepen-dently of him Reichard gave a detailed scheme of the symbolism which, according to her, sets Navajo religion apart from other Southwestern reli-gions. The author finds a system where a non-initiated observer finds none; and indeed, the Navajo himself is unaware of it.[43] With all reverence to Reichard's insights into Navajo religion, her interpretation of it is too exclu-sive to give justice to obvious facts. The service she renders us lies in her attention to symbolism as such.

Through her knowledge of Navajo religion, Reichard was able to discuss the Navajo's negative response to Christianity in an interesting study on acculturation.[44] Her interest in myths, evident in her first published paper— which dealt with the distribution of myths[45]—is best manifested in her

[38] Gladys A. Reichard, *Navajo Medicine Man: Sandpaintings and Legends of Miguelito* (New York: J. J. Augustin, 1939).

[39] Reichard, *Prayer, op. cit.*, p. 2.

[40] *Ibid.*

[41] Gladys A. Reichard, "Distinctive Features of Navaho Religion," *Southwestern Journal of Anthropology* I (1945), pp. 199–220.

[42] Frank Hamilton Cushing, *Outlines of Zuñi Creation Myths* (Washington, D.C: Bureau of Ethnology, 13th Annual Report, 1896), pp. 368ff.

[43] Gladys A. Reichard, *Navaho Religion: A Study of Symbolism*, 2 vols. (New York: Princeton University, Bollingen Series, 1950); see in particular, I, pp. 147ff.

[44] Gladys A. Reichard, "The Navaho and Christianity," *American Anthropologist* LI (1949), pp. 66–71.

[45] Gladys A. Reichard, "Literary Types and Dissemination of Myths," *Journal of American Folklore* XXXIV (1921), pp. 269–307.

analysis of Coeur d'Alene mythology (Indians of northern Idaho).[46] Here her investigations of the spread of traditions bring to mind the procedures used by Boas in his *Tsimshian Mythology.*[47]

Navajo culture and religion has been the field of interest for many other scholars, including Haile, Kluckhohn, Hill, Spencer, O'Bryan, and Aberle. Father Bernard Haile has recorded and issued several substantial collections of Navajo myths and ceremonials.[48] He has also written a book on sacrificial figures[49] and a survey of the religious concepts held by these Indians.[50] W. W. Hill has composed articles on Navajo rituals and, together with two collaborators, an interesting paper on Navajo eschatology.[51] Katherine Spencer is the author of an analysis of Navajo mythology in which she tries to find out what light this mythology can throw on Navajo values.[52] One outcome of her investigation is that violation of ritual rules brings about punishments. Aileen O'Bryan has given us an exhaustive survey of the Navajo origin myths,[53] and David Aberle a systematic investigation of the Peyote cult in the Navajo Country.[54] Among other things, Aberle correlates the level of acceptance of peyotism with the level of acculturation.

Clyde Kluckhohn was an outstanding anthropologist, and his achievements in the field of religion deserve attention. Like Reichard he was a student of Navajo society, and like her he dealt with the problem of the connection between myths and rituals. However, in contradistinction to Reichard he finds no necessary correlation between them as the drama and its text, although in most cases they are interrelated in some way. Kluckhohn elaborates here points of view which had earlier been adopted by another Navajo scholar, Matthews.[55] He finally relates Navajo myths and rituals with their "type anxiety," the concern for health.[56]

---

[46] Gladys A. Reichard, *An Analysis of Coeur d'Alene Indian Myths* (Philadelphia: American Folklore Society Memoirs XLI, 1947).

[47] See above, p. 19.

[48] Cf. Berard Haile, "Navaho Chantways and Ceremonials," *American Anthropologist* XL (1938), pp. 639–52.

[49] Berard Haile, *Navaho Sacrificial Figurines* (Chicago: University of Chicago, 1947).

[50] Berard Haile, "Religious Concepts of the Navajo Indians," *Proceedings of the Catholic Philosophical Association* X (1935), pp. 84–98.

[51] Leland C. Wyman, W. W. Hill, and Iva Ósanai, *Navajo Eschatology* (Albuquerque: New Mexico Bulletin Anthropological Series IV/1, 1942).

[52] Katherine Spencer, *Mythology and Values: An Analysis of Navaho Chantway Myths* (Philadelphia: American Folklore Society Memoirs XLVIII, 1957).

[53] Aileen O'Bryan, *The Díné: Origin Myths of the Navaho Indians* (Washington, D.C.: Bureau of American Ethnology Bulletin CLXIII, 1956).

[54] David F. Aberle, *The Peyote Religion among the Navaho* (New York: Aldine, Viking Fund Publications in Anthropology XLII, 1966).

[55] Wahington Matthews, "Some Illustrations of the Connection between Myth and Ceremony," *Memoirs of the International Congress of Anthropology* (Chicago, 1894), pp. 246–51.

[56] Clyde Kluckhohn, "Myths and Rituals: A General Theory," *Harvard Theological Review* XXXV (1942), pp. 45–79.

Kluckhohn also wrote papers on ritual participation among the Navajo and conceptions of death among Southwestern Indians.[57] An interesting article deals with what he calls the Navajo "sensitivity for categorization"; among other things, he shows here how beliefs and practices relating to the supernatural constitute a ramified system.[58] His foremost contribution to comparative religion is, besides the important investigation of myth and rite, a penetrating analysis of Navajo witchcraft.[59] In this study he shows, like Evans-Pritchard for the Azande (Africa) and Hallowell for the Saulteaux (Canada), how witchcraft is interrelated with personality disorders and how, through reduction of anxiety, it stabilizes the cultural system. This book thus synthesizes psychoanalytic, learning, and social structure theories.[60] Like all other works by Kluckhohn, it aims at explaining cultural behavior, not religion as such.

The close kinsmen of the Navajo, the Apache, have in recent times had their main interpreters in Goodwin and, after his death, in Morris Opler.[61] Grenville Goodwin is particularly known for his excellent description and analysis of Western Apache social organization, but he also treated religious themes. Thus he recorded the religion and mythology of the White Mountain Apache, and he reported on a new religion in this society.[62]

Morris Opler is, like Kluckhohn, a leading name in theoretical American anthropology. In particular, he has applied psychological points of view to Apache culture and religion. His great description of the culture of the Chiricahua Apache is a detailed study of "enculturation," that is, the process by which during his formative years an Indian grows into the cultural pattern and religious traditions of his tribe.[63] In numerous smaller papers, Opler has dealt with different facets of Apache religion, such as the sacred clowns, the mountain spirits, the concept of supernatural power, sorcery, shamanism, the idea of death, and the peyote rites. His peyote investigations also take in the Tonkawa Indians of Texas, and his analyses of the concept of death and

---

[57] Clyde Kluckhohn, "Conceptions of Death among the Southwestern Indians," *Harvard University Divinity School Bulletin* XIV (1948–49), pp. 5–19.

[58] Clyde Kluckhohn, "Navaho Categories," Stanley Diamond (ed.), *Culture in History: Essays in Honor of Paul Radin* (New York: Columbia University, 1960), pp. 65–98.

[59] Clyde Kluckhohn, *Navaho Witchcraft* (Cambridge: Papers of the Peabody Museum of American Archaeology and Ethnology XXII/2, 1944).

[60] Talcott Parsons and Evon Z. Vogt, "Clyde Kay Maben Kluckhohn 1905–1960," *American Anthropologist* LXIV (1962), p. 142.

[61] Not to be confused with Marvin Opler, a specialist on the Ute Indians who has written *inter alia* articles on Ute peyote rites and bear dances.

[62] Grenville Goodwin, "White Mountain Apache Religion," *American Anthropologist* XL (1938), pp. 24–37; Grenville Goodwin and Charles Kaut, "A Native Religious Movement among the White Mountain and Cibecue Apache," *Southwestern Journal of Anthropology* X (1954), pp. 385–404.

[63] Morris E. Opler, *An Apache Life-Way* (Chicago: University of Chicago, 1941).

the reaction to death embrace several Apache groups.[64] Opler's works on Apache shamanism include such interesting topics as the relation of shamanism to modern psychiatry and the creative role of shamanism in mythology.[65] He has published extensive collections of myths and legends of the Chiricahua, Lipan, and Jicarilla Apache.

Among the primitive Indian groups in the Southwest may also be counted the Yuman Mohave Indians. George Devereux, who is working among these Indians, is one of those scholars who, like Opler, combine an anthropological with a psychiatric approach. Among his publications are articles on puberty rites, magic, soul concepts, dreams of omens, and so-called dream learning:[66] the Mohave medicine men are supposed to acquire their knowledge about the supernatural in dreams, although they actually learn it in waking life and then experience dreams which condense or allude to this body of knowledge.

Among students who have made research particularly on the religions of the advanced agriculturists of the Southwest, the Pueblo Indians, we may here mention Bunzel, Goldfrank, Titiev, White, and Laski. Ruth Bunzel has presented the distinguishing traits of Zuni religion, particularly ritualism, mythology, and spirit (*kachina*) worship.[67] In her introduction to Zuni ceremonialism, for instance, she shows that the complexity of this ceremonialism refers to organization rather than ritual content. Esther Goldfrank first studied Cochiti ceremonial organization but later took up personality research in Hopi and (Plains) Blackfoot societies.[68] Titiev gave informed data on Hopi religion, in particular the rituals which, as in the *kachina* cult, display the patterned ideas of the yearly rhythm and the survival after death.[69]

Leslie White, the originator of the "culturalistic" theory in anthropology, should be mentioned here because of his energetic and successful

[64] Cf. Morris E. Opler, "The Lipan Apache Death Complex and Its Extensions," *Southwestern Journal of Anthropology* I (1945), pp. 122–41; "Reaction to Death among the Mescalero Apache," *Southwestern Journal of Anthropology* II (1946), pp. 454–67.

[65] Morris E. Opler, "Some Points of Comparison and Contrast between the Treatment of Functional Disorders by Apache Shamans and Modern Psychiatric Practice," *American Journal of Psychiatry* XCII (1936), pp. 1371–87; "The Creative Role of Shamanism in Mescalero Apache Mythology," *Journal of American Folklore* LIX (1946), pp. 268–81.

[66] George Devereux, "Dream Learning and Ritual Differences in Mohave Shamanism," *American Anthropologist* LIX (1957), pp. 1036–45.

[67] Ruth L. Bunzel, *Introduction to Zuni Ceremonialism, Zuni Katcinas, Zuni Origin Myths, and Zuni Ritual Poetry* (Washington, D.C.: Bureau of American Ethnology, 47th Annual Report, 1930), pp. 467ff., 837ff., 545ff., and 611ff.

[68] Esther S. Goldfrank, *The Social and Ceremonial Organization of Cochiti* (Menasha, Wisconsin: American Anthropological Association Memoirs XXXIII, 1927); "The Impact of Situation and Personality on Four Hopi Emergence Myths," *Southwestern Journal of Anthropology* IV (1948), pp. 241–62.

[69] Mischa Titiev, *Old Oraibi: A Study of the Hopi Indians of Third Mesa* (Cambridge: Papers of the Peabody Museum of American Archaeology and Ethnology XXII/1, 1944), pp. 142ff.

efforts to assemble information on rituals and religious organizations among the still very secretive Eastern Pueblo Indians, the inhabitants of the pueblos Acoma, Santa Ana, Santo Domingo, San Felipe, and Sia. The information was given in the strictest secrecy, and outside of the pueblo, and the informants' names are of course not mentioned in the books, as is otherwise the rule.[70]

Vera Laski, finally, a disciple of Ruth Underhill, is the author of a clear and informed account of the rain god ceremony in the pueblo of San Juan. She managed to get hold of the ritual texts from an elderly Indian and, according to their mutual agreement, she could publish them after his death. Besides this agrarian ceremony for the *kachina*, the dead who have developed into rain gods, Laski also presents a sketch of the (imported) shamanism, part of a hunting religion.[71]

All the writers now mentioned have profited from their area of investigation. It is certainly no mere coincidence that they have been inspired by the cultural and religious conditions in this desert province whose native inhabitants up till now have preserved so much of their old faith. Lately the Southwest has indeed played the same role as a fountain of new thoughts on religion (and culture) as did the Plains area during the Boas regime.

No other area in North America has meant so much for anthropological research in recent times as the Southwest, but seen from the angle of comparative religion the Northeast also deserves our attention. On the one hand, there are many recent important papers on Iroquois religion; on the other, research on Algonkian religions has had a certain renaissance during the last decades.

The leading name in the study of Algonkian religion after the 1920s was, beside Speck, Father John Cooper. Genuinely interested in religion, he paid particular attention to this subject during his many field expeditions among the Northern Algonkian Indians. As a theologian he was, like Father Schmidt, interested in the ideas of the Supreme Being, and wrote a paper on these beliefs among the Algonkian Cree and their neighbors.[72] It is a rewarding study, done with care and sound criticism, although the demarcation line between the Supreme Being and the Master of the Game (another well-developed Algonkian concept) is not always clearly drawn. Unlike his European colleague, however, Cooper did not engage himself in conjectural theories about the origins of the idea of God. His approach was that of the field ethnographer and historian.[73] His cautious attitude toward historical

---

[70] Leslie A. White, *The Pueblo of Santa Ana, New Mexico* (Menasha, Wisconsin: American Anthropological Association Memoirs LX, 1942), pp. 9ff.; *The Pueblo of Sia, New Mexico* (Washington, D.C.: Bureau of American Ethnology Bulletin CLXXIV, 1962), pp. 6ff.

[71] Vera Laski, *Seeking Life* (Philadelphia: American Folklore Society Memoirs L, 1958).

[72] John M. Cooper, "The Northern Algonquian Supreme Being," *Primitive Man* VI/3-4 (1933), pp. 41-111.

[73] Regina Flannery, "John Montgomery Cooper 1881-1949," *American Anthropologist* LII (1950), pp. 65f.

reconstruction in the field of culture and religion is revealed in a special monograph.[74]

Cooper also wrote an article on the Cree fear of the *witiko* (*windigo*), the cannibal monster of the hunger hallucinations, one of the first investigations of abnormal behavior in American anthropology.[75] He also composed articles on Algonkian divination procedures,[76] and on the Algonkian shaking tent ceremony.[77] He summed up his views of Algonkian religious traits and their history in a lengthy article in which he used both ecological and distributional approaches.[78]

During his later years, Cooper performed fieldwork among the Gros Ventre Indians (of Algonkian stock) on the Plains. His posthumous book on their religion, edited by his close colleague Regina Flannery, is the finest piece of work on Plains Indians religion since Lowie wrote his Crow study.[79] It is true that we miss certain essential parts of religious belief, such as the eschatology, but the detailed information on gods, spirits, and medicine men is most satisfactory.

Another specialist on the Northern Algonkian groups, particularly the Ojibway (Chippewa) and Saulteaux, is Irving Hallowell. After the completion of his classical bear ceremonial investigation, already mentioned, Hallowell turned away from studies of diffusion and became one of the prominent American experts in the field of personality and culture. Some of his papers of this type, relating to the Ojibway, are of importance to comparative religion—for instance, his study of the beliefs of the dead[80] and his

---

[74] John M. Cooper, *Temporal Sequence and the Marginal Cultures* (Washington, D.C.: Catholic University of America Anthropological Series X, 1941).

[75] John M. Cooper, "The Cree Witiko Psychosis," *Primitive Man* VI/1 (1933), pp. 20–24. A modern paper on the same subject is Morton I. Teicher, *Windigo Psychosis: A Study of a Relationship between Belief and Behavior among the Indians of Northeastern Canada* (Seattle: University of Washington, 1960).

[76] John M. Cooper, "Northern Algonquian Scrying and Scapulimancy," *Festschrift P. W. Schmidt* (Vienna: Mechitharisten-Congregations, 1928), pp. 205–17; "Scapulimancy," *Essays in Anthropology Presented to A. L. Kroeber* (Berkeley: University of California, 1936), pp. 29–43.

[77] John M. Cooper, "The Shaking Tent Rite among the Plains and Forest Algonquians," *Primitive Man* XVII/3–4 (1944), pp. 60–84.

[78] John M. Cooper, "The Culture of the Northeastern Indian Hunters: A Reconstructive Interpretation," Frederick Johnson (ed.), *Man in Northeastern North America* (Andover, Massachusetts: Papers of the Robert S. Peabody Foundation for Archaeology III, 1946), pp. 272–305. The same volume contains Regina Flannery, "The Culture of the Northeastern Indian Hunters: A Descriptive Analysis," pp. 263–71, and a diffusion study by Margaret W. Fisher, "The Mythology of the Northern and Northeastern Algonkians in Reference to Algonkian Mythology as a Whole," pp. 226–62.

[79] John M. Cooper, *The Gros Ventres of Montana: Part II, Religion and Ritual* (Washington, D.C.: Catholic University of America, Anthropological Series XVI, 1956). Cf. also "The Religion of the Gros Ventres of Montana," *Annali Lateranensi* IV (1940), pp. 97–115.

[80] A. Irving Hallowell, "The Spirits of the Dead in Saulteaux Life and Thought," *Journal of the Royal Anthropological Institute of Great Britain and Ireland* LXX/1 (1940), pp. 29–51.

rich account of the shaking tent rite.[81] One of his articles deals with the concept of sin among the same Indians.[82] Hallowell has also written a couple of articles which directly concern the structure of Saulteaux religion.[83] The psychological bias in the study of Ojibway religion is also apparent in the works of Victor Barnouw,[84] and in the form of child psychology it enters Sister Inez Hilger's description of Ojibway religious beliefs.[85]

The list of well-known contributions to our knowledge of Algonkian religions can easily be lengthened. Erminie Wheeler-Voegelin, distinguished ethnohistorian and a connoisseur not only of Algonkian but also of Californian religions (Shasta, Tübatulabal), has written a monograph on Shawnee funeral customs.[86] and, together with the linguist C. F. Voegelin, a historical article on the Shawnee great goddess.[87] She is also co-author of a study of the American Indian emergence myth.[88] Wilson Wallis, veteran from the Boas regime and specialist on Micmac (and Plains Dakota) Indians, has completed a Micmac ethnography in which much space has been given to mythology.[89] Diamond Jenness, the master of Canadian ethnography, is the author of an interesting account of Ojibway religion,[90] as well as the recorder of myths and tales about the corn goddess of the Northern Woodland area.[91] The corn ritual in the Eastern Woodlands has been

[81] A. Irving Hallowell, *The Role of Conjuring in Saulteaux Society* (Philadelphia: Publications of the Philadelphia Anthropological Society II, 1942).

[82] A. Irving Hallowell, "Sin, Sex and Sickness in Saulteaux Belief," *British Journal of Medical Psychology* XVIII (1939), pp. 191–97.

[83] See, e.g., A. Irving Hallowell, "Some Empirical Aspects of Northern Saulteaux Religion," *American Anthropologist* XXXVI (1934), pp. 389–404.

[84] Cf. Victor Barnouw, "A Psychological Interpretation of a Chippewa Origin Legend," *Journal of American Folklore* LXVIII (1955), pp. 73–85, 211–23, 341–55.

[85] M. Inez Higler, *Chippewa Child Life and Its Cultural Background* (Washington, D.C.: Bureau of American Ethnology Bulletin CXLVI, 1951); cf. also her *Arapaho Child Life and Its Cultural Background* (Washington, D.C.: Bureau of American Ethnology Bulletin CXLVIII, 1952).

[86] Erminie Wheeler-Voegelin, *Mortuary Customs of the Shawnee and Other Eastern Tribes* (Indianapolis: Indiana Historical Society, Prehistory Research Series II/4, 1944).

[87] Charles F. Voegelin and Erminie Wheeler-Voegelin, "The Shawnee Female Deity in Historical Perspective," *American Anthropologist* XLVI (1944), pp. 370–75; cf. Carl F. Voegelin, *The Shawnee Female Deity* (New Haven: Yale University Publications in Anthropology X, 1936).

[88] Erminie Wheeler-Voegelin and Remedios W. Moore, "The Emergence Myth in Native North American," *Studies in Folklore in Honor of Stith Thompson* (Bloomington: Indiana University, 1957), pp. 66–91.

[89] Wilson Dallam Wallis and R. S. Wallis, *The Micmac Indians of Eastern Canada* (Minneapolis: University of Minnesota, 1955).

[90] Diamond Jenness, *The Ojibwa Indians of Parry Island, Their Social and Religious Life* (Ottawa: Canada Department of Mines LXXVIII, 1935).

[91] Diamond Jenness, *The Corn Goddess and Other Tales from Indian Canada* (Ottawa: National Museum of Canada CXLI, 1956).

analyzed by John Witthoft, well-known archaeologist and ethnohistorian.[92]

The *midewiwin*, the medicine society of the Ojibway and neighboring tribes, has been described and commented upon by, *inter alios*, Hallowell, Asen Balikci, and Harold Hickerson.[93] The latter has an ethnohistorical approach to the origins of the ceremony. The historical perspective is also dominant in William Newcomb's paper on Delaware culture change in which he traces the growth and development of the Big House ceremony.[94] The ecological aspects of Algonkian ceremonialism have been dealt with by Gertrude Kurath, noted specialist on American Indian dances.[95] And so on. Perhaps it is also permissible to include a non-professionalist among the students of Algonkian religions, the Canadian zoologist and botanist J. J. Rousseau. Among his numerous articles are some vivid sketches of Mistassini-Montagnais and Cree religions.[96]

The main promoter of the modern studies of Iroquoian religions is the ethnohistorian William Fenton. In a long series of excellent articles he has illuminated different aspects of Iroquois culture, for instance, the medicine societies and the longhouse ceremonies.[97] His best piece of work is the book on the eagle dance which presents the phenomenology and the history of the *calumet* ritual in North America.[98] Another interesting researcher in the same field is Anthony Wallace, who combines a psychological approach with a predilection for studies of aboriginal "nativism," "revivalism," and "revitalization." He, as a matter of fact, is one of the leading theorists on the latter topic. Wallace has shown that the Iroquois attitude to dreams anticipates modern psychiatric knowlege,[99] and he has analyzed the origin legend of the

[92] John Witthoft, *Green Corn Ceremonialism in the Eastern Woodlands* (Ann Arbor: Occasional Contributions from the Museum of Anthropology of the University of Michigan XIII, 1949), pp. 31ff.

[93] Asen Balikci, "Note sur le Midewiwin," *Anthropologica*, II (1956), pp. 165–217; Harold Hickerson, "Notes on the Post-Contact Origin of the Midewiwin," *Ethnohistory* IX (1962), pp. 404–26.

[94] W. W. Newcomb, *The Culture and Acculturation of the Delaware Indians* (Ann Arbor: Anthropological Papers of the Museum of Anthropology, University of Michigan X, 1956). Cf. also Anthony F. C. Wallace, "New Religions among the Delaware Indians, 1600–1900," *Southwestern Journal of Anthropology* XII (1956), pp. 1–21.

[95] Gertrude Prokosch Kurath, *Algonkian Ceremonialism and Natural Resources of the Great Lakes* (Bangalore: Indian Institute of Culture, 1957).

[96] See, e.g., Jacques Rousseau, "Persistances Païennes chez les Indiens de la Forêt Boréale," *Cahiers des Dix* XVII (1952), pp. 183–208.

[97] William N. Fenton, "Masked Medicine Societies of the Iroquois," *Annual Report of the Smithsonian Institution . . . 1940* (Washington, D.C.: Government Printing Office, 1941), pp. 397–429; *Tonawanda Longhouse Ceremonies* (Washington, D.C.: Bureau of American Ethnology Bulletin CXXVIII/15, 1941).

[98] William N. Fenton, *The Iroquois Eagle Dance* (Washington, D.C.: Bureau of American Ethnology Bulletin CLVI, 1953).

[99] Anthony F. C. Wallace, "Dreams and the Wishes of the Soul: A Type of Psychoanalytic Theory among the Seventeenth Century Iroquois," *American Anthropologist* LX (1958), p. 234–48.

famous Six Nations confederacy as a document of a revitalization movement.[100] Other scholars who have contributed to our understanding of
Iroquois religion are Kurath (see above), Chafe, Dunning, and Deardorff.
Huron Indian religion has been treated by Hickerson and by Tooker, who
has brought together the relevant passages of the *Jesuit Relations* and other
older sources.[101] Cherokee magic has been studied by Fogelson.[102]

If, now, we turn to the Plains area, there are very few important
anthropological works on religion being published today. Cooper's paper on
Gros Ventre religion has been mentioned. There is a lot of information on
religion in such skilful ethnographical monographs as Mandelbaum's on the
Cree and Weltfish's on the Pawnee,[103] but the emphasis is as usual on culture
as a working whole. An author who links religion with social structure is
Alfred Bowers, whose treatise on Mandan ceremonialism is a scrupulous
piece of work.[104] Martha Beckwith's paper on the same subject is actually
more concerned with myths and tales.[105] Ralph Linton, the famous anthropological theoretician, studied Pawnee and Comanche religions during the
years between the wars, but his published accounts of Pawnee rituals and
the Comanche Sun Dance are rather insignificant.[106]

An interesting study of the secret societies of the Omaha Indians has
been published by Reo Fortune, the author of a well-known work on Mela-
nesian sorcery.[107] Fortune's account deviates from earlier information in
stressing the hereditary character of the secret societies and the differences
in religious beliefs between initiates and non-initiates. His evidence and
interpretation have been contested by other anthropologists (Lowie, Radin).
Alexander Lesser reached less ambiguous results in his study of the Pawnee
Ghost Dance and its associated hand game.[108] "All who joined in the games

[100] Anthony F. C. Wallace, "The Dekanawideh Myth Analyzed as the Record of a Revitalization Movement," *Ethnohistory* V (1958), pp. 118–30.

[101] Elizabeth Tooker, *An Ethnography of the Huron Indians, 1615–1649* (Washington, D.C.:
Bureau of American Ethnology Bulletin CXC, 1964), pp. 72ff.

[102] Raymond D. Fogelson, *Change, Persistence, and Accommodation in Cherokee Medico-
Magical Beliefs* (Washington, D.C.: Bureau of American Ethnology Bulletin CLXXX/21, 1961).

[103] David G. Mandelbaum, *The Plains Cree* (New York: Anthropological Papers of the American Museum of Natural History XXXVII/2, 1940); Gene Weltfish, *The Lost Universe* (New
York and London: Basic Books, 1965).

[104] Alfred W. Bowers, *Mandan Social and Ceremonial Organization* (Chicago: University of
Chicago, 1950); *Hidatsa Social and Ceremonial Organization* (Washington, D.C.: Bureau of
American Ethnology Bulletin CXCIV, 1965).

[105] Martha Warren Beckwith, *Mandan-Hidatsa Myths and Ceremonies* (New York: American
Folklore Society Memoirs XXXII, 1938).

[106] Cf., e.g., Ralph Linton, "The Origin of the Skidi Pawnee Sacrifice to the Morning Star,"
American Anthropologist XXVIII (1926), pp. 457–66.

[107] Reo Franklin Fortune, *Omaha Secret Societies* (New York: Columbia University Contributions to Anthropology XIV, 1932).

[108] Alexander Lesser, *The Pawnee Ghost Dance Hand Game: A Study of Cultural Change*
(New York: Columbia University Contributions to Anthropology XVI, 1933).

succeeded in renewing the experiences and pleasures which had attended the old rituals and ceremonies."[109] A first-class informer of Plains Indian religions was Frances Densmore, the ethnomusicologist, whose accounts of Teton Dakota and Pawnee music abound with the most interesting notes on beliefs in supernatural beings.[110] Densmore's contributions were not confined to the Plains Indians. She wrote papers on other Indian tribes as well, and not exclusively on music.[111] Her rich production encompasses articles on the Indian's belief in a connection between song and the supernatural, his communication with the dead, and his belief in the friendliness of Nature.

The Plains area is, from a distributional point of view, the focus of the modern Peyote religion. Radin was the first anthropologist who paid particular attention to Peyote;[112] he was followed by Weston La Barre who composed the first general survey of this new cult, disclosing its origin, diffusion, and elements.[113] Since then, literature on the Peyote religion and affiliated complexes has grown immensely.[114] We need here only mention names like Aberle, Campbell, Denman, Gusinde, Howard, Malouf, Opler, Petrullo, Shonle, Slotkin, Stewart, and Underhill. James Slotkin, who had devoted particular interest to Menomini peyotism, wrote a historical survey of peyotism since the fall of the Aztecs[115] and also a book which may be considered a manual for peyotists (he himself was a member of the movement).[116] It is, however, of value to students of religion on account of its containing legal texts and administrative reports. Today, peyote research may be considered a branch of science in its own right, with contributions rendered not only by anthropologists and students of religion, but also by botanists, pharmacologists, psychologists, and students of medicine. Another young religion on the Plains, the Ghost Dance, has received an account in a book by David Miller.[117]

Among the more modern students of Plains religions, Brown, Howard, Feraca, and Dusenberry deserve our attention. Joseph Brown's chief service to comparative religion is his publication of the rituals of the Oglala Dakota

[109] *Ibid.*, p. 329.

[110] Frances Densmore, *Teton Sioux Music* (Washington, D.C.: Bureau of American Ethnology Bulletin LXI, 1918); *Pawnee Music* (Washington, D.C.: Bureau of American Ethnology Bulletin XCIII, 1929).

[111] Cf. Frances Densmore, *Chippewa Customs* (Washington, D.C.: Bureau of American Ethnology Bulletin LXXXVI, 1929).

[112] See above, p. 29.

[113] Weston La Barre, *The Peyote Cult* (New Haven: Yale University Publications in Anthropology XIX, 1938).

[114] Weston La Barre, "Twenty Years of Peyote Studies," *Current Anthropology* I (1960), pp. 45–60.

[115] J. S. Slotkin, "Peyotism, 1521–1891," *American Anthropologist* LVII (1955), pp. 202–30.

[116] J. S. Slotkin, *The Peyote Religion* (Glencoe, Illinois: Free Press, 1956).

[117] David H. Miller, *Ghost Dance* (New York: Duell, Sloan and Pearce, 1959).

as told to him by one of their foremost medicine men, Black Elk.[118] It is a valuable account if we disregard the editor's own naïve footnotes (with references to parallels in Hindu rituals!).[119] More scholarly contributions to our discipline have been provided by the enthusiastic ethnohistorian James Howard, the author of some tribal monographs (Plains Ojibway, Ponca) and several minor papers on religion.[120] Stephen Feraca has composed a study of modern Dakota religion, with particular attention to the so-called Yuwipi cult.[121] Verne Dusenberry, finally, an American anthropologist who passed his final graduation at the University of Stockholm (in comparative religion), studied the Northern Plains and Southeastern Plateau Indians. His monograph on the Montana Cree Indians shows how dispersed groups of these Indians found a cultural and national focus in religion and thus brought about the persistence of old religious beliefs and values.[122] Dusenberry wrote several other papers on Plains Indian religion, all of them oriented from a deep interest in religion *in et per se*, before he met an untimely death.[123]

Besides Spier, Reichard, and Dusenberry, religious research in the Plateau area has been conducted, in particular, by DuBois and Ray. Cora DuBois, noted anthropologist, studied principally the new syncretistic religions which formed under the pressure of white encroachments. One paper summarizes a less than successful movement along the Columbia, the Feather Cult;[124] another is a detailed investigation of the Ghost Dance in 1870 (forerunner of the better-known Ghost Dance of 1889–90) and its integration with other religious cults in western Oregon, northern California, and Nevada.[125] Also Verne Ray, the leading student of the Plateau culture, has been interested in similar themes: the Spirit Dance, the Kolaskin cult, the shaking tent rite.[126]

[118] Joseph Epes Brown, *The Sacred Pipe* (Norman: Univeristy of Oklahoma, 1953). Cf. also John G. Neihardt, *Black Elk Speaks* (New York: William Morrow, 1932). A similar modern pseudo-autobiographic ethnography which throws light on Plains Indian religion is Michael Stephen Kennedy (ed.), *The Assiniboines* (Norman: University of Oklahoma, 1961).

[119] Cf. also Joseph Epes Brown, *The Spiritual Legacy of the American Indian* (Lebanon, Pennsylvania: Pendle Hill Pamphlets CXXXV, 1964).

[120] Cf., e.g., James H. Howard, "The Mescal Bean Cult of the Central and Southern Plains: An Ancestor of the Peyote Cult?" *American Anthropologist* LIX (1957), pp. 75–87.

[121] Stephen E. Feraca, *Wakinyan: Contemporary Teton Dakota Religon* (Browning, Montana: Studies in Plains Anthropology and History II, 1963).

[122] Verne Dusenberry, *The Montana Cree: A Study in Religious Persistence* (Stockholm: Acta Universitatis Stockholmiensis, Stockholm Studies in Comparative Religion III, 1962).

[123] See, e.g., Verne Dusenberry, "The Significance of the Sacred Pipes to the Gros Ventre of Montana," *Ethnos* XXVI/1–2 (1961), pp. 12–29.

[124] Cora DuBois, *The Feather Cult of the Middle Columbia* (Menasha, Wisconsin: General Series in Anthropology VII, 1938).

[125] Cora DuBois, *The 1870 Ghost Dance* (Berkeley: University of California, Anthropological Records III/1, 1939).

[126] Verne F. Ray, "The Kolaskin Cult," *American Anthropologist* XXXVIII (1936), pp. 67–75; "The Bluejay Character in the Plateau Spirit Dance," *American Anthropologist* XXXIX (1937), pp. 593–601.

In the Basin area field research has intensified since 1925, a fact which, however, does not say very much, since this area was largely unknown before this date. Paviotso and Paiute shamanism has been studied in great detail by Willard Park and Isabel Kelly.[127] A related aspect of magic, sorcery (witchcraft), was taken up by Beatrice Whiting. She demonstrates that among the Northern Paiute in Oregon the fear of sorcery is a forceful device for social control. In fact, it is the only resource of such control, since the loosely organized Paiute society does not provide for other means.[128] Other topics from this area which have been dealt with in recent times are the sun dances (Hoebel, Jones, and Shimkin), the round dances (Park, Harris) and peyotism (Aberle, Stewart).[129]

There are few modern works on Californian Indian religion of particular interest. Kroeber did his work well and, as regards fieldwork, very little remained for his successors. Still, Ann Gayton collected much valuable information from the different Yokuts groups, and she wrote an important article on their medicine men.[130] She was interested in the Ghost Dance, like her husband Leslie Spier, and published many Yokuts myths. Her article on the Orpheus myth in North America is an important diffusional study.[131] Jaime de Angulo's fascinating analyses of the religious feelings of the Achomawi appear very informed, but opinion is divided as to his trustworthiness.[132] The work by DuBois and Demetracopoulou on the Wintu, in particular their mythology, should also be mentioned here.[133]

One of Kroeber's collaborators in work among the Central Californian tribes was Edwin Loeb. Originally occupied with studies of "the blood sacrifice complex," Loeb made field trips to north central California and produced several papers on religion in this area. He described in detail the *Kuksu* cult, a secret society concerned with the formal initiation of boys.[134] He compared this and other organizations in the same area with corresponding

[127] Willard Z. Park, *Shamanism in Western North America* (Evanston, Illinois: Northwestern University Studies in the Social Sciences II, 1938); Isabel T. Kelly, *Southern Paiute Shamanism* (Berkeley: University of California, Anthropological Records II/4, 1939).

[128] Beatrice B. Whiting, *Paiute Sorcery* (New York: Viking Fund Publications in Anthropology XV, 1950).

[129] Omer C. Stewart, *Washo-Northern Paiute Peyotism: A Study in Acculturation* (Berkeley: University of California Publications in American Archaeology and Ethnology XL/3, 1944).

[130] A. H. Gayton, *Yokuts-Mono Chiefs and Shamans* (Berkeley: University of California Publications in American Archaeology and Ethnology XXIV/8, 1930).

[131] A. H. Gayton, "The Orpheus Myth in North America," *Journal of American Folklore* XLVIII (1935), pp. 263–93.

[132] Jaime de Angulo, "La Psychologie Religieuse des Achumawi," *Anthropos* XXIII (1928), pp. 141–66, 561–89. Cf. Wilhelm Schmidt's repudiation of de Angulo's theories, *ibid.*, p. 141.

[133] D. Demetracopoulou and Cora DuBois, "A Study of Wintu Mythology," *Journal of American Folklore* XLV (1932), pp. 373–500.

[134] E. M. Loeb, *The Western Kuksu Cult* (Berkeley: University of California Publications in American Archaeology and Ethnology XXXIII/1, 1932); *The Eastern Kuksu Cult* (Berkeley: University of California Publications in American Archaeology and Ethnology XXXIII/2, 1933).

organizations in southernmost South America,[135] and made a general study of secret societies and their distribution. He also developed a theory about the creator concept in north central California according to which Maya and Aztec influences may be responsible for its formation.[136] Loeb was genuinely interested in religion and religious history. In his approaches he shows a certain dependence on the theories of the Vienna school with which he was well acquainted.

California and other Western Indians are included in the diffusionistic surveys of soul-loss ideas and girls' puberty rites made by W. Elmendorf and H. E. Driver, respectively.[137] Driver makes use of the statistical devices introduced by Clements in his correlation studies (see Part III).

After the departure of Boas and Swanton from the scene of the North Pacific Coast, not much important fieldwork in religion was performed there. W. C. MacLeod wrote some articles on mortuary aspects (a theme which he also followed up in the Southeast); one of them deals with anthropophagy.[138] In the 1940s, however, ethnological activities were resumed in this area, and present-day research is characterized by names like Barnett, Clark, Drucker, Gunther, Jacobs, Lopatin, McIlwraith, McClellan, Melançon, Smith, Suttles, Swadesh, and others. Of these students, Erna Gunther has been mentioned earlier in connection with research on animal ceremonialism; more recently she has written a good survey of the so-called Shaker religion.[139] Other anthropologists who have contributed to the same general theme, modern religious syncretism, are Marian Smith, H. G. Barnett, and Wayne Suttles.[140]

More traditional rituals have been studied by Drucker and Ernst. Alice Ernst's paper on the wolf ritual of the Nootka, Makah, and Quileute gives a dramatic description of the wild rites around the Strait of Juan de Fuca.[141]

---

[135] E. M. Loeb, "The Religious Organizations of North Central California and Tierra del Fuego," *American Anthropologist* XXXIII (1931), pp. 517–56.

[136] Loeb, *ibid.*, p. 543; a different theory in his earlier article, "The Creator Concept among the Indians of North Central California," *American Anthropologist* XXVIII (1926), pp. 467–93.

[137] William W. Elmendorf, "Soul Loss Illness in Western North America," *Proceedings of the 29th International Congress of Americanists* III (1952), pp. 104–14; Harold E. Driver, *Girls' Puberty Rites in Western North America* (Berkeley: University of California Anthropological Records VI/2, 1941).

[138] William Christie MacLeod, "Mortuary and Sacrificial Anthropophagy on the Northwest Coast," *Journal de la Société des Américanistes* XXV (1933), pp. 335–66.

[139] Erna Gunther, "The Shaker Religion of the Northwest," Marian W. Smith (ed.), *Indians of the Urban Northwest* (New York: Columbia University Contributions to Anthropology XXXVI, 1949), pp. 37–76. Cf. also H. G. Barnett, n. 140 below.

[140] Marian W. Smith, "Shamanism in the Shaker Religion of Northwest American," *Man* LIV (1954), pp. 119–22; H. G. Barnett, *Indian Shakers* (Carbondale: Southern Illionis University, 1957); Wayne Suttles, "The Plateau Prophet Dance among the Coast Salish," *Southwestern Journal of Anthropology* XIII (1957), pp. 352–96.

[141] Alice H. Ernst, *The Wolf Ritual of the Northwest Coast* (Eugene: University of Oregon, 1952).

In this connection, we should also mention Margaret Lantis's study of cere-monialism in Alaska.[142]

Few modern ethnographies satisfy the student of religion more than T. F. McIlwraith's voluminous monograph on the Bella Coola Indians.[143] It is written in the best British social-anthropological tradition and contains "the interwoven social, religious, and folklore concepts of a people, the sum-total of their mental life."[144] McIlwraith did not content himself with interrogations, as most anthropologists have done in the North American field, where religions operating within the framework of aboriginal culture are largely a thing of the past. He became an observer and a partaker, and thereby secured inside information of a most valuable kind.

McIlwraith's fieldwork took place in the early twenties, before research on social structure had broken through. A conscious use of the latter term in its interrelation with ceremonialism may be found in a study by Catherine McClellan, dealing with the Tlingit Indians.[145]

Melville Jacobs is today the leading anthropological theorist on myth studies in America. He has collected, in a very scrupulous way, myths and other tales (which he carefully separates according to Indian categories) from Shahaptian Indians in Washington and Chinook and Coos-Takelman groups in Oregon. He presents them in full and interprets them in terms of values, social organization, personality structure, etc.[146] His analyses are often brilliant and engaging, but he overinterprets the text in favor of its stylistic and dramatic qualities. "I believe," he says, "that stress upon Chinook literature as a kind of theater does better justice to its content, designs, and functions."[147] The risk is, of course, as has been pointed out by Liljeblad, that the myths are only explained in their own setting without regard to the fact that they contain migrational motifs.[148] Furthermore, the psychological interpretations of the *dramatis personae* tend to overlook the divine qualities of the latter. Religion is of no major concern in these analyses.

Finally, we should mention the studies of Athapascan religions in the

[142] Margaret Lantis, *Alaskan Eskimo Ceremonialism* (New York: Monographs of the American Ethnological Society XI, 1947).

[143] Thomas Forsyth McIlwraith, *The Bella Coola Indians*, 2 vols. (Toronto: University of Toronto, 1948).

[144] *Ibid.*, I, p. viii.

[145] C. McClellan, "The Interrelations of Social Structure with Northern Tlingit Ceremonialism," *Southwestern Journal of Anthropology* X (1954), pp. 75–96.

[146] Cf. e.g., Melville Jacobs, *The Content and Style of an Oral Literature: Clackamas Chinook Myths and Tales* (New York: Viking Fund Publications in Anthropology XXVI, 1959); *The People Are Coming Soon: Analyses of Clackamas Chinook Myths and Tales* (Seattle: University of Washington, 1960).

[147] Jacobs, *The Content and Style, op. cit.*, p. 7.

[148] Sven Liljeblad, "The People Are Coming Soon: A Review Article," *Midwest Folklore* XII (1962), pp. 93–103.

interior of western Canada. With the exception of a few contributions—by Jenness on the Carrier, MacNeish on the Slave, and McClellan on the Indians of the Yukon area—almost all papers of relevance have been written by Osgood and Honigmann. Cornelius Osgood has published several ethnographical monographs on different Athapascan groups (Ingalik, Tanaina, Kutchin or Loucheux, Hare, Satudene, Dogrib, and Slave). Of these papers, his extensive account of Ingalik mental culture offers many good insights into religion, although the religious aspects are hidden in a mass of materials on knowledge, psychology, values, emotions, etc., to quote the author's own strange classification.[149] John Honigmann who is also the writer of some tribal monographs (Kaska, Slave, Sarsi) is generally known as a student of personality in culture and acculturation. Both these approaches, and distribution studies as well, figure in his article on Kaska witchcraft.[150] Honigmann has also made interesting comparisons between the northern and southern Athapascan ideas of eschatology and shamanism.[151]

Thus the American anthropologists have continued their research on Indian religions, but the old unity in methods and interests from the Boas era has disappeared, and religious investigations are, on the whole, only instruments used to illuminate other cultural topics or to illustrate anthropological methods. This does not rule out the fact that some of these investigations are rewarding even from the point of view of comparative religion, and some do reveal an interest in the religious facts as such. It is apparent, however, how many American anthropologists have left their old hunting grounds.[152] Some of them, like DuBois, Linton, and Mandelbaum have accomplished their best anthropological work outside the United States. To many American anthropologists who do not work with acculturation and personality studies, North American Indian religion has become a finished chapter.

EUROPEAN SCHOLARS

The European studies of North American religions during the last decades emerge mostly from ethnologists, students of comparative religion, and students of the history of religions (sometimes the latter two disciplines are united). These students may be classified together with the American

---

[149] Cornelius B. Osgood, *Ingalik Mental Culture* (New Haven: Yale University Publications in Anthropology LVI, 1959).

[150] J. J. Honigmann, "Witch-Fear in Post-Contact Kaska Society," *American Anthropologist* XLIX (1947), pp. 222–43.

[151] J. J. Honigmann, "Northern and Southern Athapaskan Eschatology," *American Anthropologist* XLVII (1945), pp. 467–69; "Parallels in the Development of Shamanism among Northern and Southern Athapaskans," *American Anthropologist* LI (1949), pp. 512–14.

[152] Some examples: Bunzel went to Guatemala; Mandelbaum, Opler, and Smith to India; DuBois to Indonesia; Osgood to China; Titiev to Japan; Linton to the South Seas; Park to Ethiopia; Loeb to southwest Africa.

students of the history of religions, for common to them all are the aspirations for understanding Red Man's religion in its own right, and not only as a reflection of culture or in its functioning within a social system. Here we must exclude Forde, who (in any case today), is interested in religion as a focus of social relations, and Lévi-Strauss, whose approach to mythology is structuralistic (cf. below). In the main, the students on the European continent have performed historical research, grouping religious phenomena in strata and historical complexes. Also phenomenological points of view have appeared, more particularly in Scandinavia. The historical reconstructions have dominated, since most Europeans have not had the possibility to do field research in North America, with some few exceptions (Forde, Gusinde, Lips, Cazeneuve, Rooth, Lindig, Hultkrantz).

The historical and phenomenological approaches have not been accepted by some American anthropologists. "It might be asked," says Robert Spencer, a student of modern Klamath religion, "whether the native American data lend themselves to the kind of content description which has preoccupied students of comparative religions."[153] Spencer thinks that religious data are so bound up with other social data that they cannot be isolated and formed into segments of their own. For instance, he contends that T. J. Brasser, in his ethnographic survey of North America, extrapolates the concept of religious dualism from the—according to him—social categories of moiety or rivalry.[154] It is rather surprising that some religions are allowed to stand on their own feet—for instance, Asiatic religions—whereas others, like those of North America, are denied this privilege. Lack of insight into the universality of religions as well as dogmatic views on the meaning of social structures seem to have generated this attitude.

Here is not the place to discuss how research on North American Indian religions should be made. Suffice it to say that they can be attacked from many angles profitably, and the European contributions offer, with their large perspectives and concentration on religious phenomenology, a valuable supplement to the American investigations with their different emphases. We cannot here present in detail the theoretical backgrounds of the European students, but we can give some hints as to the general traditions of research to which they belong.

In Great Britain, anthropologists and historians of religion have, for obvious reasons, paid more attention to the religions of Africa and other parts of the British Empire than to the religions of the North American Indians.[155] It is true that Canada belonged to the Empire, but the native

[153] Robert F. Spencer, "Review of W. Krickeberg et al., Les Religions Amérindiennes," American Anthropologist LXVI (1964), p. 917.

[154] Robert F. Spencer, "Review of P. van Emst (ed.), Panorama der Volken, I," American Anthropologist LXVIII (1966), p. 266.

[155] Cf. George Peter Murdock, "British Social Anthropology," American Anthropologist LIII (1951), p. 467.

religions here were studied by the Canadians themselves (Barbeau, Jenness, etc.), sometimes by methods derived from British ethnologists (McIlwraith). Nevertheless, some British researchers have written papers on North American religions. One of them is William Perry, ethnologist and historian of religion, and the last champion of the British diffusionist school.[156] In his great work, *The Children of the Sun*, devastatingly criticized by most of his colleagues, Perry tries to show the spread of such institutions and beliefs as sacral kingship, culture heroes, sky as home of the dead, human sacrifices, dual organizations, from Egypt to North America. They all form part of what is labeled the "Archaic Civilization."[157] It was exaggeration of this kind that caused the fall of the diffusionistic school.

Daryll Forde represents another, sounder, and more factual research technique. In his early days he completed, in the tradition of Boas and Kroeber, a thorough study of the Yuma Indians at the mouth of the Colorado. In this work he deals extensively with religious beliefs and ceremonies.[158] In later days, as professor of anthropology at the University of London, Forde has become known as a good africanist of the social-anthropological school. He still frequently writes on religion.

Another British americanist to be mentioned here is Barbara Aitken. Fired by Ruth Benedict's pattern analyses, she made a study of the social-psychological backgrounds of North American Indian religions. She found an important difference in religious emphasis between Pueblo and Eastern Woodlands religions: the former had a collectivistic, the latter an individualistic stamp.[159] Aitken talks of temperaments, and thereby introduces, more clearly than Benedict, a psychological factor in the configurative approach.

Professor E. O. James, the well-known historian of religion, has casually entered the North American field. There is from his pen an article on Indian types of burial, as well as an analysis of Indian soul concepts.[160]

Turning to France we may, first of all, pay tribute to Lévy-Bruhl, who in several comparative investigations, adduced North American data to build up his theories of the primitive mind and the *participations mystiques*. Jean Cazeneuve, who has recently written an excellent introduction to Lévy-Bruhl and his theories (1963),[161] has himself, in contradistinction to

---

[156] C. Joel, "William James Perry, 1887-1949," *Man* L (1956), pp. 6–7.

[157] William James Perry, *The Children of the Sun: A Study in the Early History of Civilization* (London: Methuen, 1923).

[158] C. Daryll Forde, *Ethnography of the Yuma Indians* (Berkeley: University of California Publications in American Archaeology and Ethnology XXVIII/4, 1931), in particular, pp. 176ff.

[159] Barbara Aitken, "Temperament in Native American Religion," *Journal of the Royal Anthropological Institute of Great Britain and Ireland* LX (1930), pp. 363–87.

[160] E. O. James, "The Concept of the Soul in North America," *Folk-Lore* XXXVIII (1927), pp. 338–57; "Cremation and the Preservation of the Dead in North America," *American Anthropologist* XXX (1928), pp. 214–42.

[161] Cf. also Jean Cazeneuve, "Les Zuñis dans l'Oeuvre de M. Lévy-Bruhl," *Revue Philosophique* (1957), pp. 530–38.

his master, witnessed American Indian religious ceremonials. Thus he has described in great detail the colorful Zuni Indian winter ceremony, the *shalako*, named after the six gods who then visit the pueblo, personified by masked persons.[162] The tradition from Dumézil and Mauss is today represented by the celebrated "structuralist" Claude Lévi-Strauss. His structural analysis of some Winnebago myths collected by Radin is provocative (although scarcely convincing) but disregards, like most modern structural analyses, the religious contents.[163] Marcelle Bouteiller is less prejudiced in the choice of methods in her studies of North American Indian religion. Her foremost work is a survey of North American shamanism—the most exhaustive one so far—in its relation to other forms of shamanism and to practicers of folk medicine (with examples from France).[164] She investigates the social situation of the medicine men, their acquisition of supernatural powers, and their use of these powers in curing. Bouteiller has also written a study of the role of the dead in North American native societies.[165]

Several other contributions from French authors could be mentioned, but they do not have the same importance as the writings to which we have referred.

The German-speaking countries—Germany, Austria, and (part of) Switzerland—have produced, at least if seen quantitatively, the richest literature in Europe on North American Indian religion. The culture-historical school in Vienna, as represented by Father Wilhelm Schmidt, has already been debated (see Part III). To the same school belong such scholars as Gusinde and Haekel, both of them prominent americanists, and their colleague Dangel. Martin Gusinde, the well-known specialist on the religions of the Tierra del Fuego tribes, has written a comprehensive survey of the Peyote cult and its history.[166] (Like most German papers it is, unfortunately, seldom quoted in the debate on American Indian religion in the United States.) Josef Haekel has a world-embracing interest in religious ethnology which has expressed itself in papers on Australian, Indian, Siberian, South American, and North American religions. In his attitude to North American religion he largely followed Schmidt, in his first works, but he has slowly turned away from the latter's methodological assumptions and accepts now

---

[162] Jean Cazeneuve, *Les Dieux Dansent à Cíbola* (Paris: Gallimard, 1957).

[163] Claude Lévi-Strauss, "Four Winnebago Myths: A Structural Sketch," Stanley Diamond (ed.), *Culture in History, op. cit.*, pp. 351–62.

[164] Marcelle Bouteiller, *Chamanisme et Guérison Magique* (Paris: Universitaires de France, 1950). Cf. also the same author's "Don Chamanistique et Adaptation à la Vie chez les Indiens de l'Amérique du Nord," *Journal de la Société des Américanistes* XXIX (1950), pp. 1–14.

[165] Marcelle Bouteiller, "Le Défunt dans les Sociétés Indiennes de l'Amérique du Nord," *L'Ethnographie* XLVIII (1953), pp. 23–40.

[166] Martin Gusinde, "Der Peyote-Kult," *Festschrift zum 50-Jährigen Bestandsjubilaum des Missionshaus St. Gabriel* (Wien: St. Gabriel-Studien VIII, 1939), pp. 401–99. Cf. in this connection G. Wagner, "Die Entwicklung und Verbreitung des Peyote-Kultes," *Baessler-Archiv* XV (1932), pp. 59ff.

the "direct historical approach": the religious history of the Indians is determined with the aid of written documents and archaeological facts.[167]

It is characteristic of Haekel with his masterly outlook over all American religions that even when he concentrates his research on one area, for instance the North Pacific Coast, he also includes in his historical analysis corresponding religious phenomena from neighboring areas, or even areas farther away. The topics which most often occur in his writings are the Supreme Being, totemism, secret societies, and sacred poles. The idea of the Supreme Being is treated in most of his papers;[168] like Schmidt he puts a particular weight on the overwhelming testimony of such beliefs in aboriginal North America. Haekel's earliest production refers to clan totemism among the Sioux and the widespread vision quest or individual totemism.[169] His interest in the latter theme was followed up in studies of initiation rites and their connections with secret societies.[170] The combination of initiations, secret societies, and men's club houses (sweat houses) in California inspired Haekel to diffusionistic studies of this complex.[171] Of major importance to the history of religion should be considered his investigations of the sacred pole, a feature which connects North America with both Siberia and South America and which involves the belief in the high god and the institution of the medicine man.[172] His paper on the "second self" deals with the concept of the guardian animal, sometimes called *nagual*, which is common in the American high culture but has some counterparts in North America north of Mexico.[173] Finally, in a couple of articles Haekel has discussed funeral customs on the North Pacific Coast.

Richard Dangel has tried to reconstruct the original belief in the high god (*Tirawa atius*) among the Pawnee, and thereby repudiated the idea that

---

[167] Josef Haekel, "Prof. Wilhelm Schmidts Bedeutung für die Religionsgeschichte des Vorkolumbischen Amerika," *Saeculum* VII/1 (1956), pp. 1–39.

[168] See in particular Josef Haekel, "The Concept of a Supreme Being among the Northwest-Coast Tribes of North America," *Wiener Völkerkundliche Mitteilungen* II (1954), pp. 171–83.

[169] Josef Haekel, "Totemismus und Zweiklassen-System bei den Sioux-Indianern," *Anthropos* XXXII (1937), pp. 210–38, 450–501, 795–848; "Zum Problem des Individualtotemismus in Nordamerika," *Internationales Archiv für Ethnographie* XXXV (1938), pp. 14–22.

[170] Josef Haekel, "Schutzgeistsuche und Jugendweihe im Westlichen Nordamerika," *Ethnos* XII (1947), pp. 106–22; "Initiationen und Geheimbünde an der Nordwestküste Nordamerikas," *Mitteilungen der Anthropologischen Gesellschaft in Wien* LXXXIII (1954), pp. 167–90.

[171] Josef Haekel, "Das Männerhaus im Nördlichen Kalifornien," *Mitteilungen der Anthropologischen Gesellschaft in Wien* LXX/2 (1940), pp. 144–258; "Zur Frage alter Kulturbeziehungen zwischen Alaska, Kalifornien und dem Pueblo-Gebiet," *Proceedings of the 32nd International Congress of Americanists* (1958), pp. 88–96. Cf. also his "Männerhäuser und Festplatzanlagen in Ozeanien und im Östlichen Nordamerika," *Baessler-Archiv* XXIII (1940), pp. 8–18.

[172] Josef Haekel, "Kosmischer Baum und Pfahl in Mythus und Kult der Stämme Nordwestamerikas," *Wiener Völkerkundliche Mitteilungen* VI (1958), pp. 33–81.

[173] Josef Haekel, "Die Vorstellung vom Zweiten Ich in den Amerikanischen Hochkulturen," Wilhelm Koppers (ed.), *Kultur und Sprache* (Wien: Herold, Wiener Beiträge zur Kulturgeschichte und Linguistik IX (1952), pp. 124–88.

this lofty godhead was a personification of impersonal power or, on the other extreme, a monarchical, enthroned god.[174] He has also endeavored to outline the creator beliefs in California and the idea of the Great Spirit among Algonkian tribes.[175]

Among younger members of the "Vienna school," we shall mention here Gerturde Hafner who has established the close connection between the *calumet* ("peace pipe") and the dualistic world view.[176]

In Germany, americanistic research has had a stronghold at the Frobenius Institute in Frankfurt, the center created and guided by scholars such as Frobenius and Jensen. The "culture-morphological" outlook of the Frankfurt scholars is discernible in the works of Müller, Lindig, and Schuster. Of these scholars, Müller is of particular interest to us.

Werner Müller, ethnologist and historian of religion, is the author of a comprehensive volume interpreting the religions of the Eastern Woodland Indians.[177] He is concerned with mythical and ritual patterns which he conceives as visual images ("Bilder"), and he contrasts a late, North Algonkian religion with an archaic religion among the southern, agricultural Algonkians, characterized by the conceptions of a Supreme Being attached to the pillar of the world, and a faint development of the idea of the culture hero. The same general pattern is disclosed in Müller's study of the medicine ceremony (*midewiwin*) of the Central Algonkian tribes and their Sioux neighbors: an older form of the ceremony is associated with the high god, a younger form with the culture hero.[178] The older form, which stresses the cosmic relations, has largely disappeared in the Great Lakes area but is retained in the Lenape Big House ceremony and the Arapaho Sun Dance; the younger form, now dominant in the Great Lakes area, reflects a dualistic world view and is more concerned with man than with cosmos. Müller's reconstruction is very daring but most suggestive.

The same author has given us a plastic account of Kwakiutl religion[179]— something that Boas could never achieve—and a survey of North American

---

[174] Richard Dangel, "Tirawa, der Höchste Gott der Pawnee," *Archiv für Religionswissenschaft* XXVII (1929), pp. 113–44. Cf. also Dangel, "Der Hochgott der Caddo-Gruppe," *Studi e Materiali di Storia delle Religioni* V (1929), pp. 186–213.

[175] Richard Dangel, "Die Schöpfergestalten Nordcentralkaliforniens," *Proceedings of the 22nd International Congress of Americanists* (1928), pp. 481–504; "Der Schöpferglaube der Nordcentralkalifornier," *Studi e Materiali di Storia delle Religioni* III (1927), pp. 31–54; "Kiče-Manito, der 'Grosse Geist,'" *Baessler-Archiv* XVII (1934), pp. 155–71.

[176] Gertrude Hafner, "Das Calumet und seine Beziehungen zum Nordamerikanischen Südwesten," *Proceedings of the 34th International Congress of Americanists* (1962), pp. 564–68.

[177] Werner Müller, *Die Religionen der Waldlandindianer Nordamerikas* (Berlin: Dietrich Reimer, 1956).

[178] Werner Müller, *Die Blaue Hütte: Zum Sinnbild der Perle bei Nordamerikanischen Indianern* (Wiesbaden: Franz Steiner, Studien zur Kulturkunde XII, 1954).

[179] Werner Müller, *Weltbild und Kult der Kwakiutl-Indianer* (Wiesbaden: Studien zur Kulturkunde XV, 1955).

religions.[180] The latter work suffers, however, from a rather sketchy approach and the surprising exclusion of the important Plains religions (as well as of the religions of the Southeast, the Plateau, and the Basin areas).

Of the other two scholars mentioned here, Wolfgang Lindig, a specialist on the American Southwest, has been the co-author of a presentation of the Ghost Dance,[181] whereas Meinhard Schuster has written an important article on the first-fruit rites in North America.[182]

Outside of the context of the historical schools in western Germany, Eva Lips of Leipzig has included an interesting account of Ojibway religion on Nett Lake (Minnesota) in her detailed description of Ojibway economic culture.[183]

Italian students of North American religions may be divided into two groups: the followers of the Vienna school in its old orthodox approach (Guariglia), and the followers of the important historian of religion, Pettazzoni (Pettazzoni, Lanternari, and Bianchi, of whom the latter has a mediating position).[184] The main figure is Pettazzoni; Guariglia and Lanternari have, each from his particular perspective, written chapters on North American messianism and prophetism,[185] and Bianchi has dealt with North American Indian dualism.[186] However, it is Pettazzoni who has contributed most to our subject.

Starting out as a historian of the religions of the high cultures, Raffaele Pettazzoni turned increasingly to the study of primitive religions from a comparative perspective. As is well known, his main field of interest was the idea of God, but he also paid attention to such topics as myths and the interpretation of myths. He was apparently very attracted by the religious and mythical materials of aboriginal North America, for these materials are

---

[180] Werner Müller, "Die Religionen der Indianervölker Nordamerikas," *Die Religionen des Alten Amerika* (Stuttgart: Kohlhammer, Die Religionen der Menscheit VII, 1961), pp. 171–267.

[181] Wolfgang H. Lindig and Alfons M. Dauer, "Prophetismus und Geistertanz-Bewegung bei Nordamerikanischen Eingeborenen," Wilhelm Emil Mühlmann (ed.), *Chiliasmus und Nativismus* (Berlin: Dietrich Reimer, 1961), pp. 41–74.

[182] Meinhard Schuster, "Zur Frage der Erste-Früchte-Riten in Nordamerika," *Festschrift für Ad. E. Jensen*, 2 vols. (München: Klaus Renner, 1964), pp. 611–19.

[183] Eva Lips, *Die Reisernte der Ojibwa-Indianer* (Berlin: Deutsche Akademie der Wissenschaften zu Berlin, Völkerkundliche Forschungen I, 1956), pp. 180ff,; see also, Lips, "Formen der Religiösen Verehrung des Maises bei Indianischen Bodenbauern," *Wissenschaftliche Zeitschrift der Karl-Marx-Universität* IX/2 (1959–60).

[184] See J. Henninger, "Die Historische Völkerkunde in Neuren Italienischen Publikationen," *Mitteilungen zur Kulturkunde* I (1966), pp. 53–60.

[185] C. Guariglia, *Prophetismus und Heilserwartungs-Bewegungen als Völkerkundliches und Religionsgeschichtliches Problem* (Wien: Horn, F. Berger, Wiener Beiträge zur Kulturgeschichte und Linguistik XIII, 1959), pp. 133ff.; Vittorio Lanternari, *Movimenti Religiosi di Liberta e di Salvezza dei Popoli Oppressi* (Milano: Feltrinelli, 1960), pp. 67ff., 112ff.

[186] Ugo Bianchi, *Il Dualismo Religioso* (Roma: "L'Erma" di Bretschneider, 1958), pp. 69ff.

given much weight in his phenomenological investigations.[187] In this connection we shall select two of his later works, his final treatise on the beliefs in all-knowing gods[188] and his exposition of North American Indian mythology.[189] In the former work the author wants to demonstrate the world-wide extension of "the attribute of Divine omniscience considered as an ideological complex and as a religious experience." He makes use of a phenomenological interpretation, based on formal typology, but his results involve historical considerations. Thus, Pettazzoni opposes the Lord of the Beasts, Supreme Being of the primitive hunters and gatherers, with the Sky god of the more advanced hunters. He does so in partial agreement with Kroeber, adducing the North American data.[190] His book on North American myths and legends is voluminous and may be used as a reference work, although with caution, for it contains several factual mistakes.[191] Let us, finally, mention a short paper on Californian creation mythology in which Pettazzoni argues against the frequent use of the term *creatio ex nihilo* in connection with the creation acts by the Californian high gods.[192]

Turning now to Belgium and the Netherlands, we observe that research on North American religions came to a peak here in the years between the world wars. That was the time when Nieuwenhuis wrote on the American Indian spirit concept, Locher on the two-headed monster of the North Pacific Coast, and van Deursen on the religious facets of the culture hero. In his article on the spirit concept, Nieuwenhuis, proceeding from his findings among the Malay peoples, ascribed different psychological meanings to the American Indian concepts of soul and spirit.[193] Locher interpreted Kwakiutl religion in terms of a closed religious system, with the double-headed serpent as the fundamental concept.[194] Boas protested vigorously against this

---

[187] Cf., e.g., Raffaele Pettazzoni, *Essays on the History of Religions* (Leiden: Brill, Studies in the History of Religions I, 1954), in particular the articles on mythology, pp. 11–23, 24–36.

[188] Raffaele Pettazzoni, *The All-Knowing God: Researches into Early Religion and Culture* (London: Methuen, 1956); the theme was first dealt with in Pettazzoni, *Dio: Formazione e Sviluppo del Monoteismo Nella Storia delle Religioni* I (Roma: Società Editrice Athenaeum, 1922).

[189] Raffaele Pettazzoni, *Miti e Leggende*, III: *America Settentrionale* (Torino: Unione Tipografico-Editrice Torinese, 1953).

[190] The North American data may be found in *ibid.*, chapter 22, pp. 354ff.; cf. also the Epilogue, pp. 433ff.

[191] Cf. Renato Boccassino, "La Religione dei Primitive," G. Castellani (ed.), *Storia delle Religioni* (Torino: Unione Tipografico, 1962), I, p. 213.

[192] Raffaele Pettazzoni, "L'Idée de Création et la Notion d'un Être Createur chez les Californiens," *Proceedings of the 32nd International Congress of Americanists* (1958), pp. 238–44.

[193] A. W. Nieuwenhuis, "The Differences between the Conception of Soul (Animus) and of Spirit (Spiritus) among the American Indians," *Proceedings of the 21st International Congress of Americanists* (1924), pp. 125–39.

[194] Gottfried Wilhelm Locher, *The Serpent in Kwakiutl Religion: A Study in Primitive Culture* (Leiden: n.p., 1932).

interpretation.[195] However, the basic theme, religious beliefs operating as systems or configurations, seems quite acceptable today. The most important work of the period was van Deursen's study of the culture hero, the *Heilbringer*.[196] Here is the old theme from Breysig's time appearing again, the religious position of the enigmatic culture hero.[197] A thorough perusal of the rich North American traditional material has convinced van Deursen that the culture hero is a mediator between God and humanity, that he is no object of religious veneration, and that his origin may be sought in a historical hero, a chief, medicine man, or prophet.

After the last war, few papers of interest to an americanist have appeared in Holland. From Belgium we may report on a short article on American Indian "salvation" rituals (the Ghost Dance, the *midewiwin*) by Annie Dorsinfang-Smets.[198]

Denmark has seen a long line of eskimologists who have written excellent monographs on Eskimo religion, for instance, Knud Rasmussen. They will not be discussed here except insofar as they have contributed to our understanding of North American Indian religion. Kaj Birket-Smith, the present dean of eskimologists, has provided us with a sketch of Chipewyan religion (Manitoba).[199] He has also, together with the American archaeologist Frederica de Laguna, written a detailed survey of the religion of the Eyak Indians in Alaska.[200] His comparative investigations in the latter part of this work and in the second part of his monograph on the Caribou Eskimo furnish us with excellent syntheses of the distribution of religious and ritual features in native North America.[201] The diffusionist approach was also taken by Gudmund Hatt, who enriched our knowledge of North American mythology with two important papers. One was a study of Asiatic influences on myths and myth motifs in the Americas,[202] the other an investigation of

---

[195] Franz Boas, Review of Locher in Franz Boas, *Race, Language and Culture* (New York: Free Press, 1940), pp. 446–50.

[196] Arie van Deursen, *Der Heilbringer: Eine Ethnologische Studie über den Heilbringer bei den Nordamerikanischen Indianern* (Groningen: J. B. Wolters, 1931).

[197] See above, p. 14.

[198] Annie Dorsinfang-Smets, "La Recherche du Salut chez les Indiens d'Amérique," *Annales du Centre d'Etude des Religions* II (1962), pp. 113–25.

[199] Kaj Birket-Smith, *Contributions to Chipewyan Ethnology* (Copenhagen: Gyldendal, Reports of the Fifth Thule Expedition 1921–24 VI/3, 1930).

[200] Kaj Birket-Smith and Frederica de Laguna, *The Eyak Indians of the Copper River Delta, Alaska* (Copenhagen: Levin & Munksgaard, E. Munksgaard, Det Kongelige Danske Videnskabernes Selskab, 1938).

[201] Kaj Birket-Smith, *The Caribou Eskimos: Material and Social Life and Their Cultural Position* (Copenhagen: Gyldendal, Reports of the Fifth Thule Expedition 1921–24 V/1-2, 1929), II: Analytical Part.

[202] Gudmund Hatt, *Asiatic Influences in American Folklore* (Copenhagen: Levin & Munksgaard, E. Munksgaard, Det Kongelige Danske Videnskabernes Selskab, Historisk-Filologiske Meddelelser XXXI/6, 1949).

the corn mother concept and associated myths in America and Indonesia.[203] The author considers here that pre-Columbian agriculturalists once crossed the Pacific and brought both food plants and myths and rites from Indonesia. He also distinguishes between different forms of the corn mother myth in North America.

In Sweden the research on North American religion has also been very active during the last decades. Albin Widén wrote an article on the concept of God among the Lenape, criticizing Father Schmidt's use of sources and general results.[204] Gösta Kock attacked van Deursen's idea of the culture hero as a mediator and thought it possible to derive the culture hero concept from the concept of the supernatural lord of animals.[205] Arvid Wachtmeister wrote a substantial monograph on the North American ideas of the reincarnation and transmigration of souls, a paper which is our foremost investigation of the topic (although unfortunately only published in Swedish).[206] Ivar Paulson, the well-known specialist on Finno-Ugric and Siberian religions, collocated the North American material informing us about the ritual preservation of animal bones,[207] and also published a short article on the elevation of bear skulls in northern Europe, Siberia, and North America.[208] Anna Birgitta Rooth has written a preliminary account of the world-origin myths in North America, their classification and distribution.[209]

To these scholars may also be added the author of this series of articles. My production may be divided into two groups: one which comprises comparative works on North American Indian religion and mythology, and another one composed of articles on my field studies of Shoshoni and Arapaho Indians (Wyoming). To the first category belongs my investigation of the soul conceptions in aboriginal North America, a paper in which the dualism of these soul conceptions and their importance in shamanism, eschatology and animal-guardian beliefs is stressed.[210] Another comparative work is the study of the North American Orpheus tradition, considered in its historical,

---

[203] Gudmund Hatt, "The Corn Mother in America and in Indonesia," *Anthropos* XLVI (1951), pp. 853–914.

[204] Albin Widén, "Om Gudsbegreppet hos Lenape," *Ethnos* II (1937), pp. 252–65.

[205] Gösta Kock, "Is 'der Heilbringer' a God or Not?" *Ethnos* VIII/1–2 (1943), pp. 61–77; "Der Heilbringer, Ein Beitrag zur Aufklärung seiner Religonsgeschichtlichen Voraussetzungen," *Ethnos* XXI/1–2 (1956), pp. 118–29.

[206] Arrid Wachtmeister, *Själavandringsföreställningar hos Nordamerikas Indianer* (Stockholm: Natur och Kultur, 1957).

[207] Ivar Paulson, "Zur Aufbewahrung der Tierknochen im Nördlichen Nordamerika," *Mitteilungen aus dem Museum für Völkerkunde in Hamburg* XXV (1959), pp. 182–88.

[208] Ivar Paulson, "Die Rituelle Erhebung des Bärenschädels bei Arktischen und Subarktischen Völkern," *Temenos* I (1965), pp. 150–69.

[209] Anna Birgitta Rooth, "The Creation Myths of the North American Indians," *Anthropos* LII (1957), pp. 497–508.

[210] Åke Hultkrantz, *Conceptions of the Soul among North American Indians* (Stockholm: Statens Etnografiska Museum, Monograph Series I, 1953).

functional, and religious aspects.[211] Arctic and subarctic North American religion in its relation, ecological and historical, to north Asiatic and north European religions has been made the object of a particular investigation.[212] To the field reports of the second category belong a series of articles on myths and ceremonies, vision quests, medicine men, and religious concepts. One article deals with the organization of religious beliefs in configurations and patterns.[213] Finally, my phenomenological interpretations of American Indian religions, including some historical perspectives, have been summarized in a separate volume.[214]

Before ending this historiographic survey, we shall once more take cognizance of research made in the United States. Our road leads to Chicago where Mircea Eliade, the distinguished historian of religions, has inaugurated vital research on primitive religions. Since Eliade has a European background and his discipline represents an outgrowth of European tradition, it seems justifiable to discuss him and his center in this connection. Eliade has substantially contributed to the research on North American Indian religions in several of his numerous publications. Here we should particularly mention his well-known book on shamanism in which he has much to say about North American medicine men and their rituals.[215] A pupil of Eliade's, Mac Linscott Ricketts, has written a study on that controversial figure, the culture hero, in which he assumes a pre-religious origin of this personage.[216] To this author, the culture hero is a reflection of man himself as a godless humanist.

This survey has concentrated on European and American research. Let us not forget, however, that also in other quarters of the world the aboriginal religions of North America are beginning to attract attention, for instance in Japan (unfortunately the present author has no knowledge of Japanese, in which the relevant contributions appear). This international interest in different parts of the world promises that in the future a many-sided and critical research will successfully contribute in lifting the veil of the religious secrets of the North American Indians.

[211] Åke Hultkrantz, *The North American Indian Orpheus Tradition* (Stockholm: Statens Etnografiska Museum Monograph Series II, 1957).

[212] Åke Hultkrantz, "Type of Religion in the Arctic Hunting Cultures: A Religio-Ecological Approach," Harald Hvarfner (ed.), *Hunting and Fishing* (Luleå: Norbottens Museum, 1965), pp. 265–318.

[213] Åke Hultkrantz, "Configurations of Religious Belief among the Wind River Shoshoni," *Ethnos* XXI/3–4 (1956), pp. 194–215.

[214] Åke Hultkrantz, *Les Religions des Indiens Primitifs de l'Amérique: Essai d'une Synthése Typologique et Historique* (Stockholm: Acta Universitatis Stockholmiensis, Stockholm Studies in Comparative Religion IV, 1963).

[215] Mircea Eliade, *Shamanism: Archaic Techniques of Ecstasy* (New York: Bollingen Series LXXVI, 1964), in particular pp. 288ff.

[216] Mac Linscott Ricketts, "The North American Indian Trickster," *History of Religions* V (1966), pp. 327–50.

THE CONTRIBUTION OF THE STUDY
OF NORTH AMERICAN INDIAN RELIGIONS
TO THE HISTORY OF RELIGIONS

INTRODUCTION

Some years ago a leading American authority in the field of religion, Professor Wilfred Cantwell Smith, remarked in a provocative article that the study of non-Christian religions should be entirely dedicated to the great contemporaneous traditions, Islam, Hinduism, Buddhism and so forth. In his estimation the religions of smaller ethnic groups should be omitted, and he praised those textbooks which avoid tribal religions in favor of a more exhaustive treatment of the living world religions. The motivation for this reasoning was simple enough: tribal religions were judged as crude remnants of past religious traditions which have no importance for the world of today. Nor could the study of these religions increase our understanding of the "we/they orientation" which is, according to Smith, of supreme interest to modern religionists. Moreover, Smith's demand that any statement about a religion should be approved by its devotees could not be satisfied if it originated from representatives of a tribal religion.[1]

It is perfectly clear that this position, if accepted, implies that the study of aboriginal North American religions should be of no concern to the historian of religion. These religions may be labeled tribal, or "primitive"—that is, molded in a formerly primitive technological milieu.[2] They are only embraced by small minorities of people, and they play an insignificant role in the world at large. It is, on the other hand, less conspicuous why their adherents would not lend themselves to a we/they interpretation. (I wish Dr. Smith could have listened to my discussions with a Shoshoni medicine man on the validity of religious beliefs.) It is furthermore enigmatic why they could not communicate in terms of the researcher's way of dealing with their religion—if this should prove necessary.[3] Smith's views remind us of those American anthropologists who discard the study of tribal societies as

---

[1] Wilfred Cantwell Smith, "Comparative Religion: Whither—and Why?" Mircea Eliade and Joseph M. Kitagawa (eds.), *The History of Religions: Essays in Methodology* (Chicago: University of Chicago, 1959), pp. 37–38.

[2] The term *primitive religion*, when met in this article, should be understood in this sense.

[3] It seems less meaningful in religious research to make the condition that the student's results should be accepted by members of the religious community involved. What if they demand that the researcher should share their particular convictions?

romantic antiquarianism and speak in favor of more research on modern complex civilizations.[4] Perhaps we can discern the American drive for more "practical" research, an extroverted outlook on the world, behind the screen of similar pronouncements.

This indifference to studies of tribal religions has also been obvious in European history of religions until recent times. As may emerge from a perusal of readers and textbooks in the discipline, for a long time the material and ideas have been taken primarily from the so-called civilizations (or the old high cultures in the Near East, India, and China, and their successors) as well as from the cosmopolitan cultures that were the cradles of the present great world religions. These religions are of course of utmost importance, but they constitute a part of the many religions which, in different places and at different times, have accompanied humanity. Any phenomenology of religion which does not take into closer account religious forms among preliterate peoples gives a false picture of the religious world. Fortunately, however, the widening world scene in our time has more and more aroused scientific interest in some of these neglected religions, in particular, African religions and modern syncretistic religions built up on the ruins of tribal religions. There is the prospect that in the future, and contrary to the opinion exposed at the beginning of this paper, historians of religions will come increasingly to observe the "primitive religions" in their multiformity.

In this perspective, the North American Indian religions, which vary so drastically in quality, deserve a wider attention. For a long time they have been the almost exclusive hunting ground of American anthropologists. Certainly, American anthropologists have contributed many fine insights to our store of religious knowledge. We are reminded specifically of Boas's analyses of Kwakiutl religion, Lowie's and Radin's influential papers on Crow and Winnebago religions, Fletcher's investigations into Teton Dakota, Omaha and Pawnee religions, Hewitt's penetration of Iroquois religious ideas, Benedict's survey of guardian-spirit conceptions, Hallowell's presentation of the bear cult, and others.[5] However, all of these contributions belong to the first decades of our century. Later anthropologists have been less occupied with American Indian religion and, if they have dealt with religion at all, they have often done it with a sociological or psychoanalytic bias. It is important therefore that historians of religion, with their interest in religion *in et per se*, step in on the scene. Together with a new generation of anthropologists they may open new vistas on American Indian religions.

Until now North America has been a field for extra trips of historians of religion who have been specialists in other subjects. Pettazzoni, who wrote

[4] See the discussion of "Urgent Anthropology" in *Current Anthropology* XII (1971), pp. 243–54.

[5] Cf. above, chapters 1–4.

books and articles on North American mythology and particularly the trick-ster figure, was first a prominent classic scholar.[6] E. O. James, who composed an article on animistic beliefs in North America, is a learned compiler of European religions of the past, and a general phenomenologist.[7] Eliade, also a well-known phenomenologist of religion, and a good Indologist, has treated American shamanism in a famous monograph.[8] Bianchi, authority on Gnosticism, has included a chapter on the North American trickster and culture hero in a study of dualism.[9] This has been the pattern. What is needed, however, is full-time specialists on North American religions. They may call themselves anthropologists or historians. (In Europe historians of religion refer to themselves as anthropologists, or are trained in both subjects.) Regardless of nomenclature, the important thing is that they concentrate their attention on North American Indian religion and orient their descriptions and analyses around the form and content of religion. There are at present several researchers in both America and Europe who seem to move in this direction. (Some of them will be mentioned later on.) Their task is both interesting and rewarding. North American religion cannot be considered a marginal area in religious studies any longer. Aboriginal North America is and has been the home of hundreds of religions which are interesting in themselves and have importance for the knowledge of religious expressions. It seems that the new research on these religions should be correlated with the early twentieth-century phase, when the theories and methods of religious studies were stimulated by the research focusing on North American Indians.

The renewed interest in North American aboriginal religion has several sources, besides the general concern for peoples outside the Euro-American sphere and the observation of new hybrid religious forms in these areas. One is the reawakening of the Indians themselves to new national consciousness, or supernational feelings—called pan-Indianism. They have shown us how a traditional religion can constitute a focus of ethnic identity, and an inter-tribal Peyote ritual can create a bond of commonness and unity between separate tribes. Another source is the growing realization among educated people that in many respects these religions attain a loftiness and a dignity that even surpass that of some of the supposed "higher" religions. The high-god concept and the beautiful symbolism bear witness to this. Finally, the modern concern with ecological problems invites us to a closer observation of the Indians on the religioecological level: the harmonious combination of

---

[6] Raffaele Pettazzoni, *Miti e Leggende, III, America Settentrionale* (Torino: Unione Tipografico-editrice Torinese, 1953), and *The All-Knowing God: Researches into Early Religion and Culture* (London: Methuen, 1956), pp. 354–403.

[7] E. O. James, "The Concept of the Soul in North America," *Folk-Lore* XXXVIII (1927), pp. 338–57.

[8] Mircea Eliade, *Shamanism: Archaic Techniques of Ecstasy* (New York: Pantheon, Bollingen Series LXXVI, 1964), pp. 288–322.

[9] Ugo Bianchi, *Il Dualismo Religioso* (Rome: "L'Erma" di Bretschneider, 1958), pp. 69–138.

nature and religion that they have achieved impresses every outsider. They evidence in their way of living and in their religion that human beings have to live with nature, and not against it, as is the case in our modern technocratic societies.

Let us now take a closer look at the contributions that the present research on North American religion has made to the history of religions, and also discuss some contributions which may be forthcoming.

RESEARCH ON TRADITIONAL RELIGION

A major task of modern research will be to supply more knowledge on traditional religious forms in aboriginal North America, with the clear intention of making this area one of the great and well-known provinces in the history of religions. In Joseph Brown's words, we shall "give to the American Indian heritage its rightful place among the great spiritual traditions of mankind."[10]

Now, in anthropological circles it has long been considered that this work has been done and is finished. For instance, the research on Plains Indians and their religions had its high time in the beginning of this century, during the days when Dorsey, Wissler, Kroeber, Lowie, Grinnel and other field ethnographers were active here. Their ethnography was a "salvage ethnography," saving the remnants of old Plains religions and often building ritual reconstructions on hearsay and oral tradition. So it is undoubtedly true that such work has belonged to the past. Nevertheless, two things are forgotten in this connection. First, the traditional religions live on, sometimes have even been invigorated. For instance, the Sun Dance has returned in places where it had dropped out as a consequence of the government's prohibition (now repealed) against it. Indeed, lately the Sun Dance has spread to tribes who either have not had it before or, as among the Crow, had lost their old form of Sun Dance.[11] Dusenberry has coined the term "persistence" to describe this force of nativism and traditionalism which makes the old religion the core of ethnic existence.[12] Second, the ethnographical sources compiled by Wissler et consortes often reveal an irritating barrenness when it comes to descriptions and analyses of religion. For instance, the Sun Dance is treated as a ritual complex where the religious motivation and symbolism is disregarded.[13] In other words, the most important aspects of the ceremony

[10] Joseph Epes Brown, *The Spritual Legacy of the American Indian* (Wallingford, Pennsylvania: Pendle Hill Pamphlet CXXXV, 1964), p. 27.

[11] Fred W. Voget, "Individual Motivation in the Diffusion of the Wind River Shoshone Sundance to the Crow Indians," *American Anthropologist* L (1948), pp. 634–46.

[12] Verne Dusenberry, *The Montana Cree: A Study in Religious Persistence* (Stockholm: Acta Universitatis Stockholmiensis, Stockholm Studies in Comparative Religion III, 1962).

[13] Cf. Fred Eggan, "Social Anthropology and the Method of Controlled Comparison," *American Anthropologist* LVI (1954), p. 57; Åke Hultkrantz, "The Study of North American Indian Religion: Retrospect, Present Trends and Future Tasks," *Temenos* I (1965), p. 88.

have been overlooked.

Facts like these encourage us to pursue two lines of research on Plains religions: first, continued field investigations, and second, further comparative analyses of existing documents. Both procedures complement each other. The field investigations provide us with new religious materials, and may help to clarify old issues and earlier unclear information. The comparative analyses may reveal to us living religion behind the sterile facts of ethnographical publications, and thus fertilize and stimulate the field investigations. It goes without saying that the engagement of educated Indians in both approaches would give the work increased value.

There are some modern publications which testify to the new interest in field investigations of Plains Indian religions. Gros Ventre religion has been covered in a volume by the late Father John Cooper;[14] aspects of Arapaho religion were published by Sister Inez Hilger;[15] and the main tribal mysteries of the Cheyenne Indians have been described in a beautiful work by Father Peter Powell.[16] Dusenberry's monograph on Plains Cree religion has already been mentioned. The Siouan religions have been studied quite intensely. Alfred Bowers has disclosed the religious and ceremonial organization of the Mandan and Hidatsa.[17] The great ceremony of the Mandan has won further attention by Ewers's republication, in a lavishly illustrated volume, of Catlin's famous *O-kee-pa* from 1867.[18] Joseph Brown's book *The Sacred Pipe* is perhaps at present the most widely read work on Plains Indian religion. It contains excellent materials on Oglala Dakota rites and beliefs dictated to Brown by Black Elk, the most renowned of Dakota medicine men in later times.[19] Brown is now preparing an analysis of Oglala religion built upon his field experience.[20]

It is significant that comparative analyses of ethnographical records from

[14] John M. Cooper, *The Gros Ventres of Montana* I (Washington, D.C.: Catholic University of America Anthropological Series XVI, 1956).

[15] M. Inez Hilger, *Arapaho Child Life and Its Cultural Background* (Washington, D.C.: Bureau of American Ethnology Bulletin CXLVIII, 1952).

[16] Peter J. Powell, *Sweet Medicine: The Continuing Role of the Sacred Arrows, the Sun Dance, and the Sacred Buffalo Hat in Northern Cheyenne History*, 2 vols. (Norman: University of Oklahoma, 1969). It is a strange coincidence that all these authors have a professional religious background. People engaged in ecclesiastical work seem at present to be more intrigued by traditional religions than are the numerous anthropologists.

[17] Alfred W. Bowers, *Mandan Social and Ceremonial Organization* (Chicago: University of Chicago, 1950), and *Hidatsa Social and Ceremonial Organizaion* (Washington, D.C.: Bureau of American Ethnology Bulletin CXCIV, 1965).

[18] George Catlin, *0-kee-pa: A Religious Ceremony and Other Customs of the Mandans*, John C. Ewers (ed.) (New Haven: Yale University, 1967).

[19] Joseph Epes Brown, *The Sacred Pipe: Black Elk's Account of the Seven Rites of the Oglala Sioux* (Norman: University of Oklahoma, 1953).

[20] It would be a great service to the study of religion if the valuable manuscripts on Dakota religion prepared or inspired by Deloria, Bushotter, and other Dakota Indians could be published.

the Plains area, for the most part, have been undertaken by European Americanists. The reasons are obvious: they have fewer opportunities to conduct field
research in America, and are therefore often forced to fall back upon literary
sources. Besides, at least on the continent, their research traditions guide them
to comparative library research. These works fall in two categories: regional
monographs and thematic investigations. To the former belongs the thoughtful
study of the religions of the Sioux tribes by Werner Müller (a good example of
where symbolistic studies can lead us).[21] To the same range of studies may also
be counted several small but important articles, such as Ewers's description of
the Assiniboin bear cult on the northern Plains,[22] Dräger's analyses of Sun
Dance paintings[23] and Hartmann's discussion of the Gros Ventre high-god
concept.[24] Hultkrantz's survey of Plains-Prairie religion may also be included
here.[25] Among the thematic investigations may be mentioned some recent
studies of visionary and guardian-spirit experiences which indeed testify to a
renewed interest in a field eariler analyzed by Wissler, Lowie, Benedict, and
Blumensohn. Here belongs Coale's study of the guardian-spirit ideas among a
tribe with a late influx of Plains-culture characteristics, the Nez Perce,[26]
Arbman's exhaustive survey of fasting experiences in their connections with
theory on ecstasy,[27] and Albers and Parker's analysis of the relations between
visionary experiences and sociopolitical structures on the Plains.[28] Closely
related to these studies are a couple of new investigations of the Spirit Lodge,
or Shaking Tent, a shamanistic ceremony.[29] Other thematic research enter-
prises comprise Lindig's comparative monograph on Omaha and Iroquois
societies: secret societies, age societies, military societies in their religious and

[21] Werner Müller, *Glauben und Denken der Sioux: Zur Gestalt Archaischer Weltbilder* (Berlin: Dietrich Reimer, 1970).
[22] John C. Ewers, *Indian Life on the Upper Missouri* (Norman: University of Oklahoma,
1968), pp. 131–45.
[23] L. Dräger, "Einige Indianische Darstellungen des Sonnentarzes aus dem Museum für
Völkerkunde in Leipzig," *Jarbuch des Museums für Völkerkunde zu Leipzig* XVIII (1961), pp.
59–86.
[24] Horst Hartmann, "Die Gros Ventres und Ihr Hochgott," *Zeitschrift für Ethnologie* XCIII
(1968), pp. 73–83.
[25] Åke Hultkrantz, *Prairie and Plains Indians* (Leiden: Brill, Iconography of Religions X/2,
1973).
[26] George L. Coale, "Notes on the Guardian Spirit Concept among the Nez Perce," *Internationales Archiv für Ethnographie* XLIII (1958), pp. 135–45.
[27] Ernst Arbman, *Ecstasy or Religious Trance* II (Stockholm: Svenska Bokförlaget, 1968), pp.
573–605.
[28] Patricia Albers and Seymour Parker, "The Plains Vision Experience: A Study of Power and
Privilege," *Southwestern Journal of Anthropology* XXVII (1971), pp. 203–33.
[29] Åke Hultkrantz, "Spirit Lodge, a North American Shamanistic Séance," Carl-Martin
Edsman (ed.), *Studies in Shamanism* (Uppsala: Scripta Instituti Donneriani Aboensis I, 1967), I,
pp. 32–68, and Claude E. Schaeffer, *Blackfoot Shaking Tent* (Calgary, Alberta: Glenbow-
Alberta Institute, 1969).

historical aspects,[30] and Hultkrantz's comparisons of Shoshoni and Dakota high-god concepts.[31]

This short and certainly not complete survey of present activities in the field of Plains Indian religion could easily be supplemented with similar surveys of other North American Indian religious areas, such as the Southwest, the Plateau, the Eastern Woodlands, and so on. The last years have seen publications of such importance as a new treatise on Havasupai religion and mythology,[32] Codere's edition of Boas's manuscripts on Kwakiutl religion[33] and an assortment of new interpretations of the Great Medicine Society among the Central Algonkian and Northeastern Siouan tribes.[34] This work clearly demonstrates that research on traditional Indian religion is no finished chapter but, on the contrary, a living current activity. We recognize not only that fieldwork and comparative literary research continue, but that they have gained a distinctive depth and qualitative intensification.

No doubt the collaboration of students of religion in these tasks has meant the introduction of new angles of scientific exploration in americanistic studies. As distinct from most anthropological studies, emphasis has been placed on religion as such. Whereas too many anthropologists view religion as a mere mechanism for providing social and cultural values, historians of religions tend healthily to regard religion as a means in itself, as the adequate instrument of *homo religiosus*. In this connection we should be aware of the functionalistic fallacy as first discussed by Gellner and expounded for religionists by Penner: the use and function of a religious phenomenon is not the same as its explanation and meaning.[35] The reductionist theory has to be abolished if we shall be able to arrive at a real understanding of American Indian religion as a value system and symbolic structure.

[30] Wolfgang Lindig, *Geheimbünde und Männerbünde der Prärie- und der Waldland-Indianer Nordamerikas* (Wiesbaden: Franz Steiner, Studien zur Kulturkunde XXV, 1970).

[31] Åke Hultkrantz, "The Structure of Theistic Beliefs among North American Plains Indians," *Temenos* VII (1971), pp. 66–74.

[32] Carma Lee Smithson and Robert C. Euler, *Havasupai Religion and Mythology* (Salt Lake City: Anthropological Papers of Utah University LXVIII, 1964),

[33] Franz Boas, *Kwakiutl Ethnography*, Helen Codere (ed.) (Chicago: University of Chicago, 1966).

[34] See Harold Hickerson, "Notes on the Post-Contact Origin of the Midewiwin," *Ethnohistory* IX (1962), pp. 404–23; Harold Hickerson, "The Sociohistorical Significance of Two Chippewa Ceremonials," *American Anthropologist* LXV (1963), pp. 67–85; Werner Müller, *Die Blaue Hütte* (Wiesbaden: Franz Steiner, 1954); Annie Dorsinfang-Smets, "La Recherche du Salut chez les Indiens d'Amérique," *Annales du Centre d'Etude des Religions* II (1962), pp. 113–25; and J.-L. Michon, "La Grande Medicina degli Ojibwa," *Conoscenza Religiosa* II (1970), pp. 177–246. Cf. also Ruth Landes, *Ojibwa Religion and the Midewiwin* (Milwaukee: University of Wisconsin, 1968).

[35] Hans H. Penner, "The Poverty of Functionalism," *History of Religions* XI (1971), pp. 91–97. Cf. Melford E. Spiro, "Religion: Problems of Definition and Explanation," Michael Banton (ed.), *Anthropological Approaches to the Study of Religion* (London: Tavistock, A. S. A. Monograph III, 1966), pp. 85–126.

PHENOMENOLOGICAL RESEARCH

The intensified research on North American Indian religions opens new vistas not only for our understanding of these religions in their ethnographical frame but also for our general understanding of religious forms. The results gained by americanists may provide correctives to the phenomenological perspectives on religion. Until recently these perspectives have been largely molded by the impressions and experiences the authors of phenomenological works have had from studies of the religions of the civilizations.

It is unnecessary here to point out what stimulation the phenomenology of religion once received from the discovery and discussions of concepts like *orenda, manitou,* and *wakanda,* or the elucidation of totemistic ideas, guardian spirit notions and high-god conceptions with the *creatio ex nihilo* motif, or the differentiation between shamanistic thinking and layman thinking, between the the devoted religious persons and the "intermittently religious" (Radin). Indeed, some Indian concepts became the point of departure for new terms in the history of religions, just as once *totemism* had been formed from the Agonkian *totam.* Thus, scholars like Pfister and von Sydow used the term *orendism* (from Iroquois *orenda*) to denote the belief in impersonal power, also labeled *dynamism;* and Ankermann found the word *manituism* (from Algonkian *maitou*) a fitting term for the belief in guardian spirits, also called *individual totemism.*[36] However, during the last fifty years phenomenology of religion has gained more insights from the studies of the so-called high religions. One historian of religions has expressed the matter thus that for him issues like impersonal power, taboo, and soul beliefs have been left behind, or replaced by concepts like myth and rite, sacral kingship and high-god beliefs. All of these concepts are relevant to the Near Eastern religions.[37]

And yet, North American Indian religions have even more to offer to the phenomenologist. It may be, as Müller considers, that some of the old formulations from the study of American and other primitive religions were "desiccated" and less rewarding.[38] The modern contribution of americanistic studies to the phenomenology of religion has less to deal with new concepts and new terms than with new contents and new dimensions. It is a well-known fact that a specialist in a certain religion tries to see all other religions in the light of his own findings. It is therefore important that phenomenology of religion, now largely imbued with the particular insights of Orientalists, is

---

[36] Cf. Carl Wilhelm von Sydow, *Selected Papers on Folklore* (Copenhagen: Rosenkilde and Bagger, 1948), pp. 147–48, 151–53, 163–65; and B. Ankermann, "Die Religion der Naturvolker," A. Bartholet and E. Lehmann (eds.), *Chantepie de la Saussaye's Lehrbuch der Religionsgeschichte* I (4th ed.; Tubingen: J. C. B. Mohr, 1925), p. 172.

[37] George Widengren, *Religionens Ursprung* (2d ed.; Stockholm: Aldus/Bonniers, 1963), p. 85.

[38] Werner Müller, "Die Pawnee in Nebraska: Lebensbild eine Naturvolkes," *Antaios* XI (1970), pp. 412–39, esp. p. 412.

complemented with the specific experiences of americanists. Indeed, some of the current concepts of the history of religions—like the formulation of the connections between myth and rite, or the dimensions of the high-god concept—would have to be changed in most textbooks if they were compared with the interpretations of North American Indian materials.

On this point I shall restrict myself to adduce my own reactions as an americanist, not because I consider my own work among North American Indians to be any way more important than that of my colleague americanists, but because it is easier to judge the phenomenological approaches against the background of one's own results in the field. I should like to enumerate the following topics in the phenomenology of religion as being in need of revision in view of my findings:

1. *The importance of self-sacrifice, mutilation, and sufferings as means of creating a bond with the supernatural powers.* Although the "blood sacrifice complex," to quote Loeb,[39] has a restricted distribution among hunters and gatherers it expresses an attitude that has its counterpart in these cultures and probably also underlies such cosmogonic tales as Jensen's *Hainuwele* or immolation myth.[40] Man's greatest gift is to offer himself, under pain. Plains Indians are aware of the deep connection between such rituals and the crucifixion of Christ.

2. *The cosmic symbolism of rituals.* North American ceremonialism is sometimes dismissed with phrases like "repetitive," or "complicated without meaning." In actual fact, however, it reflects an intricate cosmic symbolism, and every move has its own import within the symbolic pattern. The realization of symbolic structure sheds light on the meaning of ceremonies. It is therefore desirable that this aspect of rituals will be observed more in the phenomenology of religions.

3. *The symbolism of ritual objects.* The straightforward praying to a cultic image is less frequent in aboriginal North America. For instance, prayers are given in connection with the opening of a medicine bag, or tribal bundle, but they are not directed to the bundle as such: they are directed to the supernatural powers which it represents. Medicine objects are no *Abgötter*. The venerative attitude, without real cult of the sacred object, is worth observing and should be recorded in phenomenological manuals.

4. *The fundamental importance of "animalism"—the conception of supernatural powers in animal forms—in precivilized societies.* In North American hunting cultures the supernatural beings express themselves predominantly in animal disguise, and the animals are symbolically related to

---

[39] E. M. Loeb, *The Blood Sacrifice Complex* (Menasha, Wisconsin: American Anthropological Association Memoir XXX, 1923).

[40] Adolf E. Jensen, *Myth and Cult among Primitive Peoples* (Chicago: University of Chicago, 1963), pp. 83–190.

the supernatural world.[41] The supernatural master of animals, in particular, plays an important role.[42] Here is a concept of world-wide distribution that deserves fuller treatment in the phenomenology of religion. The importance of what Findeisen called "the animal stratum" (*Tierschicht*) for the development of religious ideas cannot on the whole be neglected.[43]

5. *The idea of the culture hero*. In spite of the fact that Breysig called attention to the culture hero (*Heilbringer*) some seventy years ago, this figure is seldom introduced in phenomenological works on religion. Where he appears authors are often confused as to his functions and general import. The typical culture-hero concepts belong to Africa, Oceania, and North America, but aspects of the idea are also met elsewhere, for instance, in Greek and Scandinavian religions. The North American data are eminently suited to outline the most characteristic features of the culture hero: his appearance in mythology (primarily), his trickster aspect, his opposition to the Creator, his possible relations to the master of the animals, etc.

6. *The nature of the high god*. On the whole, historians of religion have been too rigorous in discriminating between the Supreme Being and other divine beings. Thus they have created a gap between monotheism and polytheism. The facts do not speak in favor of this interpretation. Although developed forms of monotheism or polytheism occur in the high civilizations, the incipient form of theism includes both unity (one god) and pluralism (a host of divinities and spirits), depending upon the situation of beliefs or dominant patterns of thought.[44]

7. *The independent nature of the myth*. The majority of historians of religions seem to consider that myths complement cults and beliefs to make up an integrated picture of religion, and that myths are cultic texts. (This is the opinion at least, of the British and Scandinavian myth-and-ritual schools.) I challenge both these interpretations, if they claim to cover all the mythic material. It is true that myths *may* complement cults and beliefs, that they *may* be cultic texts; but the North American mythologies also tell us that myth and religion may be separate entities. Sometimes they appear as segments of belief that almost exclude each other.[45]

[41] Cf. Joseph Epes Brown, "The Unlikely Associates: A Study in Oglala Sioux Magic and Metaphysics," *Ethnos* XXXV (1970), pp. 5–15, and Åke Hultkrantz, "Attitudes to Animals in Shoshoni Indian Religion," *Studies in Comparative Religion* IV (1970), pp. 70–79.

[42] Åke Hultkrantz, "The Owner of the Animals in the Religion of the North American Indians: Some General Remarks," Åke Hultkrantz (ed.), *The Supernatural Owners of Nature* (Stockholm: Acta Universitatis Stockholmiensis, Stockholm Studies in Comparative Religion I, 1961), pp. 53–64.

[43] Hans Findeisen, *Das Tier als Gott, Dämon und Ahne* (Stuttgart: Kosmos, 1956), p. 75.

[44] I have elaborated this observation more closely in Åke Hultkrantz, "The Structure of Theistic Beliefs among North American Plains Indians," *Temenos* VII (1971), pp. 66–74.

[45] Åke Hultkrantz, "An Ideological Dichotomy: Myths and Folk Beliefs among the Shoshoni Indians of Wyoming," *History of Religions* XI (1972), pp. 339–53.

HISTORICAL RESEARCH

The last hundred years has seen an immense accumulation of documents relating to North American Indians. Together with older materials—traveling accounts, government reports, missionary documents, etc.—they constitute excellent source material for the reconstruction of historical events and historical sequences within the field of religion. First of all, such reconstructions sharpen our knowledge of what actually happened in North American Indian religious history. Secondly, they give the general historian of religion a distinct idea of how religious processes have taken form in preliterary milieus in the past—a good substitution for the guesswork that took place in the old evolutionistic era and that occurs even today, here and there, in professional circles. Thirdly, despite the lack of pre-Columbian documents, the material at hand is sufficient to allow us to establish distributional series and chronological sequences which have importance for the general study of religions. North American religions can be linked historically to religious phenomena and patterns not only in Siberia but in the world at large.

The reconstruction of North American Indian religious history has three major roads to follow:

1. Reconstruction through analysis of archaeological materials. A good example is offered in Howard's recent presentation of the "Southern Death Cult" in the prehistoric Mississippian-Southeastern region.[46]

2. Reconstruction through studies of documents from the historical era. A model for such research may be found in Fenton's classical volume on the character and distribution of the Calumet ceremonies and the Iroquois Eagle Dance.[47]

3. Reconstruction through oral testimony from Indian informants. This method once relied upon by such a distinguished anthropologist as John Swanton was later discarded by Lowie, Steward, and other authorities.[48] Recently, however, students like Euler, Pendergast, and Meighan have reassessed the reliability of oral information.[49] It is apparently possible to trust Indian memory for three generations back in time. Together with documentary materials, oral testimony may supply reliable information for a longer span of time. We have examples of this in the reconstructions that have been

---

[46] James H. Howard, *The Southeastern Ceremonial Complex and Its Interpretation* (Columbia: Missouri Archaeological Society Memoir VI, 1968).

[47] William N. Fenton, *The Iroquois Eagle Dance: An Offshoot of the Calumet Dance* (Washington, D.C.: Bureau of American Ethnology Bulletin CLVI, 1953),

[48] Cf. Robert H. Lowie, *Lowie's Selected Papers in Anthropology*, Cora DuBois (ed.) (Berkeley: University of California, 1960), pp. 202–10.

[49] Cf. Robert C. Euler, "Ethnographic Methodology: A Tri-Chronic Study in Culture Change, Informant Reliability, and Validity from the Southern Paiute," Carroll L. Riley and Walter W. Taylor (eds.), *American Historical Anthropology, Essays in Honor of Leslie Spier* (Carbondale: Southern Illinois University, 1967), pp. 61–67.

made of the succession of keepers of tribal *palladia* among Plains Indian tribes: the keepers of the Kiowa Sun Dance doll, and of the Cheyenne sacred arrows and medicine hat.[50]

Religiohistorical reconstructions are essential because religion is a product of tradition, and religious data can only be grasped in their historical framing. Religious culture embodies, in a sense, the traces of past religious developments. Radin introduced an approach that has been rather overlooked but still is rewarding in this connection: "reconstruction from internal evidence."[51] The makeup of a culture or a religion, or parts of it, conveys significant information about religious trends in bygone times. The tensions between different patterns in the Plains Shoshoni religion reveal its complex origins.[52]

Particularly rewarding for the Old World history of religions is the documentation of the dissemination of religious traits in North America. Some of these traits join America with Siberia,[53] and others with Europe and the Near East (like the myth of the Earth Diver, the concept of the world tree, the bear cult).[54] Here we encounter world-wide connections which, as a consequence, force us to reevaluate the history of religions even in Southwest Asia. For example, it is not possible any longer to trace religious dualism from Iran when the myth of the divine rival twins is found from the Finns and Slavs to the Lenni Lenape (Delaware) at the North American Atlantic Coast.[55]

The studies of diffusion do more than demonstrate the connections between religious ideas or rituals in the New and Old Worlds. They also tell us that North American religions belong fundamentally to a cultural stratum that may be termed Mesolithic or Late Paleolithic, which stratum constitutes an outgrowth of Arctic culture.[56] The general relations between American and Eurasian religions are thereby defined.

---

[50] Wilbur S. Nye, *Bad Medicine and Good: Tales of the Kiowas* (Norman: University of Oklahoma, 1962), pp. 51–56; and Powell, *Sweet Medicine, op. cit.*

[51] Paul Radin, *The Method and Theory of Ethnology* (New York and London: McGraw-Hill, 1933), pp. 183–252.

[52] Åke Hultkrantz, "Religion und Mythologie der Prärie-Schoschonen," *Proceedings of the 34th International Congress of Americanists* (1962), pp. 546–54.

[53] See the trait list in Åke Hultkrantz, "Type of Religion in the Arctic Hunting Cultures: A Religio-Ecological Approach," Harold Hvarfner (ed.), *Hunting and Fishing, Nordic Symposium of Life in a Traditional Hunting and Fishing Milieu* (Luleå: Norbottens Museum, 1965), pp. 265–318.

[54] General information in Gudmund Hatt, "Asiatic Influences in American Folklore," *Det Kongelige Danske Videnskabernes Selskab, Historisk-Filologiske Meddelelser* XXXI/6 (1949). Later studies by Count, Haekel, Hultkrantz, Müller, Paulson and others strengthen Hatt's arguments and deal with other religious traits as well.

[55] Earle W. Count, "The Earth-Diver and the Rival Twins," Sol Tax (ed.), *Indian Tribes of Aboriginal America* (Chicago: University of Chicago, 1952), pp. 55–62.

[56] Cf. Weston La Barre, *The Ghost Dance: Origins of Religion* (New York: Doubleday, 1970), pp. 121–60.

RESEARCH ON THE STRUCTURE AND FUNCTION OF RELIGION

The field studies of North American Indian religions furnish the investigators with a key to the understanding of the interplay between religion on one side and culture, society, and ecology on the other. The field scene is a valuable laboratory where different theories may be tested and different interrelationships investigated. Here again the *point de repère* is religion, and the results are designed to throw light on the structure and function of religion.

North American Indian data are significant for this kind of research for the following reasons: the societies are small and well circumscribed, direct observation is possible in most particulars, and the role of religion is easy to survey. The field analyses of the relations between religion and society are numerous,[57] but most often focus on the contribution religion makes to society, not the other way round. It is characteristic, for instance, that moiety systems are seen as social systems only, whereas to the student of religion they reveal religious functions and, very often, religious motivations. Indeed, as Müller has suggested, even the kinship structure expresses values that govern religious emotions and religious ideals.[58] Here is a new frontier of religious research which has scarcely been opened as yet.

The same judgment applies to the studies of the interactions of religion and ecology. There is a growing understanding among americanists of the dependence that aboriginal cultures and societies owe to the surrounding nature. By making close analyses of the interplay between religion and nature in the same societies we can stimulate the discussion in the history of religions of the principal import of such relations. It seems that this issue has been almost completely neglected. This is unfortunate, for, basically, the social and cultural ideas that feed religion in tehnically less-developed cultures are dependent upon environmental factors.

RESEARCH ON RELIGIOUS ACCULTURATION

Closely allied with the tasks just referred to are the analyses of syncretism or, as it may also be called, religious acculturation. Through careful observations in the field of present-day religious situations, the student becomes equipped with tools to analyze this specific form of culture contact. Viewed formally, such contact has always taken place, except in isolated marginal societies. Practically speaking, however, it is preferably the modern contact situations that lend themselves to thorough scrutiny. In studying the clash between traditional tribal religion and Christianity among North American Indian groups, we are provided with observations of regularities

[57] A sample of titles in Hultkrantz, "The Study of North American Indian Religion," *op. cit.*, esp. p. 98.
[58] Müller, *Glauben und Denken, op. cit.*, pp. 162–71.

of religious process that may serve other operational investigations in other parts of the world and at other times. Indeed, we may also be able to formulate some principles of religious process.

The acculturation studies which may be said to have started with Mooney's famous paper on the Ghost Dance (1896) have been coming since the 1930s when their theoretical importance was first appreciated. By now there is vast literature on religious acculturation in North America.[59] In this regard the following topics may be singled out as being particularly significant for the history of religions:

1. Research on prophetic and messianic movements, mainly the Ghost Dance and associated cults (the Plateau Prophet Dance, Puget Sound Shakerism). Most of these movements now belong to the past. Recently Jorgensen has ranged the Plains Sun Dance among them.[60]

2. Research on other new, mixed religions, such as the partly aboriginal, partly Christian Peyote Cult.[61]

3. Research on the progressive history of syncretism in particular tribal societies. Works in this field include thematic studies like Walker's paper on Nez Perce religious acculturation which registers the influence of factionalism, sects, and political parties on religious development.[62]

As mentioned earlier there are also tendencies of contraacculturation, represented by revivalism ("nativism") and persistence of traditional religious patterns.

The studies of religious acculturation in North America are important because they illustrate emergent forms of religion. Weston La Barre has chosen the title *The Ghost Dance* for his provocative work on the origins of religion, wherein North American Indian religion plays a decisive role.[63]

RESEARCH ON RELIGIOUS PERSONALITIES

It remains to be said that data from Indian North America provide material for the study of religious personalities, medicine men, prophets, and cult leaders. Fifty years ago, Radin's monograph on a Winnebago creative individual formed a new genre of religioethnographical literature, and names like "Crashing Thunder," "Gregorio the Hand-Trembler" and "Black

---

[59] Cf. bibliographic notes in Hultkrantz, "The Study of North American Indian Religion," *op. cit.*, p. 98f., 108ff. See also Bernard J. Siegel (ed.), *Acculturation: Critical Abstracts, North America* (Stanford, California: Stanford Anthropological Series II, 1955).

[60] Joseph G. Jorgensen, *The Sun Dance Religion: Power for the Powerless* (Chicago: University of Chicago, 1972).

[61] Cf. Weston La Barre, "Twenty Years of Peyote Studies," *Current Anthropology* I (1960), pp. 45–60. A major work is David F. Aberle, *The Peyote Religion among the Navaho* (New York: Viking Fund Publications in Anthropology XLII, 1966).

[62] Deward E. Walker, *Conflict and Schism in Nez Perce Acculturation: A Study of Religion and Politics* (Seattle: Washington State University, 1968).

[63] La Barre, *The Ghost Dance, op. cit.*

Elk" are imprinted forever in the treasury of religious autobiographies.[64] They show, most convincingly, that grappling with theological problems is not unique to "civilized" man. The makers of dogma, as well as the mystics and the doubters of the Old World, all have their counterparts in the New World.

The earlier writers on Amerindian religions often lacked sensistivity and empathy in depriving the aborigines of more subtle religious expressions. The growing concern with the Indian as a human being has brought about a better understanding of him as *homo religiosus*. It is most urgent that those involved in religious research among American Indians evince *Einfühlung*, respect the Sacred, and try to read its meaning. In so doing they enhance the importance of their research as a contribution to the history of religions.

---

[64] A selection of sources in Hultkrantz, "The Study of North American Indian Religion," *op. cit.*, pp. 99–100.

THE STUDY
OF NATIVE AMERICAN RELIGIONS TODAY[1]

THE ISSUE

The insight has slowly dawned on the scholarly world that American Indian religions are not just a thing of the past, something we can look up in Catlin's, Grinnell's, Morgan's, Fewkes's or Boas's works. These religions are alive; they continue to flourish, sometimes in traditional forms, and sometimes in new appearances. Christianity is often part of the picture, constituting a segment of the Indian religious fabric, but characteristically clothed in an Indian cloak. The common religious heritage from the past is strengthened at religious conferences, like the annual reunions of American religious leaders and medicine men on the Stoney Reservation in Alberta.[2] In books published by Indian spokesmen for old traditional religions the inherited religious values are emphasized. In short, we meet an Indian population in growing religious self-consciousness and in rapid religious expansion. Whatever the forms, the past is nourishing the present.

This fascinating and dynamic situation should indeed stimulate the research on American Indian religions. There is today a growing concern with North American Indian religion, not least among professional students of religion, and this tendency seems stronger today than, say, fifteen years ago. The tenacity and even renascence of individual Indian religions has definitely spurred American students to new field work and new theoretical studies. It is perhaps less certain that European students, with their strong historical and comparative tendencies, have been influenced to the same extent. Still, the new interest in American Indian medicines and ethnobotany in Europe is certainly part of the trend. Moreover, there is reason to expect that the vital persistence of Indian traditional religions will animate more profound research on the earlier epochs of these religions.

It is my intention to give in the following an overview of the present state of studies on North American Indian religions. I have earlier made

---

[1] This chapter is an extended and updated version of a paper that was read at the symposium on "The Study of Native American Religions, and the Study of Religion, and the Humanities," arranged by the Department of Religious Studies, University of California, Santa Barbara, January 17–19, 1980.

[2] Chief John Snow, *These Mountains Are Our Sacred Places* (Toronto: Samuel-Stevens, 1977), pp. 142ff.

similar summaries of the research situation.[3] This time I shall shift the emphasis from what has been achieved to the ways of research. The overall goal is, as I see it, to link our work to the international study of religion. It is interesting to see how far that general purpose has been realized through the work hitherto done, and how it can be furthered through continued endeavors. In short: I shall dwell on the aims of these studies, what meaning we can attach to them. In order to be able to do so I shall first summarize what happened in the field since my earlier survey articles were published.

RECENT RESEARCH TOPICS

The following survey of recent writings on North American Indian religions will deal mainly with the literary activity during the 1970s and the early 1980s. A comparison of these writings with earlier literary work on the subject will enable us to define major trends in scholarship on these religions. There is of course a host of papers on religious aspects in many local publications. Only a few of them will be discussed here. I am forced to make a selection, and I can only hope that this selection will be representative of contemporary scholarship.

1. *General surveys of Native American religions.* There are now some new publications that examine North American religions in a summarizing way. Here should be mentioned Robin Fox's general article on North America in *Historia Religionum*, a handbook on the earlier and present religions of the world.[4] Here belong also my lengthy paper on American Indian religions in *Theologische Realenzyklopädie* and my book *The Religions of the American Indians* whose first part describes and analyzes the North American Indian religions.[5] Sam Gill has recently written another survey.[6] The Gill and Hultkrantz books show interesting varying emphasis in their treatment of native religions (cf. below). In this connection could also be mentioned Alice Marriott and Carol Rachlin's summary representation of the mythology of the American Indians.[7]

A fine selection of articles on Indian religions has been collected and published by Dennis and Barbara Tedlock.[8] Other recent anthologies contain

---

[3] Åke Hultkrantz, "The Study of North American Indian Religion: Retrospect, Present Trends and Future Tasks," *Temenos* I (1965), pp. 87–121; see above, chapters 1–4.

[4] J. Robin Fox, "Religions of Illiterate Peoples: North America," C. J. Bleeker and George Widengren (eds.), *Historia Religionum* II (Leiden: Brill, 1971), pp. 592–608.

[5] Åke Hultkrantz, "Amerikanische Religionen," *Theologische Realenzyklopädie* II/3–4 (Berlin: Walter de Gruyter, 1977), pp. 402–50, and *The Religions of the American Indians* (Berkeley: University of California, 1979).

[6] Sam D. Gill, *Native American Religions: An Introduction* (Belmont, California: Wadsworth, 1982).

[7] Alice Marriott and Carol K. Rachlin, *American Indian Mythology* (New York: Mentor, 1972).

[8] Dennis Tedlock and Barbara Tedlock (eds.), *Teachings from the American Earth: Indian Religion and Philosophy* (New York: Liveright, 1975).

articles by the important German scholar Werner Müller and the present author.[9] Republications of such classics as Daniel Brinton's study of religion and mythology in America[10] are a measure of the reawakened interest in Indian spiritual traditions. There is also now a textbook on past and present-day beliefs and rituals among North American Indians, composed by and for Navajo Indians.[11] Finally, the extent of European scholarly interest in North American Indian religions may be studied in a recent volume, *North American Indian Studies: European Contributions.*[12]

 2. *Area Studies.* Until recently regional surveys have been rather rare, probably because the concept of culture area has largely fallen into disuse (as a consequence of the relinquishment of diffusion studies). Two books deserve mentioning, one on the mythology of the Plains Indians, the other on Eastern Woodlands religions and mythology.[13] Other books are an introduction to Prairie and Plains Indian religions and a presentation of the ritual drama in the Southwest.[14] We find also papers on the Plains Indian berdache institution, Great Basin religion and ecology, religious authority among the Algonkian Indians, eschatology among the Algonkians in Eastern Canada, and beliefs in a supernatural home of animals in the woodland tribes of Canada.[15] In two monographs Anna Birgitta Rooth has investigated Alaska Indian myths and the puberty rites of Northern Athapascan girls.[16]

 [9] Werner Müller, *Neue Sonne - Neues Licht: Aufsatze zu Geschichte, Kultur und Sprache der Indianer Nordamerikas* (Berlin: Dietrich Reimer, 1981); Åke Hultkrantz, *Belief and Worship in Native North America*, Christopher Vecsey (ed.) (Syracuse: Syracuse University, 1981).

 [10] Daniel G. Brinton, *Myths of the Americas* (New York: Rudolf Steiner, 1976; reprint of *Myths of the New World*, 1868).

 [11] Peggy V. Beck and A. L. Walters, *The Sacred: Ways of Knowledge, Sources of Life* (Tsaile, Arizona: Navajo Community College, 1977).

 [12] Pieter Hovens (ed.), *North American Indian Studies: European Contributions* (Göttingen: Edition Heredot, 1981).

 [13] Alice Marriott and Carol K. Rachlin, *Plains Indian Mythology* (New York: Mentor, 1977); Elisabeth Tooker (ed.), *Native North American Spirituality of the Eastern Woodlands: Sacred Myths, Dreams, Visions, Speeches, Healing Formulas, Rituals and Ceremonies* (New York: Paulist, 1979).

 [14] Åke Hultkrantz, *Prairie and Plains Indians* (Leiden: Brill, Iconography of Religions X/2, 1973); Charlotte J. Frisbie (ed.), *Southwestern Indian Ritual Drama* (Albuquerque: University of New Mexico, 1980).

 [15] James Steel Thayer, "The Berdache of the Northern Plains: A Socioreligious Perspective," *Journal of Anthropological Research* XXXVI (1980), pp. 287–93; Åke Hultkrantz, "Religion and Ecology among the Great Basin Indians," Agehananda Bharati (ed.), *The Realm of the Extra-Human, Ideas and Actions* (The Hague: Mouton, 1976), pp. 137–50; Lothar Dräger, "Chieftanship and Religious Authority among the Central Algonkin," Hovens, *op. cit.*, pp. 37–58; Åke Hultkrantz, "The Problem of Christian Influence on Northern Algonkian Eschatology," *Studies in Religion* IX (1980), pp. 161–83; Johanna Herweg, "The Conception of the Supernatural Home of Animals for the Déné and Algonkin," Hovens, *op. cit.*, pp. 67–76.

 [16] Anna-Birgitta Rooth, "The Complexity of Girls' Puberty Rites among the Athabascan Indians," *Proceedings of the 38th International Congress of Americanists* II (1970), pp. 267–73, and *The Alaska Expedition 1966: Myths, Customs and Beliefs among the Athabascan Indians*

It is possible that the interest in regional anlyses will grow with the publication of the estimated twenty volumes of the new *Handbook of North American Indians*. The first volumes of this work present regional surveys of conspicuous religious items such as the so-called "cults" (an unfortunate term!)—Kuksi, Hesi, Jimsonweed—in California, the secret society or "midewiwin" in the Northeast and the culture-hero mythology of the Southwest.[17]

3. *Tribal investigations.* The majority of the published works during the period deal with religions or aspects of religions of particular tribes. In some cases excellent analyses of tribal religions may be found in tribal monographs composed by anthropologists. If first of all we turn to whole presentations of tribal religions and begin with the high north, we find the following works: my own paper on Hare religion, Irving Goldman's interpretation of Kwakiutl religion, based on material originally collected by Boas, Koozma Tarasoff's description of Cree religion and ceremonialism in southern Saskatchewan, Ruth Landes's monograph on Ojibway religion, James Walker's excellent account of Oglala Dakota religion collected from his field notes at the turn of the century, William Powers's study of the same religion, a book that deals more with social organization than with religion, Werner Müller's thoughtful presentation of the religions of the Plains Sioux, Peter Powell's remarkably well-informed works on Cheyenne traditional religion, Alfonso Ortiz's clever, acclaimed investigation of Tewa world view and ritualism, Sam Gill's introduction to Navajo religion and Lowell John Bean's instructive study of Cahuilla religion.[18] Travis Hudson has published important information on Chumash religion, mainly taken from the voluminous

and the Eskimos of Northern Alaska (Lund: Acta Universitatis Lundensis, 1971).

[17] Lowell John Bean and Sylvia B. Vane, "Cults and Their Transformations," *Handbook of North American Indians* VIII (Washington, D.C.: Smithsonian Institution, 1978), pp. 662–72; Robert E. Ritzenthaler, "Southwestern Chippewa," *Handbook of North American Indians* XV (Washington, D.C.: Smithsonian Institution, 1978), pp. 743–59; Richard J. Parmentier, "The Pueblo Mythological Triangle: Poseyemu, Montezuma, and Jesus in the Pueblos," *Handbook of North American Indians* IX (Washington, D.C.: Smithsonian Institution, 1979), pp. 609–22.

[18] Åke Hultkrantz, "The Hare Indians: Notes on Their Traditional Culture and Religion, Past and Present," *Ethnos* XXXVIII (1973), pp. 113–52; Irving Goldman, *The Mouth of Heaven: An Introduction to Kwakiutl Religious Thought* (New York: John Wiley and Sons, 1975); Koozma J. Tarasoff, *Persistent Ceremonialism: The Plains Cree and Saulteaux* (Ottawa: Canadian Ethnological Service Paper LXIX, 1980); Ruth Landes, *Ojibwa Religion and the Midewiwin* (Madison: University of Wisconsin, 1968); James R. Walker, *Dakota Belief and Ritual*, Raymond J. DeMallie and Elaine A. Jahner (eds.) (Lincoln: University of Nebraska, 1980); William K. Powers, *Oglala Religion* (Lincoln: University of Nebraska, 1977); Werner Müller, *Glauben und Denken der Sioux* (Berlin: Dietrich Reimer, 1970); Peter J. Powell, *Sweet Medicine: The Continuing Role of the Sacred Arrows, the Sun Dance, and the Sacred Buffalo Hat in Northern Cheyenne History*, 2 vols. (Norman: University of Oklahoma, 1969), and *The People of the Sacred Mountain* (San Francisco: Harper and Row, 1981); Alfonso Ortiz, *The Tewa World* (Chicago: University of Chicago, 1969); Sam D. Gill, *Songs of Life: An Introduction to Navajo Religious Culture* (Leiden: Brill, Iconography of Religions X/3, 1979); Lowell John Bean, *Mukat's People: The Cahuilla Indians of Southern California* (Berkeley: University of California, 1972).

unpublished material collected by the late John P. Harrington.[19]

As pointed out, some ethnographical tribal monographs have fine expositions of tribal religions. James Howard's book on the Shawnee is particularly good on religion and ceremonialism, and Carobeth Laird's volume on the Chemehuevi gives us an inside view of their religion.[20] The *Handbook of North American Indians* contains some valuable sketches of native religions, for instance, the short papers on Zuni and Hopi religion in Volume IX, on the Southwest.[21]

There is a great variety of publications on selected aspects of Indian religions. Here is a sample. Starting again from the north we find that the Ridingtons have written a fascinating paper on religious ideas among the Beaver Indians.[22] Shamanism and initiation rites among the Haida have been discussed in a paper on ecstasy.[23] Calvin Martin's investigations of the relationship between the Algonkian hunter, the wild animals and the masters of these animals will probably become a classic in its genre.[24] The same goes for Adrian Tanner's detailed and intriguing study of the religious ideology around the game animals among the Mistassini Cree.[25] Selwyn Dewdney's interesting book on the sacred scrolls of the "midewiwin" society of the Ojibway has evoked a vivid discussion.[26] In a paper on the Chippewa (Ojibway) Drum society we are told that it supplants the "midewiwin" society in our times and strengthens both kinship bonds and religious beliefs.[27] Another Ojibway ritual complex, the "wabeno" cult, has been interpreted as an adversary of the "midewiwin."[28] Some Canadian anthropologists have dedicated their time and interest to the study of the symbolism of rock drawings.

[19] Travis Hudson *et al.*, *The Eye of the Flute: Chumash Traditional History and Ritual* (Santa Barbara: Museum of Natural History, 1977).

[20] James H. Howard, *Shawnee! The Ceremonialism of a Native American Tribe and Its Cultural Background* (Athens: Ohio University, 1981); Carobeth Laird, *The Chemehuevis* (Banning, California: Malki Museum, 1976).

[21] Louis A. Hieb, "Hopi World View," and Dennis Tedlock, "Zuni Religion and World View," *Handbook of North American Indians* IX (Washington, D.C.: Smithsonian Institution, 1979), pp. 577–80 and 499–508.

[22] Robin Ridington and Tonia Ridington, "The Inner Eye of Shamanism and Totemism," *History of Religions* X (1970), pp. 49–61.

[23] Hans-Joachim Schepker, "Forms of Ecstasy in the Traditional Culture of the Haida Indians," Hovens, *op. cit.*, pp. 99–108.

[24] Calvin Martin, *Keepers of the Game: Indian-Animal Relationships and the Fur Trade* (Berkeley: University of California, 1978).

[25] Adrian Tanner, *Bringing Home Animals: Religious Ideology and Mode of Production of the Mistassini Cree Hunters* (London: C. Hurst, 1979).

[26] Selwyn Dewdney, *The Sacred Scrolls of the Southern Ojibway* (Toronto: University of Toronto, 1975).

[27] Vivian Róhrl, "Some Observations on the Drum Society of Chippewa Indians," *Ethnohistory* XIX (1972), pp. 219–25.

[28] Rolf Krusche, "The Wabeno Cult as an Adversary of the Midewiwin," Hovens, *op. cit.*, pp. 77–98.

In one such paper it is argued that these drawings mainly illustrate the shaman's art.[29]

Delaware folk medicine is described in a handy little book, a reprint from 1942 under a new title.[30] The author is an Indian, and so is Thomas McElwain who in two books has analyzed, in a structuralistic perspective, Seneca myths and myth-telling, and present-day religion in a mixed Indian community in the Alleghenies.[31]

As could be expected many investigations on tribal religious facets concern the Plains area. It is interesting to observe that the Dakota Sioux, for a long time neglected in research on Plains religions, recently have been a focus of particular attention. Besides Müller's and Powers's contributions, mentioned above, there are important investigations like Joseph Epes Brown's penetrating and painstaking study of Oglala animal concepts, Louis Kemnitzer's analyses of the Dakota "yuwipi" ceremony, Thomas Lewis's scrutiny of Oglala Sun Dance structure, Darcy Paige's recounting of and commenting upon an account of the Sioux Sun Dance in the 1860s, Raymond DeMallie and Robert Lavenda's article on the Dakota concept of power, and Thomas Mails's comprehensive volume on Dakota Indian Sun dancing.[32] Among other publications on Plains religions two papers on the Blackfoot Indians deserve our attention, Claude Schaeffer's study of the Shaking Tent and John Hellson's presentation of a religious society.[33] Werner Müller has written a thought-provoking article on Pawnee world view, and the present author has discussed

[29] Joan Vastokas and Romas K. Vastokas, *Sacred Art of the Algonkians: A Study of the Peterborough Petroglyphs* (Peterborough, Ontario: Mansard, 1973).

[30] Gladys Tantaquidgeon, *Folk Medicine of the Delaware and Related Algonkian Indians* (Harrisburg: Pennsylvania Historical and Museum Commission Anthropological Series III, 1972).

[31] Thomas McElwain, *Mythological Tales and the Allegany Seneca* (Stockholm: Stockholm Studies in Comparative Religion XVII, 1978), and *Our Kind of People: Identity, Community and Religion on Chestnut Ridge* (Stockholm: Stockholm Studies in Comparative Religon XX, 1981).

[32] Joseph Epes Brown, "The Unlikely Associates: A Study in Oglala Sioux Magic and Metaphysics," *Ethnos* XXXV (1970), pp. 5–15; Louis S. Kemnitzer, "Cultural Provenience of Objects Used in Yuwipi: A Modern Teton-Dakota Healing Ritual," *Ethnos* XXXV (1970), pp. 140–75, and "Structure, Content and Cultural Meaning of Yuwipi: A Modern Dakota Healing Ritual," *American Ethnologist* III (1976), pp. 261–80; Thomas Lewis, "The Oglala (Teton Dakota) Sun Dance: Vicissitudes of Its Structure and Function," *Plains Anthropologist* XVII (1972), pp. 44–49; Darcy Paige, "George W. Hill's Account of the Sioux Sun Dance of 1866," *Plains Anthropologist* XXIV (1979), pp. 99–112; Raymond J. DeMallie, Jr. and Robert H. Lavenda, "*Wakan*: Plains Siouan Concepts of Power," Raymond Fogelson and Richard N. Adams (eds.), *Anthropology of Power* (New York: Academic, 1977), pp. 153–65; Thomas E. Mails, *Sunancing at Rosebud and Pine Ridge* (Sioux Falls, South Dakota: The Center for Western Studies, Augustana College, 1978).

[33] Claude E. Schaeffer, *Blackfoot Shaking Tent* (Calgary: Glenbow-Alberta Institute Occasional Paper V, 1969); John C. Hellson, "The Pigeons, a Society of the Blackfoot Indians," Earle H. Waugh and K. Dad Prithipaul (eds.), *Native Religious Traditions* (Waterloo, Ontario: Wilfred Laurier University for the Canadian Corporation for Studies in Religion VIII, 1979), pp. 181–220.

Shoshoni relations to the animals and the religio-ecological integration of the Sheepeater Indians.[34]

Now as earlier the Southwestern Indian religions attract the interest of students of American religions—for old traditional religions are still much alive here. Navajo religion is a particularly popular object of research. For some time now Karl Luckert has published a series of books on Navajo religion, several of them in the particular series that he has founded, *American Tribal Religions*. Thus, a book by the famous Navajo specialist, Father Berard Haile, on the Navajo Waterway ceremony was published in this series.[35] Luckert has more recently edited another book by Haile, on the Emergence Way.[36] Luckert has himself been the author of several studies on Navajo ceremonialism and also written a most interesting paper on the traditions of the Navajo hunter.[37]

Materials collected by Father Berard Haile form the basis of the monograph on the Navajo Mountainway that was composed by the grand old man of Navajo anthropological studies, Leland Wyman.[38] A separate line of research is represented by Charlotte Frisbie who as a woman scholar has had good opportunities to watch Navajo female puberty rites.[39]

In a sequence of excellent papers Sam Gill has interpreted important aspects of Navajo religion, in particular prayer and sand-painting rituals. While in her days Gladys Reichard emphasized that Navajo prayer should be regarded as the "compulsive word" Gill interprets it as a messenger to the Holy People, and characterizes it as a language of creation.[40] Proceeding from the structure of the prayer Gill has tried to find a road to understand Navajo religion as an integrated whole.[41] The same author has also written a

[34] Werner Müller, "The Pawnee View of the World: A Sacred Reality," Hovens, *op. cit.*, pp. 29–58; Åke Hultkrantz, "Attitudes to Animals in Shoshoni Indian Religion," *Studies in Comparative Religion* IV/2 (1970), pp. 70–79, and "Accommodation and Persistence: Ecological Analysis of the Religion of the Sheepeater Indians in Wyoming, U.S.A.," *Temenos* XVII (1981), pp. 35–44.

[35] Berard Haile, *Waterway: A Navajo Ceremonial Myth* (Flagstaff: Museum of Northern Arizona, American Tribal Religions V, 1979).

[36] Berard Haile, *The Upward Moving and Emergence Way* (Lincoln: University of Nebraska, 1981).

[37] Karl W. Luckert, *Navajo Mountain and Rainbow Bridge Religion* (Flagstaff: Museum of Northern Arizona, American Tribal Religions I, 1977), *A Navajo Bringing-Home Ceremony* (Flagstaff: Museum of Northern Arizona, American Tribal Religions III, 1978), *Coyoteway: A Navajo Holyway Healing Ceremonial* (Tucson: University of Arizona, 1979), and *The Navajo Hunter Tradition* (Tucson: University of Arizona, 1975).

[38] Leland C. Wyman, *The Mountainway of the Navajo* (Tucson: University of Arizona, 1975).

[39] Charlotte J. Frisbie, *Kinaaldá: A Study of the Navaho Girl's Puberty Ceremony* (Middleton, Connecticut: Wesleyan University, 1967).

[40] Sam D. Gill, "Prayer as Person: The Performative Force in Navajo Prayer Acts," *History of Religions* XVII (1977), pp. 143–57.

[41] Sam D. Gill, *Sacred Words: A Study of Navajo Religion and Prayer* (Westport, Connecticut: Greenwood, 1981).

couple of perceptive studies on sandpaintings and their religious import.[42]

Among other papers on Southwestern Indian religions there is an important collection of articles on Pima medicine men and their concepts of disease.[43] Ruth Underhill, the well-known veteran anthropologist who was recently hailed by the Papago people as their true historiographer, is responsible for a book on Papago annual celebrations.[44]

Several new studies concern Californian Indian religions, for instance, Richard Applegate's paper on guardian spirits in the south-central area and Zigmond's article on supernatural beings among the Kawaiisu Indians in southern Sierra Nevada.[45] Theodora Kroeber has edited the Yurok myths left by her celebrated husband, Alfred Kroeber.[46] It is an imposing monument for one of the great scholars in the field. Let us finally include in this review of papers a stimulating book on Huichol religion, Barbara Myerhoff's description of a sacred expedition for Peyote.[47]

4. *Comparative phenomenological research.* Phenomenology is as we know a particular branch of the studies on religion, but the term is used here to include social anthropological works of a similar kind (often with structural or functional implications). There are indeed few papers covering the whole North American scene. We notice that Deward Walker has edited a volume on witchcraft and sorcery.[48] Werner Müller has written an article on the connections between New Year rituals and shamanic revivification rituals in North America.[49] Also covering the whole of North America are a couple of investigations by the present author on divination and ancestor worship.[50] I have also outlined the basic features of myths and rituals in

[42] Sam D. Gill, "It's Where You Put Your Eyes," *Parabola* IV/4 (1979), pp. 91–97, and "Whirling Logs and Coloured Sands," Waugh and Prithipaul, *op. cit.*, pp. 151–63.

[43] Donald M. Bahr *et al.*, *Piman Shamanism and Staying Sickness* (Tucson: University of Arizona, 1974).

[44] Ruth M. Underhill *et al.*, *Rainhouse and Ocean: Speeches for the Papago Year* (Flagstaff: Museum of Northern Arizona, American Tribal Religions IV, 1979).

[45] M. Zigmond, "The Supernatural World of the Kawaiisu," Thomas Blackburn (ed.), *Flowers of the Wind* (Ramona, California: Ballena, Anthropological Papers VIII, 1977), pp. 59–95; Richard Applegate, *'Atishwin: The Dream Helper in South-Central California* (Ramona, California: Ballena, Anthropological Papers XIII, 1978).

[46] Alfred Louis Kroeber, *Yurok Myths* (Berkeley: University of California, 1976).

[47] Barbara G. Myerhoff, *Peyote Hunt. The Sacred Journey of the Huichol Indians* (Ithaca: Cornell University, 1974).

[48] Deward E. Walker, Jr. (ed.), *Systems of North American Witchcraft and Sorcery* (Moscow: Anthropological Monographs of the University of Idaho I, 1970).

[49] Werner Müller, "'Neue Sonne, Neues Licht': Stirb- und Werdeformeln in Nordamerika," *Leben und Tod in den Religionen, Symbol und Wirklichkeit* (Darmstadt: Wissenshaftliche, 1980), pp. 335–50.

[50] Åke Hultkrantz, "La Divination en Amérique du Nord," André Caquot and Marcel Leibovici (eds.), *La Divination* II (Paris: Universitaires de France, 1968), pp. 69–149, and "The Cult of the Dead among North American Indians," *Temenos* XIV (1979), pp. 97–126.

North America—as I see them—in two survey articles.[51]

Some phenomenological studies have a restricted regional scope. Thus, some authors have concentrated on the beliefs in God in the Plains area.[52] One investigator has found that the complexity of Plains tribal bundle systems corresponds to the level of organizational complexity of the tribes.[53] In the same way a study on the vision experience of the Plains Indians stresses social but not religious values.[54] Other works which may be labeled phenomenological have been registered below, under studies of symbolism and meaning.

5. *Historical research.* Several papers are "historical" in the sense that they point at historical connections in the past (through diffusion or common origins), or reveal a successive series of events, implied or hypothetical. To these we may count Balaji Mundkur's discussion of snake worship in the Americas, paralleled by an investigation on the same theme by Luckert.[55] The ties between Eurasian and North American religious complexes, once a particular interest of Lowie's, were recently the object of an article by the present author.[56] Wolfgang Lindig has demonstrated the historical growth of secret cultic societies among the Omaha and Iroquois in an impressive volume.[57] Travis Husdon and Thomas Blackburn's paper on ritual complexes in South-Central California is a careful delineation of old religious patterns in a little known area.[58] Peter Powell's interesting recounts of Cheyenne religious history from oral sources have already been mentioned.

A good deal of the historical investigations are "ethnohistorical" in so far as they concern known historical events or a fixed chronology. For example, John Ewers has made an excellent reconstruction of Blackfoot religion in

[51] Åke Hultkrantz, "Myths in Native North American Religions" and "Ritual in Native North American Religions," Waugh and Prithipaul, *op. cit.*, pp. 77–96 and 135–47.

[52] Horst Hartmann, "Die Gros Ventres und Ihr Hochgott," *Zeitschrift für Ethnologie* XCIII (1968), pp. 73–83; Åke Hultkrantz, "The Structure of Theistic Beliefs among North American Plains Indians," *Temenos* VII (1971), pp. 66–74; Paul B. Steinmetz, *Pipe, Bible and Peyote among The Oglala Lakota: A Study in Religious Identity* (Stockholm: Stockholm Studies in Comparative Religion XIX, 1980).

[53] Jeffrey R. Hanson, "Structure and Complexity of Medicine Bundle Systems of Selected Plains Indian Tribes," *Plains Anthropologist* XXV (1980), pp. 199–216.

[54] Patricia Albers and Seymour Parker, "The Plains Vision Experience: A Study of Power and Privilege," *Southwestern Journal of Anthropology* XXVII (1971), pp. 203–33.

[55] Balaji Mundkur, "The Cult of the Serpent in the Americas: Its Asian Background," *Current Anthropology* XVII (1976), pp. 429–55; Karl W. Luckert, *Olmec Religion: A Key to Middle America and Beyond* (Norman: University of Oklahoma, 1976).

[56] Åke Hultkrantz, "North American Indian Religions in a Circumpolar Perspective," Hovens, *op. cit.*, pp. 11–28.

[57] Wolfgang Lindig, *Geheimbünde und Männerbünde der Prärie- und der Waldlandindianer Nordamerikas* (Wiesbaden: Franz Steiner, Studien zur Kulturkunde XXIII, 1970).

[58] Travis Hudson and Thomas C. Blackburn, "The Integration of Myth and Ritual in South-Central California: The 'Northern Complex,'" *The Journal of Californian Anthropology* V (1978), pp. 225–50.

1846 and 1847 through the study of pictographs on blankets, or "wintercounts."[59] Another instance is Michael Hittman's reconstruction of the 1870 Ghost Dance at Walker River;[60] for other contributions to the history of the Ghost Dance, see below, under studies of religions in transition. Perhaps I should also mention my study of the Shoshoni chief and medicine man Yellow Hand, my reconstruction of the way in which the fear of geysers in the Yellowstone area has been communicated to us, and my analysis of the origins of the Plains Sun Dance.[61] Many anthropological books and articles on tribes and local groups contain important information on historical religious facts. Some historical research has a partly archaeological slant and will be treated next.

6. *Ethnoastronomy.* This is a new branch of studies which also involves research on cosmology and religious geography. The foremost expert on American ethnoastronomy is Anthony Aveni who has published two standard books on the subject.[62] Thomas and Alice Kehoe and John Eddy have written extensively on the possibilities of astronomical interpretation of Plains stone monuments, such as the Big Horn Medicine Wheel; Travis Hudson has disclosed what there is to be known of the astronomy of the Chumash Indians; and Werner Müller has examined American Indian observations on the correspondences between time and space.[63] An interesting riddle remains unsolved, the question of a possible relation between astronomical observations and religious practice. An approach to this problem may be found in an article by Lynn Ceci in which she tackles the meaning of the Pleiades for the agricultural calendar as reflected in myths.[64]

[59] John C. Ewers, "A Unique Pictorial Interpretation of Blackfoot Indian Religion in 1846–1847," *Ethnohistory* XVIII (1971), pp. 231–38.

[60] Michael Hittman, "The 1870 Ghost Dance at the Walker River Reservation: A Reconstruction," *Ethnohistory* XX (1973), pp. 247–78.

[61] Åke Hultkrantz, "Yellow Hand, Chief and Medicine-man among the Eastern Shoshoni," *Proceedings of the 38th International Congress of Americanists* I (1970), pp. 293–304; "The Fear of Geysers among Indians of the Yellowstone Park Area," Leslie B. Davis (ed.), *Lifeways of Intermontane and Plains Montana Indians* (Bozeman, Montana: Museum of the Rockies Occasional Papers I, 1979), pp. 33–42, and "The Development of the Plains Indian Sun Dance," Giulia Piccaluga (ed.), *Perennitas* (Rome: Edizioni dell'Ateneo, 1980), pp. 225–43.

[62] Anthony F. Aveni (ed.), *Archaeoastronomy in Pre-Columbian America* (Austin: University of Texas, 1975), and *Native American Astronomy* (Austin: University of Texas, 1977).

[63] John A. Eddy, "Astronomical Alignment of the Big Horn Medicine Wheel," *Science* CLXXXIV (1974), pp. 1035–43; Travis Hudson, "Die Astronomie der Chumash-Indianer (Kalifornien)," *Ethnologia Americana* XV/2 (1978), pp. 846–51; Travis Hudson and Ernest Underhay, *Crystals in the Sky: An Intellectual Odyssey Involving Chumash Astronomy, Cosmology and Rock Art* (Ramona, California: Ballena, Anthropological Papers X, 1978); Werner Müller, "Raum und Zeit in Sprachen und Kalendern Nordamerikas und Alteuropas," *Anthropos* LVII (1962), pp. 568–90, LXVIII (1973), pp. 156–80, and LXXIV (1979), pp. 443–64.

[64] Lynn Ceci, "Watchers of the Pleiades: Ethnoastronomy among Native Cultivators in Northeastern North America," *Ethnohistory* XXV (1978), pp. 301–17.

7. *Studies of religions in transition.* Occasional references to the theme of religious acculturation and syncretism may be found in many papers on culture change, and besides there are a good many special studies of religions in transition. There is now an excellent and almost exhaustive bibliography on this subject. The author of this work, Harold Turner, has also provided an interpretation of these new religions from a missiological point of view.[65] Another theoretical approach along similar lines has been presented by Joseph Cahill.[66] In particular three phenomena in recent North American religious development have been discussed as results of acculturation: the Ghost Dance and its precursors, the Peyote Cult, and what has been labeled the Sun Dance religion.

The nature of the Prophet Dance, the source of the Ghost Dance according to the late Leslie Spier, is debated in an article by Deward Walker.[67] Among the papers on the Ghost Dance proper may be noted a psychological study of the "prophetic process" in the 1890 Ghost Dance, a description of the Ghost Dance of the Pai, an account on a Ghost Dance survival among the Pomo, the study on the Ghost Dance process by Hittman earlier referred to, and my analysis of the changing meaning of the Ghost Dance.[68] In this connection should also be mentioned Weston La Barre's provocative and learned treatise, *The Ghost Dance*, which however also deals with other new religious movements, and old as well, in a comparative perspective.[69]

The Peyote Cult is the object of a new and enlarged edition of La Barre's classical monograph[70] and plays a dominant role in Steinmetz's book earlier referred to. Another expert on Peyote, Omer Stewart, who is preparing a monumental work on the history of Peyote, has published some articles of great interest on this cult, for example, a discussion of the relative time depths of the Ghost Dance and Peyotism, and on methods in the study

[65] Harold W. Turner, *Bibliography of New Religious Movements in Primal Societies.* II: *North America* (Boston: G. K. Hall, 1978), and "Old and New Religions among North American Indians: Missiological Impressions and Reflections," *Missiology* I (1973), pp. 47–66.

[66] Joseph Cahill, "An Amerindian Search: Propaideutic to the Study of Religion in Transition," *Studies in Religion* V (1975), pp. 286–99. A Polish ethnologist regards the development of native religions in their relation to ethnicity: Mirosława Posern-Zielińska, "Native Religions and Ethnic Identity of the American Indians," Hovens, *op. cit.*, pp. 183–99.

[67] Deward E. Walker, Jr., "New Light on the Prophet Dance," *Ethnohistory* XVI (1969), pp. 245–55.

[68] Thomas W. Overholt, "The Ghost Dance of 1890 and the Nature of the Prophetic Process," *Ethnohistory* XXI (1974), pp. 37–63; Henry F. Dobyns and Robert C. Euler, *The Ghost Dance of 1889 among the Pai Indians of Northwestern Arizona* (Prescott, Arizona: Prescott College, 1967); Clement W. Meighan and Francis A. Riddell, *The Maru Cult of the Pomo Indians: A California Ghost Dance Survival* (Los Angeles: Southwest Museum Papers XXIII, 1972); Hultkrantz, *Belief and Worship, op. cit.*, pp. 264–81.

[69] Weston La Barre, *The Ghost Dance: Origins of Religion* (Garden City, New York: Doubleday, 1970).

[70] Weston La Barre, *The Peyote Cult* (4th enlarged ed.; Hamden, Connecticut: Archon, 1975).

of Peyotism.[71] The present author has composed a short article on the motivations behind the spread of Peyote in the United States.[72]

The Sun Dance of the Plains Indians has usually been considered as a native religious complex of a certain age (cf. above, under historical research), but Joseph Jorgensen defines the "Sun Dance Religion" as a recent case of acculturation among the Shoshoni, Bannock and Ute.[73] Certainly, on the Plains the Sun Dance has turned into a symbolic means of ethnic resistance.[74] Also older acculturative sequences have been analyzed, such as the Delaware (Lenape) revivalism two hundred years ago.[75]

In the last analysis all Indian religions during the past four hundred years may be looked upon as religions in transition, religions which directly or indirectly have been under a strong Christian impact. Walker's book on Nez Perce acculturation and my own treatise on Wind River Shoshoni religious change demonstrate the increasing trend of religious syncretism during the last hundred and fifty years.[76] For a study of the aboriginal Ojibwa religion and its fragmenting transformations over the past four centuries, see the new monograph by Vecsey.[77] Margaret Blackman's account of creativity in Northwest Coast ceremonialism gives further perspectives on the process of acculturation.[78] Related to these studies are the studies of persistence and counter acculturation. Medicine's study just referred to is a good example. Pamela Amoss has demonstrated how old Salish ceremonials still persist, and how an old cultic complex has become reinvigorated by taking up symbols belonging to Indian shakerism.[79]

---

[71] Omer C. Stewart, "The Peyote Religion and the Ghost Dance," *The Indian Historian* V/4 (1972), pp. 27–30, and "Anthropological Theory and History of Peyotism," *Ethnohistory* XXVI (1979), pp. 277–81.

[72] Åke Hultkrantz, "Conditions for the Spread of the Peyote Cult in North America," Haralds Biezais (ed.), *New Religions* (Stockholm: Scripta Institui Donneriani Aboensis VII, 1975), pp. 70–83.

[73] Joseph G. Jorgensen, *The Sun Dance Religion: Power for the Powerless* (Chicago: University of Chicago, 1972).

[74] Bea Medicine, "Native American Resistance to Integration: Contemporary Confrontations and Religious Revitalization," *Plains Anthropologist* XXVI (1981), pp. 277–86.

[75] Charles E. Hunter, "The Delaware Nativist Revival of the Mid-Eighteenth Century," *Ethnohistory* XVIII (1971), pp. 39–49.

[76] Deward E. Walker, Jr., *Conflict and Schism in Nez Perce Acculturation: A Study of Religion and Politics* (Pullman: Washington State University, 1968); Åke Hultkrantz, "Pagan and Christian Elements in the Religious Syncretism among the Shoshoni Indians of Wyoming," Sven S. Hartman (ed.), *Syncretism* (Stockholm: Scripta Institui Donneriani Aboensis III, 1969), pp. 15–40.

[77] Christopher Vecsey, *Traditional Ojibwa Religion and Its Historical Changes* (Philadelphia: American Philosophical Society, 1983).

[78] Margaret B. Blackman, "Creativy in Acculturation: Art, Architecture and Ceremony from the Northwest Coast," *Ethnohistory* XXIII (1976), pp. 387–413.

[79] Pamela Amoss, *Coast Salish Spirit Dancing: The Survival of an Ancestral Religion* (Seattle: University of Washington, 1978), and "Symbolic Substitution in the Indian Shaker Church," *Ethnohistory* XXV (1978), pp. 225–49.

The direct influence of Christian missions on Native American Religion is a theme that increasingly draws scholarly attention. It is particularly rewarding to read Elizabeth Graham's investigation of the role played by missionaries in the transformation of Indian religion in southern Ontario.[80] She shows, for instance, how the name of God has changed under missionary impact. The general theme of the relations between natives and missionaries has now been thoroughly discussed in a treatise by Henry Bowden.[81] Volume 21 of *Ethnohistory* contains several articles describing the relations between Christian missionaries and Red Indians: one on the Praying Indians of Massachusetts, another on the breakdown of the Spanish missions in California, a third one on missionary impact among the Haida, and a fourth one on anti-missionary feelings among the Cherokee in the 1820s.[82] Also the Canadian journal *Studies in Religion* dedicated a number to the same general theme in connection with the meeting in Winnipeg of the Fourteenth International Congress of the International Association for the History of Religions. Among the articles may be mentioned John Grant's paper on the relations between missionaries and prophets among the Cree and their neighbors, Norman Williamson's study of one such Cree prophet, Guy Laflèche's reflections on the misunderstanding between medicine men and missionaries in New France, Jordan Paper's presentation of an Ojibway shaman who, under the influence of new spiritual conditions, turned into an individualistic mystic, and finally a couple of investigations of the changing eschatological beliefs among the northern Algonkians.[83] Of particular interest is a paper by Kenneth Morrison in which he delineates the traditional mythological patterns through which the Abnaki understood their Catholicism.[84]

8. *Studies of symbolism and meaning.* The symbolist anthropological

---

[80] Elizabeth Graham, *Medicine Man to Missionary: Missionaries as Agents of Change among the Indians of Southern Ontario, 1784–1867* (Toronto: Peter Martin, 1975).

[81] Henry Warner Bowden, *American Indians and Christian Missions: Studies in Cultural Conflict* (Chicago: University of Chicago, 1981).

[82] Kenneth M. Morrison, "'That Art of Coyning Christians': John Eliot and the Praying Indians of Massachusetts," *Ethnohistory* XXI (1974), pp. 77–92; George Harwood Phillips, "Indians and the Breakdown of the Spanish Mission System in California," *Ethnohistory* XXI (1974), pp. 291–302; John R. Henderson, "Missionary Influences on the Haida Settlement and Subsistence Patterns, 1876–1920," *Ethnohistory* XXI (1974), pp. 303–16; William G. McLoughlin, "Cherokee Anti-Mission Sentiment, 1824–1828," *Ethnohistory* XXI (1974), pp. 361–70.

[83] John Webster Grant, "Missionaries and Messiahs in the Northwest," *Studies in Religion* IX (1980), pp. 125–36; Norman James Williamson, "Abishabis the Cree," *Studies in Religion* IX (1980), pp. 217–45; Guy Laflèche, "Le Chamanisme des Amérindiens et des Missionnaires de la Nouvelle-France," *Studies in Religion* IX (1980), pp. 137–60, Jordan Paper, "From Shaman to Mystic in Ojibwa Religion," *Studies in Religion* IX (1980), pp.185–99; Hultkrantz, "The Problem of Christian Influence," *op. cit.*; Jean Baribeau, "L'Influence de l'Évangélisation sur la Conception de la Vie et de la Mort chez les Têtes-de-Boule au Dix-Neuvième Siècle," *Studies in Religion* IX (1980), pp. 201–16.

[84] Kenneth M. Morrison, "The Mythological Sources of Abenaki Catholicism: A Case Study of the Social History of Power," *Religion* XI (1981), pp. 235–63.

approach was introduced by Claude Lévi-Strauss whose tetralogy *Mythologiques* concluded with a volume from the 1970s,[85] deals with South and North American myths. His dialectic structuralism has attracted many Americanists but is vividly refuted by Raoul and Laura Makarius.[86] Laura Makarius has, by the way, published a mythological study of the North American culture hero and trickster whom she interprets as a mythological projection of a human violator of taboos.[87] Among other symbolic investigations could be ranged the earlier mentioned papers by Goldman and Ortiz and a linguistic-philosophical contribution to Navajo religious thought by Gary Witherspoon.[88]

Whereas structuralists like Claude Lévi-Strauss have asked for the meaning of myths and ceremonies beyond the understanding of the Indians themselves, a reawakened interest in the meaning that the Indians themselves attach to their beliefs is spreading among scholars. Most studies are still under development, or exist in manuscript form. However, enough is known of the new trend to allow the following remarks.

One part of these studies concerns interpretations of Indian symbolism. The earlier works of Mircea Eliade and Werner Müller[89] have meant much for the growth of this direction of research. The aforementioned papers by Joseph Brown and Sam Gill are fine examples of this kind of work. Other papers written in the same spirit concern Sun Dance symbolism and Iroquois masks.[90] More studies are coming.

Closely allied to these studies are the investigations on the Indian's connection with Nature which, in the last analysis, is closely affiliated with his religious philosophy. Werner Müller paved the way here with a theoretical study in Eliade's *Festschrift*, followed by two books in the German language on the North American Indian's feelings for his natural surroundings.[91] It

---

[85] Claude Lévi-Strauss, *L'Homme Nu* (Paris: Plon, 1971).

[86] Raoul Makarius and Laura Makarius, *Structuralisme ou Ethnologie* (Paris: Editions Anthropos, 1973).

[87] Laura Makarius, "The Crime of Manabozo," *American Anthropologist* LXXV (1973), pp. 663–75; cf. "Le Mythe du 'Trickster,'" *Revue de l'Histoire des Religions* CLXXV (1969), pp. 17–46.

[88] Gary J. Witherspoon, *Languare and Art in the Navajo Universe* (Ann Arbor: University of Michigan, 1977).

[89] See, e.g., Werner Müller, "The 'Passivity' of Language and the Experience of Nature: A Study in the Structure of the Primitive Mind," Joseph M. Kitagawa and Charles H. Long (eds.), *Myths and Symbols. Studies in Honor of Mircea Eliade* (Chicago: University of Chicago, 1969), pp. 227–39.

[90] Åke Hultkrantz, "The Traditional Symbolism of the Sun Dance Lodge among the Wind River Shoshoni," Haralds Biezais (ed.), *Religious Symbols and Their Functions* (Stockholm: Scripta Instituti Donneriani Aboensis X, 1979), pp. 70–95; Fred Miller, "The Crow Sun Dance Lodge: Form, Process, and Geometry in the Creation of Sacred Space," *Temenos* XVI (1980), pp. 92–102; Thomas McElwain, "Methods in Mask Morphology: Iroquoian False Faces in the Ethnographical Museum, Stockholm," *Temenos* XVI (1980), pp. 68–83.

[91] Müller, "The 'Passivity' of Language," *op. cit.*; *Geliebte Erde: Naturfrömmigkeit und*

should be pointed out, however, that some years earlier Joseph Brown had handled the same subject.[92] Calvin Martin's aforementioned investigations of the relations between the hunter and his game in north-eastern North America has stimulated continued research and debate.[93] The present author has contributed with a model of the interconnections between nature-feeling and religious thought;[94] however, the classic introduction to the subject will be found in an article by Christopher Vecsey where he gives a survey of the Indian's and the white man's reaction to Nature in North America.[95]

9. *Psychological investigations.* It is rather surprising to find that very few writings on the North American Indians during the last decade may be characterized as psychological in scope. However, there are some good papers by scholars like Bryce Boyer, Alan Dundes and Weston La Barre which more or less have applied psychoanalytical methods on religion. Thus, Boyer has looked into the minds of Apache medicine men, and tried to reveal the Apache personality through analysis of religion and folklore; Dundes has made an interesting psychoanalytic interpretation of the roots of the Kwakiutl potlatch; and La Barre has in several papers worked out the close connections between shamanism, psychotropics and psychoanalysis.[96]

Among other authors with the same kind of scientific direction we may mention the psychiatrist Wolfgang Jilek whose analysis of the Salish Spirit Dance gives evidence of its therapeutic value and its role in revitalizing the old culture.[97] Daniel Merkur offers a psychoanalytic explanation of the Navajo Coyoteway ritual.[98] In some psychoanalytically inclined anthropological works religious phenomena are dealt with as cultural epiphenomena. A psychological document of another emphasis is David Jones's portrait of a

Naturhass im Indianischen und Europäischen Nordamerika (Bonn: Bouvier Verlag Herbert Grundmann, 1972), and *Indianische Welterfahrung* (Stuttgart: Ernst Klett, 1976); cf. *Neue Sonne–Neues Licht, op. cit.*

[92] Joseph Epes Brown, *The Spiritual Legacy of the American Indian* (Wallingford, Pennsylvania: Pendle Hill Pamphlets, 1964).

[93] Cf. Shepard Krech III (ed.), *Indians, Animals, and the Fur Trade: A Critique of Keepers of the Game* (Athens: University of Georgia, 1981).

[94] Åke Hultkrantz, *Belief and Worship, op. cit.*, pp. 117–34.

[95] Christopher Vecsey, "American Indian Environmental Religions," Christopher Vecsey and Robert W. Venables (eds.), *American Indian Environments: Ecological Issues in Native American History* (Syracuse: Syracuse University, 1980), pp. 1–37, 175–84. This volume contains several other contributions indirectly bearing on the theme of nature and religion.

[96] L. Bryce Boyer, *Childhood and Folklore: A Psychoanalytic Study of Apache Personality* (New York: The Library of Psychological Anthropology, 1979); Alan Dundes, "Heads or Tails: A Psychoanalytic Study of Potlatch," *The Journal of Psychological Anthropology* II (1979), pp. 395–424; Weston La Barre, *Culture in Context: Selected Writings of Weston La Barre* (Durham: Duke University, 1980), e.g.

[97] Wolfgang C. Jilek, *Salish Indian Mental Health and Culture Change: Psychohygienic and Therapeutic Aspects of the Guardian Spirit Ceremonial* (Toronto: Holt, Rinehart and Winston, 1974).

[98] Daniel Merkur, "The Psychodynamics of the Navajo Coyoteway Ceremonial," *Journal of Mind and Behavior* II (1981), pp. 243–57.

Comanche medicine woman, an excellent description of her ways and her religio-magical techniques.[99] Carlos Castaneda's books on the teachings of a supposed desert medicine man, the Yaqui Don Juan, have evoked great public interest.[100] The presumed shamanic consciousness that here is exposed has however little in common with what we know of the psychic experiences of other North American medicine men. Whatever reality these books describe it is not that of the Yaqui medicine man as Ralph Beals and others have testified.

10. *Indian autobiographies.* This is an interesting genre which was first tried by Paul Radin sixty years ago: the Indian tells his story to a white man who edits and publishes it. Besides Neihardt's famous but somewhat spurious book on Black Elk—now in a new edition—there are some few good autobiographies (in the sense here described) that deserve mentioning, one by the Crow Two Leggings, another by the Minniconjou Dakota John Fire Lame Deer, and a third by the Navajo Frank Mitchell.[101]

11. *Apologetic studies.* Under this heading two kinds of propagandistic studies will be presented, works by Indians in defense of their native religions, and works of Christian theology. Since this kind of writing only too often has a restricted empirical value, only a most selected sample will be given.

To the first category belong Vine Deloria's books, in particular his monumental *God is Red.*[102] Its publication has given rise to some discussion among religionists.[103] Another representative work has been written by the Stoney (Assiniboin) Chief John Snow who, without abandoning his Christian faith (he is a clergyman), defends the traditional beliefs and rituals of his people.[104] In a highly apologetic book William Coffer (or Koi Hosh, of mixed Cherokee and Choctaw descent) vindicates the autochthony of American Indians on the American earth by the proofs of the evidence given by

[99] David E. Jones, *Sanapia: Comanche Medicine Woman* (New York: Holt, Rinehart and Winston, 1972).

[100] Carlos Castaneda, *The Teachings of Don Juan: A Yaqui Way of Knowledge* (Berkeley: University of California, 1968), *A Separate Reality, Journey to Ixtlan, Tales of Power,* and *The Second Ring of Power* (New York: Simon & Schuster, 1971, 1972, 1974, 1977); cf. Richard de Mille (ed.) *The Don Juan Papers: Further Castaneda Controversies* (Santa Barbara: Ross-Erikson, 1980).

[101] Peter Nabokov (ed.), *Two Leggings: The Making of a Crow Warrior* (New York: Thomas Crowell, 1967); Richard Erdoes (ed.), *Lame Deer, Seeker of Visions: The Life of a Sioux Medicine Man* (New York: Simon & Schuster, 1972); Charlotte J. Frisbie and David P. McAllester (eds.), *Navajo Blessingway Singer: The Autobiography of Frank Mitchell 1881–1967* (Tucson: University of Arizona, 1978).

[102] Vine Deloria, Jr., *God is Red* (New York: Grosset and Dunlap, 1973).

[103] Joseph Cahill, "Vine Deloria: An Essay in Comparison of Christianity and Amerindian Religions," *Journal of the American Academy of Religion* XLV (1977), pp. 419–46.

[104] Snow, *These Mountains Are Our Sacred Places, op. cit.*

American Indian creation myths.[105]

To the second category may be referred a host of missionary writings and in particular Carl Starkloff's interpretation of Arapaho religion, the religion of the sacred center.[106]

CHANGING PERSPECTIVES

This list of publications, although admittedly selective, ought to give an impressive picture of the variety of themes and the diversity in approaches taken in recent research on North American Indian religions. A comparison with earlier publications as listed in my historical bibliographical survey above demonstrates that, while there is certainly in the majority of papers a continuation of previous research lines, some trends are definitely new. In particular I should like to point out the following features as examples of the changing winds:

1. There are some new branches of learning, such as ethnoastronomy, analyses of the impact on traditional religions from missions and missionaries, and studies of symbolism and meaning. Research on these subjects occurred occasionally in the past, but was neither frequent nor pursued intentionally.

2. New perspectives are applied. For instance, Indian religions are looked upon as far as feasible from inside, from the Indian point of view; studies in symbolism, direct responses in interviews and information in Indian autobiographies furnish the foundation of such research. Furthermore, the interconnections between man and Nature have become a favorite theme. They may concern the impact of Nature on man (the religio-ecological approach), the emergence of a sacred landscape, or man's religious attitude to Nature. Finally, there is an Indian-white religious dialogue going on, and theological interpretations turn up in the debate.

3. A new category of scholars and authors joins the academic discussions, the Indians themselves. It is true that in the past Indians took part in research on their traditional religions; names like J. N. B. Hewitt (Seneca), William Jones (Fox) and George Hunt (Kwakiutl) come to mind. However, the present trend is that large groups of highly educated Indians specialize in the field of American Indian religions and assume academic offices at the universities. A good example is Dr. Ines Talamantez, professor of Native American Religions at the University of California in Santa Barbara, and co-sponsor of the 1980 symposium on native religions at the latter place. Being a Mescalero Apache she dedicates herself to studies in Southwestern, and particularly Apache, rituals and symbols. It seems reasonable to presume

---

[105] William E. Coffer, *Spirits of the Sacred Mountains: Creation Stories of the American Indian* (New York: Van Nostrand, 1978).

[106] Carl Starkloff, *The People of the Center: American Indian Religion and Christianity* (New York: Seabury, 1974).

that only the Indians themselves—Indians who have been reared in the old tribal traditions and speak the language of their ancestors—are able to supply the profound and hidden treasures of Indian religions.

One means of furthering research on American Indian religions during the 1970s has been the arrangement of multidisciplinary symposia on the subject. It all began with the section on American Indian religions organized by Joseph Epes Brown for the Los Angeles congress on religion in 1972. As the first professor of Native American Religions in the United States, Brown has had a leading, and most inspiring role in the development of the discipline. His well-written book, *The Sacred Pipe*, has long been a classic in its field and is now spread all over the earth in a series of translations.[107]

Brown's initiative proved successful, and it was later followed up by other scholars. Thus, in 1973 the philosopher of religion, Walter Capps, assembled a group of scholars on Native North American Religion for a symposium at Santa Barbara, California; the papers were later issued in book-form.[108] Four years later a similar symposium took place at Tempe, Arizona, under the guidance of Sam Gill who also edited the papers.[109] The next symposium was held in September 1977 in Edmonton, Alberta, at the instigation of Earle Waugh, professor in Religious Studies there. Here, for the first time, Indians and scholars were brought together; the scholars read their papers which were criticized by elders from selected Indian tribes. The papers and the Indian commentaries were later published.[110] The symposium on American Indian Environments that was arranged by Christopher Vecsey in April 1979 at Hobart and William Smith Colleges also touched on native religions, as was indicated earlier. There followed the above-mentioned symposium at Santa Barbara in January 1980, of which the present chapter was a part. At the IAHR meeting in Winnipeg the same year a section was organized on Northeastern Indian religions.

It is certainly no coincidence that all these symposia were arranged by students of religion. Anthropologists are not uninterested in the subject of religion, but they concentrate on the universal, principal aspects of religious behavior, and mostly prefer to see it as a symbolic expression of culture or social structure and social relations. Students of religion, on the other hand, have lately become aware of the immense dynamic power of American indigenous religions, and are eager to incorporate this vast area of research with their own discipline.

Since this expansion of religious studies has repercussions in the ways in

[107] Joseph Epes Brown, *The Sacred Pipe: Black Elk's Account of the Seven Rites of the Oglala Sioux* (Norman: University of Oklahoma, 1953).

[108] Walter Holden Capps (ed.), *Seeing with a Native Eye: Essays on Native American Religion* (New York: Harper & Row, 1976).

[109] Sam D. Gill (ed.), *The Religious Character of Native American Humanities* (Tempe: Arizona State University, 1977),

[110] Waugh and Prithipaul, *op. cit.*

which research is molded, we have reasons to look closer into the differences between the disciplines concerned.

TRENDS WITHIN VARIOUS DISCIPLINES

Until recently most work on Amerindian religions was performed by anthropologists and, up to 1960, by folklorists. For a long time these disciplines shared the historical and genetic outlooks on religion with the history of religions, and many accounts on native religions by such anthropologists as Lowie, Radin and Speck could just as well be regarded as contributions to the history of religions. However, new perspectives in American anthropology after about 1925, and a more conscious folkloristic approach during the decades that followed, changed the directions of studies in these disciplines considerably. Anthropologists now treated religion more consciously as a piece of culture, and their colleagues in folklore replaced religion with a folkloristic vision of myths, tales and customs. A vacuum ensued, and the students of religion could step in. Coming from the preoccupation with Christianity and other "high" religions of the Old World they first of all only tried to find suitable parallels to religious phenomena in Europe and Asia. After about 1950 a change set in, the students of religion became themselves specialists in the americanist field, first in Scandinavia and Germany, later on in the United States and Canada.

Today most work on North American Indian religions is done by anthropologists and students of religion (and in several cases the scholars involved are qualified both as anthropologists and students of religion), whereas the contributions from folklorists are sparse. The research results are colored by the methodological assumptions and approaches of the respective disciplines. The positions of these subjects vis-à-vis religion may be briefly characterized as follows:

1. *Anthropology.* There are at present two trends in the anthropological outlook on religion. The majority of researchers still consider religion as a cultural reflection and thoroughly integrated part of culture. To these students, religion as such is often done away with, and dissolved into world view, ritual, and mythology. The perspective tends to become reductionistic; religious expressions are traced back to sociological and psychological conditioning factors. It is enigmatic how this view of religion could be vindicated. American Indians motivate their whole culture in all its phases, and all their cultural behavior, with reference to religious precepts; religion is diffused in everything. If through anthropological operations their religion is reduced to something else the meaning of existence for the Indian believers will not be understandable to students.

Fortunately, there is a growing group of anthropologists who hold different views. Their contributions are classified under labels as Ethnoscience, Ethnosemantics or simply New Ethnography, and they build on an intensive investigation of concepts and beliefs, an "emic" methodology as understood by Kenneth Pike.[111] In other words, here is recommended a procedure that has long been practiced among students of religion! Even more important is the growing insight among some anthropologists that religion has a determining, forming influence on culture as a whole. Discussing the methodological strategies to give an adequate account of the Indians of the Southeast Charles Hudson writes:

> I take the "neointellectualist" point of view that as social anthropologists we ought to regard the beliefs of preliterate people as serious attempts at explanation and not merely as bits of custom to be explained away by one or another of our theories. . . . Because I assume that the beliefs of the Southeastern Indians ought to be taken seriously, I begin the synchronic reconstruction with an analysis of their belief system—rather than ending with it, as is so often done. It is by absorbing something of their view of the world that we can see the sense of their social institutions.[112]

This pronouncement gives a promising perspective for future anthropological research on native religions.

2. *Folklore*. There has been little folkloristic research done on Native American Religions after 1960. For a long time the picture has been rather chaotic: religious beliefs and observations have been dissolved into meaningless superstitions, myths and other tradition categories judged only in their formal expressions (as narrative genres) or as keys for psychoanalytical interpretations. Since about 1960 the predominant idea has been structuralism.[113] The major weakness of this approach is its negligence of the religious values of myths and legends assigned to them by the believers themselves. We may ask, how can we ever understand the message of a myth by simply analyzing its structural composition, but at the same time ignoring its meaning as explained through its relation to a ritual or a sacred situation, or through the very words of the believers themselves?

When this has been said it should be acknowledged that we find folklorists who follow other paths. Some are anthropologists who occasionally dip into folklore, like the recently deceased Melville Jacobs; others are folklorists by profession, like Barre Toelken. These authors have looked deeper into the perceptions and belief systems of native Americans than the often superficial structuralists.

3. *Studies in religion*. When scholars from the departments of religion have engaged themselves in the study of native American religions their emphasis has naturally been different from that of their colleagues in folklore

---

[111] Cf. Pertti J. Pelto, *Anthropological Research: The Structure of Inquiry* (New York: Harper & Row, 1970).

[112] Charles Hudson, *The Southeastern Indians* (Knoxville: University of Tennessee, 1976), pp. vii–viii.

[113] Claude Lévi-Strauss, *Mythologiques*, 4 vols. (Paris: Plon, 1964–71); Alan Dundes, *The Morphology of North American Indian Folktales* (Helsinki: FF Communications CXCV, 1964).

and, particularly, anthropology.[114] For these scholars religion as such is in focus, and it is appreciated as the major meaningful factor in human existence. This is a solid way of approach, for it is consonant with how the Indians themselves understand their situation. However, many anthropologists oppose these studies. They claim that the problems that have been chosen are irrelevant, that the concepts applied are old-fashioned, that description is preferred to analysis, that the outlook is Christian and that religious concepts related to Christian beliefs are at the heart of interest. Although these objections are a consequence of the anthropological outlook they are partly valid, and students of religion would benefit from taking them into account.

Due to historical and ideological circumstances studies in religion are pursued within three different traditions of learning:

a. *Theology*. Religious texts and occurrences are interpreted from a consistent Christian point of view that is anchored with the dogma of a particular Christian denomination. We leave theology aside here.

b. *Religious studies in the United States, Canada and Britain*. Religious ideas and patterns are expounded so that their meanings are revealed. The major question is how we all may be enlightened by the values and attitudes expressed in these ideas and patterns. Briefly put, what have Indian religions to give us?

c. *History of religions in America and Europe*. Historical and phenomenological perspectives of native American religions are presented, and investigations are both place-bound and comparative. Interest is focussed on meaning, variety of forms, historical processes, and connections with other religions.

Much because of the diverging traditions of research, students of religion often differ sharply in their approaches and methods, ask different questions, speak past each other. It is possible to discern two basic approaches, two separate traditions which are sustained by a difference in outlook between Europeans and Americans.[115] In a review of an archaeological work the American anthropologist James Judge has pointed out a major factor in the separate development of humanistic disciplines in Europe and North America:

> In emphasizing the social utility of scholarship, Trigger isolates an important dichotomy between American and European archaeologists. The latter, perhaps because of a long tradition of intellectualism, justify their profession in terms of its being a legitimate quest for knowledge in its own right. In contrast,

[114] Historians of religions consider themselves anthropologists. See, e.g., Åke Hultkrantz, "History of Religions in Anthropological Waters: Some Reflections against the Background of American Data," *Temenos* XIII (1977), pp. 81–97, esp. p. 86, n. 18. Some of them have, like myself, a double training in the disciplines of religion and anthropology. In this context, however, I mean by anthropologists those students working within the discipline of anthropology who consider themselves anthropologists.

[115] See Hultkrantz, "The Study of North American Indian Religion," *op. cit.*, pp. 90ff.

American archaeologists seem dominated by a pervasive quest for relevancy of their discipline and need to justify it in terms of its contribution to codifying laws of human behavior.[116]

The European interest in the study in *et per se*—a heritage from ancient Greece—provides for disinterested (if the term is allowed) studies in native religions, whereas Americans seek for the practical, pragmatic application of Amerindian studies. This application may concern American Indians—to support their realization of their religious heritage, their building up of a common religious consciousness. Or it may concern the vast majority of Americans whose religious life can profit from the widening perspectives provided by the knowledge of native American religions.

There is another important difference between religious research in America and Europe: even the methodological concepts and key words are disjunctive. This is of course no drawback in itself if scholars on both sides of the water learn each other's technical languages.

Despite these differences between the branches of learning in the studies of religion it seems that all students of religion specializing in the North American field may give considerable and substantial contributions to research on native religions. Some are extraordinarily well equipped through their familiarity with their subject, or their close connections with native ethnic groups. Some give promise for the future but are perhaps as yet hampered by a lack of relevant ethnographical knowledge. Many obviously need the training in field work and background knowledge that anthropological courses can supply.

Let us finally ask ourselves in what particular way students of religion can supplement anthropological work on North American Indian religions. After what has been said in the foregoing the answer should be rather obvious: by concentrating on religious values and avoiding reductionistic speculations. To repeat, most anthropologists still seem to take it for granted that religion is an illusion of the mind and therefore they dismiss religion as an empirical category. This is a very subjective position. Whatever answer we give to the problem of the truth of religion, religion plays an overwhelmingly important role in human life and should be appreciated accordingly. It is essential that we try to understand Indian religions in their own right, as testimonies of the expressions of the human spirit in existential issues. Phenomenologically religion manifests the modes of man's relationship to the supernatural world he believes in. It displays a series of patterns, or structures, whose ideological existence we shall miss if we understand religion as just a conglomerate of diverse mental features that can be reduced to something else, non-religious. Religious man makes use of symbols for religious communication, largely taken from the world around him. To penetrate the

---

[116] W. James Judge, "Review of Bruce Trigger, *Time and Traditions: Essays in Archaeological Interpretation*," *American Anthropologist* LXXXI (1979), p. 660.

nature of these symbols and their meaning we can also use anthropological methods, but we should then avoid the fallacy that they may lead up to: that religion is a product of social institutions or psychic anxieties.

Provided native religious research follows the methodological lines presented here I think there will be a fruitful cooperation between anthropology, folklore and studies in religion in the future. For there is no doubt that research on North American Indian religions would gain in depth and dimension if it appeared as a multidisciplinary enterprise.

SOME TASKS OF FUTURE RESEARCH

I shall now suggest some future lines of research on native American religions. This is a delicate task in view of my own affinity to European research traditions in the history of religions and anthropology. I cannot expect that my specific research interests will be shared by my American colleagues whose learned traditions are partly different. If personally cognizant of my spiritual heritage, I side with the history of religions, this is due to two circumstances. First of all, history and phenomenology, the two perspectives implied in this discipline, have the greatest intellectual appeal to me. Secondly, the religio-historical approach has a strict empirical framework and a set of methods that should guarantee reasonably objective results. I am afraid that where the precise logical and empirical apparatus fails the field is open for subjective evaluations and chatty accounts. Very frequently one can observe the tendency, when native American religions are discussed, to prefer value judgments to scientific analysis. No wonder that the composers of articles and books on Indian religions are often called "writers" and "authors" but seldom "scholars." A sound religio-historical analysis, coupled with anthropological insights, is according to my understanding the best guarantee for a scholarly treatment of these religions.

One of our foremost tasks must be to ensure that studies of Amerindian religions receive a general respectability and scientific standing which— perhaps—as yet they do not have. I see three different moves that may implement this aim:

1. We need a central platform for our research, a forum for our scientific endeavors and exchange of ideas. I suggest we join in the effort to create a *Journal of North American Indian Religions*, a journal where publications could be submitted to scientific control, but free from the impact of ideological and political pressure groups. I think this is a vital point. Without a medium of its own the research on native religions will be little observed by other research groups and, as it were, lack an institutional center.

2. Students of native American religions should also feel it incumbent on themselves to make an inventory of extant archival documents on these religions and to publish them to the benefit of their research. It is a little

observed fact that an enormous treasure of written field notes and manu-scripts on native religions are preserved in museums, research institutions and official and private archives all over North America. It is a must for students of these religions to make these documents available for publica-tion. We are still in the position to achieve good field research, particularly on religious change, but the bulk of information rests unconsulted, not to say unknown, in the archives. No complete information on North American religions can be achieved without access to this most important material.

3. Great efforts should be concentrated on elevating the research on native religions to a scientific level equal with that of the studies of Old World religions. It is also necessary to link the studies of native religions to the study of the religious traditions of the Old World.

This means not only that we shall try to arrive at a better chronology for Amerindian religions—the old documents at our disposal should be helpful in this respect—but also that these religions are given better cover-age. In spite of all that has been written on native religions we have only little inside knowledge of them. We know the myths, we know the rites, we know the outer shell of these religions, but mostly we are little informed about basic religious sentiments and belief contents. The reasons for this ignorance are several. One is that anthropologists in the past were fascinated by the rituals but lacked interest for the associated belief systems—witness their writings on the Sun Dance of the Plains Indians. Another reason may be that North American Indians had no dominating complex of religious beliefs like shamanism in Siberia or the sacred kingship in the Near East. Religious ideas were more diffuse and therefore did not attract the attention of anthropologists.

Perhaps there is also a need for more systematic research, with sharply defined problems within an empirical framework. There has been a ten-dency for students of religion to focus their writings on general philosophi-cal, even normative questions, or on vague psychological arguments scarcely anchored in the facts at their disposal. Reflections on the Indian outlook on man, life and nature could of course be most valuable. However, before we can approach such subjects we are obliged to make a careful research on the facts in their setting, perhaps on their entourage in various tribal religions. We must prefer such time-consuming investigations to "deep" thoughts!

I have already outlined some possible paths to choose in modern investi-gations of native North American religions.[117] The eleven categories of research lines that have been presented in this chapter provide further sug-gestions. Perhaps most of them could be digested in the following manner, thus summarizing my recommendations for future research:

a. Regional studies of tribes or areas, to complete our knowledge of religious symbols and religious values. The final aim would be to fill an

---

[117] See above, pp. 96ff.

empty room in the history of religions, thereby creating possibilities for more comprehensive comparative studies of religion. From another point of view such regional studies should serve the interests of American Indians eager to know their ethnic and religious past.

b. Particular studies to search for deeper religious perspectives, such as analyses of religious concepts, investigations of symbolic connections between man and the Universe, or portraits of religious individuals. In sum, more concentration on ideas, beliefs, values than hitherto, without for that matter passing over the classic genres of investigation, myths and rituals (which to some writers seem to constitute the specific contents of religions).

c. Applied religious studies, that is, studies to gain practical experiences of the ways in which Indian religions can contribute to the understanding of Indian problems in modern times. I am here referring to, for instance, Indian political ambitions and missionary activities from different religious denominations.

d. Studies of nativistic religious tendencies and syncretistic movements, perhaps also of the agnosticism and transformation of religious values in modern times.

These suggestions seem to me to take care of the interests both in the history of religions and the discipline of religious studies.

It is obvious that the best work on the *field* level can now be done by scholars who are themselves Indians, and the next best by non-Indian Americans who have the study material easily at hand. Europeans like myself can primarily contribute with *comparative* analyses and surveys, unless they have conducted field research among Indians.

The majority of viable methods have been conceived by anthropologists and should be used in such a way that religion, not culture or society, stands in the center. As I have emphasized earlier, this does not mean to say that the researcher should not strive for a thorough knowledge of the culture or society in question—religious facts are always more or less integrated in a sociocultural framework. There are many possible methodological inroads— such as phenomenology, symbolic analysis, functionalism-structuralism, configuration research, ecology, history, archaeology and acculturation analysis. Whatever way we choose, we should always aim at a *cognitive* approach. In this manner we come closer to an understanding of the meaning of religion and the deep-structured values that keep all beliefs and rites together.

As I see it we should ultimately come to grips with what beliefs and rites express, and not just register them or see them as functions of the culture, or parts of the cultural structure. This may be done in two ways:

1. Religious expressions are arranged according to their ecological, cultural and sociological integration. Thus, through religious ecology we arrive at an anlysis of religious forms which enables us to reduce those aspects of a concept that are due to direct or indirect impact of the environment.

Culture-historical and sociological screens may be removed in similar ways. What remains is the inmost religious contents: a cognition of divine-spiritual presence, and experiences of faith, trust, security, apathy, anxiety, fear or horror in face of the supernatural. The particular values of a religion will be illuminated.

2. Each religious idea, each religious rite is placed in a functional connection with a master concept that motivates them all. Conceptions arranged around such leading ideas form belief complexes, or religious segments. Shamanism, for instance, is such a combining structure of conceptions and rites. Within the structure all elements correspond to each other, for instance, soul beliefs—soul flight—diagnosis of disease—curative operations—guardian spirits—world tree. In this way each belief complex stands out as a holistic, meaningful pattern, and each religion is composed of such patterns which makes it a meaningful answer to the existential problems of the individual.

These are examples of cognitive approaches oriented from the point of view of religion. Something similar could be done, with advantage, in the study of North American Indian religions. Ours is a fascinating subject. May our research profit from the joy we feel in our difficult but rewarding endeavors.

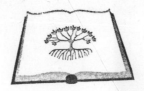